DREAMING OF HOME

HOW WE TURN FEAR into PRIDE, POWER, and REAL CHANGE

CRISTINA JIMÉNEZ

ST. MARTIN'S GRIFFIN
NEW YORK

For a teaching and discussion guide,
please visit academic.macmillan.com

Published in the United States by St. Martin's Griffin,
an imprint of St. Martin's Publishing Group

EU Representative: Macmillan Publishers Ireland Ltd., 1st Floor,
The Liffey Trust Centre, 117–126 Sheriff Street Upper, Dublin 1, D01 YC43

For information, address St. Martin's Publishing Group,
120 Broadway, New York, NY 10271.

www.stmartins.com

Designed by Meryl Sussman Levavi

The Library of Congress Cataloging-in-Publication Data
is available upon request.

ISBN 978-1-250-27566-0 (hardcover)
ISBN 978-1-250-37036-5 (trade paperback)
ISBN 978-1-250-27567-7 (ebook)

First St. Martin's Griffin Edition: 2026

10 9 8 7 6 5 4 3 2 1

More Praise for *Dreaming of Home*

***Time*, Best New Books in May**
***Ms.*, May 2025 Reads**
***Book Riot*, Best New Books in May**
***Daily Kos*, New Nonfiction**

"While [Jiménez] hopes her book inspires readers to believe in the potential for collective action, she highlights the centrality of another theme: 'finding home even when that place you consider home tells you it doesn't want you.'" —*Publishers Weekly*

"A captivating and strong debut. An emotional and inspirational recounting of the modern American immigrant rights movement . . . An invitation for readers to organize and dream of a more just place for all." —*Kirkus Reviews*

"Jiménez's story is one of transformation that is more than personal; it reaches the character of the United States . . . For readers who remain interested in America as an equitable, inclusive community of diverse backgrounds, classes, faiths, genders, races, and immigrants." —*Library Journal*

"Powerful . . . Weaving personal experience with broader social justice movements, Jiménez sheds light on the trauma of immigration, the racial and economic inequities undermining US communities, and the resilience of those who fight for a better future . . . An inspiring testament to perseverance and collective power." —*Booklist*

"At its core, *Dreaming of Home* is about reminding readers that change is possible . . . In a moment when immigrant communities are once again under political attack, Cristina Jiménez is choosing to fight with her story—one that proves the power of organizing is as urgent now as ever." —*Fierce*

"We all need to hear Cristina's story of moving from the shadows of a broken system to leading a movement that changed history."

—Heather McGhee, advocate and *New York Times* bestselling author of *The Sum of Us*

"Cristina came of age building a powerful movement of young people, fighting for their place in America. Her version of the American dream will be full of wisdom for this era."

—Ai-jen Poo, author, organizer, and president of the National Domestic Workers Alliance and executive director of Caring Across Generations

"You cannot write the modern history of the immigrant rights movement—and, in turn, the evolution of racial and social justice—without the leadership of Cristina Jiménez."

—Jose Antonio Vargas, Pulitzer Prize–winning journalist, founder of Define American, and author of *Dear America: Notes of an Undocumented Citizen*

"Cristina Jiménez is documenting her life journey as an immigrant and, in doing so, recording the journey of those who haven't been acknowledged. We don't count, we aren't history unless we tell our own stories."

—Sandra Cisneros, poet, writer, and author of *The House on Mango Street*

"Jiménez is a writer of thunderous skill and grace whose remarkable book reminds us, time and again, how important the values of compassion and generosity truly are. Cristina's story is as inspirational as it is prescient for anyone whose voice is striving to be heard in a calamitous time. What's in these pages demonstrate what values define a true American voice: empathy, imagination, fearlessness. Read this book and fill yourself with hope."

—Brando Skyhorse

To all migrants and refugees in the US and around the world, this book is for you. I wrote these pages to remind you that you are worthy of dignity, freedom, safety, and love. Wherever your journey takes you, you belong.

To my son, Itzae, you are my guide and my home.

We can disagree and still love each other unless your disagreement is rooted in my oppression and denial of my humanity and right to exist.

—James Baldwin

CONTENTS

DREAMING OF HOME

PROLOGUE

My brother, Jonathan, and I jokingly call him the Hulk. Papi, Fausto Jiménez, a former wrestler, is short and muscular with bulky arms and a wide back, the brown of his skin perfected by the intense noon sunlight we had back in Quito, Ecuador, the middle of the world. A jokester and a lover of pasillos, a genre of Indigenous Ecuadorian music, he wakes up every Monday at four in the morning to go to his construction job where he stays for the week. He drives about sixty miles from our apartment in Queens, New York, to Dover, New Jersey, in his old dark-purple Mitsubishi Eclipse, blasting pasillos from Julio Jaramillo and Carmencita Lara. Our family can't really afford for Papi to drive back and forth every day. Not only because of the cost of gas and tolls, but also because of the risk of deportation. We are undocumented and living in America in the aftermath of the terrorist attacks of 9/11.

Politicians use the "war on terror" to turn Muslims and immigrants of color, US citizens and noncitizens alike, into suspects. We become the targets of increased police surveillance, racial profiling, detention, deportation, violence, and hate. In Washington, President George W. Bush creates the Department of Homeland Security (DHS), and in our state, politicians jump on the anti-immigrant bandwagon and deny Papi and other undocumented New Yorkers the right to a driver's license. So, in this environment, something as simple as getting to work becomes risky business. But we don't have a lot of options. Finding another job as an undocumented immigrant when immigrants are seen as a threat is nearly impossible, so if you've got a job, you keep it. Papi risks deportation every time he drives to work to sustain our family. To minimize the threat, Papi stays in Dover for the week on a couch in a four-bedroom house he shares with thirteen other undocumented immigrants. They are from Ecuador and Honduras. Some of them work for the same construction company building housing for seniors.

Every Friday after work, Papi takes the I-80 east toward the George Washington Bridge heading back to Elmhurst, Queens. He gets home exhausted, with just enough energy to take off his dirty clothes and eat dinner before going to bed. On one of those Fridays, he realizes he got the wrong change after paying the toll at the bridge, so he pulls off to the side of the road to go back to the tollbooth to get his money—pretty innocuous stuff, but Papi didn't see the cop. Lights flash and then he hears those four words that can start a chain of events that has led to parents being disappeared without a trace: "License and registration, please." Papi is paralyzed with fear. He thinks this is it—this is the moment he will get deported. His mind flashes back to all that our family has sacrificed, leaving our loved ones and all we knew behind to come to this country seeking a better life. Papi's hands shake as he struggles to find his old license. He hands it to the cop, but the cop tells him he needs a valid license. Papi tells him he doesn't have one. The cop adjusts his sunglasses and, with an almost sarcastic tone, tells Papi, like he's a child, "Don't you know it's against the law to drive without a valid license?" Papi doesn't say a word. Any word or move could make matters worse. The cop tells him to get out of the car and puts him in the back of the police vehicle, leaving the Mitsubishi sitting there on the side of the road. At the station, Papi is allowed to make one phone call. He calls me panicked. "Help me, mija," he cries in anguish.

We've all heard the stories; we know the risks. But this was actually happening, and the news hits me like a punch in the gut. I think this could be the last time Papi is in the US. I may not see him ever again. I'm so afraid that my hand holding the phone starts to shake uncontrollably. But as I listen to what he is telling me, I take a deep breath and remember that I'm not alone. I quickly pull myself together and remind him that he has the right to remain silent and refuse to sign anything without the presence of a lawyer. I know that local police and immigration agents intimidate people (or even lie) to get them to sign their own "voluntary" deportation. "No matter what they tell you or how hard they try to intimidate you, don't say or sign anything," I tell him. I'm in action mode, and as I talk to him on speaker, I text immigrant rights organizers, asking for help getting a lawyer to rush to the police station. Javier Valdés from the New York Immigration Coalition (NYIC) texts me back: "We got you." He assures me our community will do everything they can to get Papi released before the NYPD gets immigration agents involved and it's too late. Javier and I both know that every second counts.

I hear Papi struggling to communicate with the cop in his broken English, so I ask him to put me on the phone with the officer. "My name is Cristina Jiménez, and I'm his daughter," I tell him. I go on to state Papi's rights and tell him that a lawyer is on their way to the station right now. One of our family friends who is a US citizen and speaks English (and who has a car—a rarity for New York City folks) also heads to help Papi. Before the lawyer even makes it to the precinct, the cop releases Papi when our family friend arrives. "Just go," he tells him and hands over a $180 ticket for driving without a license. I will never know what went through the cop's mind when he decided to let Papi go. But what I do know for sure is that the community of friends and immigrant justice organizers that I activated in that moment protected my dad and our family from the threat of deportation and the crushing possibility of us not seeing him again. It's what we do.

I wasn't always the young immigrant woman with the courage to confront the police and fight deportations. I grew up feeling afraid and ashamed—ashamed of the dark color of my skin, my Indigenous features, and of being poor, in a family that struggled to put food on the table. Don't get me wrong—I was proud of my parents' sacrifices and their courage to leave everything behind to seek a better life in the US. But once we got here, I struggled with loneliness and shame about my accent and being undocumented. We were a family that walked on eggshells, in constant fear of making the slightest slipup that could lead to racial profiling, deportation, and our family being broken apart by a heartless and senseless tangle of immigration laws and racism. I found my voice and power when I met a community of undocumented youth and immigrant justice organizers who fight to stop deportations and empower undocumented immigrants to speak up for their rights and dignity. In this community, I learned how everyday people impacted by injustice can come together, take collective action, and create change. I was undocumented, but became unafraid. *Dreaming of Home* is about this journey of transformation.

Like generations of immigrants who came before us, my family came to this country dreaming of America's promise—the American dream. We built a new life here and became a part of the fabric of this nation. But as undocumented immigrants, we were put in the position of living half a life, in constant risk as we strove, robbed of our dignity and freedom, made to feel unwanted and hated in the country we call home. Still, this isn't the only side of America I've gotten to know. As I've grown up and built a life organizing in social justice movements, I've met everyday Americans, both immigrants and nonimmigrants, who speak up in the face of injustice, pushing this country to live up to its aspirational values of freedom, justice, and equality for all. These are the Americans who stopped the deportation of my soulmate, Walter, and made the story of our family possible. This is the America that gives me hope and confidence that together we can build a country where you and I—all of us, regardless of background, race, ethnicity, class, gender, faith, and immigration status—can belong, live freely, and thrive.

1

HOME 1

Cristina, Ligia (mom), and Estefania (sister) at Cristina's kindergarten Christmas celebration, Quito, Ecuador, 1989 (courtesy of the author)

No one leaves home unless home is the mouth of a shark.

—Warsan Shire

We don't have much, but we have an abundance of love. I'm the oldest, followed by my baby sister, Estefania. My parents work hard to provide for our family. Papi, Fausto, is a security guard for a bank, and Mami, Ligia, works both as a seamstress and at home taking care of Estefania and me. Mami cooks, cleans, and somehow also manages to sew dresses and suits for her clients. Like families around us, my parents make just enough money to pay for rent, food, and my school's tuition—that's it.

We live in a tenement house on Avenida Brasil in the north of Quito, Ecuador. Our neighborhood is crammed tight with single-family homes and tenement houses interspersed by abandoned commercial space. The house we live in has two apartments with their own bathrooms and one communal bathroom for the five families that rent small apartments. Like many of the houses around us, the run-down place was never finished; its white concrete walls are smeared with gray cement, making them look like they're five hundred years old. We live under the gaze of the landlady, Señora Marcela, who lives in a separate brand-new three-story house with bright salmon-colored walls and big windows from which she peeks at our every move. When more than one tenant is washing clothes in the courtyard at the same time, Señora Marcela cuts the water off. I am so scared of her that every time we pass by her house, I stare at my shoes.

Our small apartment has one bedroom, a living room, and a kitchenette with an unfinished concrete floor. The four of us sleep in the bedroom. We jam two beds and Estefania's wooden crib in there, leaving just enough space between the beds for us to walk through sideways. The wooden floors in the living room and bedroom are kept so shiny I can always see my reflection. This is how Mami likes it. She can't change many things—the power outages, the mean landlady, not being able to get a job at a tailoring shop because she has two daughters to take care of—but she can ensure her home is always clean. "Ser pobre no es motivo para ser sucio" (Being poor is no reason to be dirty), she says while meticulously cleaning the floor and scrubbing the counters. With her small but mighty body, Mami moves the two beds, the sofa, and the large wooden cabinet in the living room all by herself to make sure every corner of the floor is shiny as a new car.

And while Mami keeps our little apartment spotless, the

places just outside of our door never fail to remind us of our station in life. We share a communal bathroom up the stairs from one of the courtyards with four other families, but Mami is adamant about us not using it. I agree. The toilet doesn't flush, the sink doesn't have running water, and the whole room smells like hundreds of people have peed all over the floor. Every time I pass by, I feel close to throwing up. But the dangers aren't only sanitary; Mami also keeps us out of the communal bathroom to protect us from the viejos—the creepy old men who just hang out around the bathrooms and in the courtyards, staring at me and other girls in the tenement house, especially when we wear shorts or skirts. We always make sure to run away.

Having no actual bathroom, our family uses red plastic potties, and we bathe in a large green plastic bin in our kitchenette. I feel ashamed when I realize that none of my school friends use plastic potties at home. When my friends talk about going to each other's homes to work on school projects together, I just keep quiet and go along, never inviting friends over to my place. Life isn't easy, but we get by, and even as a young girl I know that some people have it much worse, so I am grateful for all that we have.

Papi grew up homeless after his mother, my abuelita Julia, fled from her husband and marriage, leaving her children behind when Papi was only four years old. As a child, he sold candy and newspapers and begged outside restaurants for food. Some days he was lucky to get leftovers, while many days he had nothing to eat. He lived on the streets of Quito until a friend of the family took him and his brother to a shelter for homeless children. Abuelita Julia reunited with them when Papi was thirteen years old, eventually moving into the one-bedroom apartment that is now our home. Every time I feel ashamed of where we live, I remind myself that at least our family has a roof over our heads and food. Still, I dream of having our own bathroom one day.

When I think of my childhood in Quito, I have vivid memories of sunny mornings and cold, rainy afternoons when Mami's sewing is interrupted by our neighbor, Señora Maria, who sells fruits and vegetables at the neighborhood's street market, shouting, "Vecinas! Llueve! La ropa!" (Neighbors! It's raining! The clothes!)

"Señora Maria shouts like she is at the mercado!" Mami complains, but Señora Maria certainly is reliable! She is married to one of the viejos in the building, and they have three teenage kids and an old gray dog, named Rufo, that pees everywhere. On hearing Señora Maria's alarm, Mami and all the women in the tenement house run to the courtyard to bring in the clean laundry drying on the line. I hear the women giggling, wooden and plastic clothespins cracking, dogs barking, then only the sizzle of rain.

In the afternoons, Mami transforms our living room into her seamstress workshop. While Estefania sleeps in her crib, Mami sets up her Singer sewing machine and ironing board in between the couch and the large wooden cabinet where we store our tableware. I love to be Mami's assistant. One afternoon, she asks me to look for the plastic case where she stores buttons. I stand on tiptoes to reach down to the bottom of the tall plastic bin where she stores her tools. The case has a pink clip and looks like a tiny closet with square compartments where buttons are organized by color and size. But instead of grabbing it, I notice a brown book with gold lining on the edges. The book feels heavy in my hands as I pick it up, and it looks fancy and official but also precious and as though it needs to be handled with care—not too different from the Bibles delicately held by priests at Quito's top Catholic church, La Catedral. I run my finger along the gilded edge and glance over at Mami as I open it and see that it's full of beautiful drawings. I skim through it, pausing to admire the sketches of elegant bras, lingerie, and couture dresses. "Whose is this, Mami?" I ask.

"Oh, it's mine. That's the project I worked on to graduate from sewing school," she explains.

I am in awe that Mami has drawn such beautiful things like those worn by models and celebrities on TV. "You're a talented designer, Mami!" I say, looking at her with pride and a big smile. Mami doesn't say a word. She just looks down while tracing yellow chalk on black silk for a dress she is sewing for a client. But as I'm sitting on the floor feeling energized by this holy book filled with an outpouring of my mami's creativity, the mood in the room changes. I don't know why Mami doesn't seem as delighted as I am. "Why didn't you continue sketching these beautiful dresses?" I ask.

"No me gusta coser," she says with a sigh. Yet sewing is what she does almost every afternoon to help sustain our family. "I really wanted to go to college to become a history teacher, but I couldn't," Mami explains. Abuelita Esther, who lost her husband and raised her children on her own, didn't have enough money to pay for all thirteen of her children to go to school, and culturally, a college education was prioritized for men. When Mami was twelve years old, Abuelita told her that women needed to learn an oficio, a trade. She had two options: sewing or hairdressing. Mami chose sewing first and then decided to go to cosmetology school, becoming a hairdresser and working in a beauty salon until she had me. When Mami graduated from sixth grade, Abuelita Esther arranged for her to start working for the neighborhood's seamstress. "Your abuelita tried her best," Mami says with a brittle voice. Her gaze focuses on the black silk. I feel sad. I wonder how different Mami's life would be if she had the opportunity to continue school. I wonder what kind of history teacher she would have been and what the talented artistry of those pages could have become if it had been nurtured.

Mami breaks the silence. "Mija, tienes que estudiar. Tienes que llegar a la universidad y ser una profesional. La educación te dará una mejor vida. No quieres terminar como yo" (Darling, you must study. You must make it to college and become a professional. Education will give you a better life. You don't want to end up like me), she tells me. She is mostly right. I don't want to wind up in a tenement house without a bathroom and running water. But she's my mom and when I see her courage and resilience, hear her laughter, and experience her love and cooking, she's who I want to be when I grow up. When Mami says this to me, I understand why she is so persistent about me doing well in school. I understand why she rips the pages from my notebook when she thinks my handwriting isn't clear enough, why she pushes me to finish my homework even when the electricity goes out and I can barely see, and why she stays up with me at night to study for social studies exams. The exams require me to memorize all the key leaders and dates of the Inca Empire. (More than twenty years later, I still remember their names—like Pachacuti, ruler of the kingdom of Cuzco, and his son Túpac Yupanqui, who in 1463 extended the empire northward along the Andes through Ecuador.) Mami can't change the past, but she is determined to shape our future.

Only when I finish my homework does Mami let us watch TV. As Estefania grows older and we can play together more, we turn our small living room into a pretend TV studio. Like most children in Ecuador in the late '80s and early '90s, my sister and I are devoted fans of Xuxa and *El Show de Yuly*. Xuxa is from Brazil, and Yuly is originally from Peru but lives in Ecuador. They are the embodiment of beauty in the country's eyes: white, tall, and blond. Quite a contrast to our short legs, black hair, and brown skin. We are mesmerized by them and want to be like them—an aspiration put on TV in a country made up mostly of people who could never achieve it. Yuly records her show with a live audience of hundreds of children. Yuly and her "Yulyets," a group of backup dancers, perform musical acts and dances and showcase games with children on set. Yuly's outfits become a fashion trend among girls in Ecuador. She wears Reebok high-top aerobic sneakers with miniskirts or leggings and colorful headbands with her hair up in a ponytail. None of us can afford Reeboks, but we do our best to copy the looks.

Some afternoons when Mami doesn't sew, we walk two blocks to Abuelita Esther's house to play with our cousins. There are ten of us—Estefania, Jorgito, me, Anita, Claudia, Andres, Pablito, Gaby, Vanesa, and Daniel, ranging in age from four to fifteen. Those afternoons are so fun! Literally all of us somehow fit on Abuelita's squeaky bed to watch our favorite cartoon series, *ThunderCats*. Together we build a spaceship, like the one the ThunderCats use, with fabrics and old wood panels Abuelita Esther stores on her terrace. While we play, Abuelita Esther makes sopa de fideo (noodle soup), a perfect hot meal for Quito's chilly mountain evenings. When we are tired of running around, we gather in her kitchen with our moms—Tías Nely and Susana, who are sisters-in-law; and Tía Fany, the oldest sister; Mami; Tía Sarita; and Tía Marianita, the youngest of all the sisters. For real, there are about twenty of us squeezed around a long wooden table. We look like tomatoes at the market, tightly packed together in small boxes, but in these moments, we couldn't be happier. Abuelita Esther serves up big bowls of hot soup for everyone. The air is filled with the delicious smell of onion and cilantro. The warm, soft pasta and potatoes nearly melt in my mouth.

Those fun afternoons of play and sopa de fideo at Abuelita Esther's house soon become something of the past. Our family is growing. We move farther away from Abuelita Esther's house to a bigger apartment that has not one but TWO full bathrooms! The new apartment is farther away from the center of the city and owned by a friend of our family who agrees to rent it to us at an affordable price. Soon after, when I'm ten years old, we welcome our new baby brother, Jonathan. He is a little bundle of joy that makes everyone feel happier. I'm a proud oldest sister.

But the joy of my brother's arrival is saddened by a devastating change in my six-year-old sister's health. Estefania develops a severe pain in her chest, and I can see a visible lump that is clearly getting bigger. I delicately run my little finger over it, and Mami pushes my hand away. Our family routine becomes interrupted by trips to the clinic for multiple tests—tests that we can't afford, of course. One day, Papi, Mami, and Estefania go together to meet with the doctors while I stay home taking care of Jonathan, who is only a few months old. Up to now, everyone's been trying to keep a positive attitude, but this time, when they get home with puffed-up eyes, I know it's bad news. Estefania has been diagnosed with Ewing sarcoma, a rare cancerous tumor mostly found in children. She needs to start chemotherapy treatment immediately. "Tenemos que mantener la fe y orar. La esperanza es lo último que se pierde," Mami tells me. I hold on to her words, keeping faith and hope, as if they were a life buoy in the middle of an ocean storm.

Estefania and Mami go away to the hospital for a few weeks for chemotherapy treatment. During this time, Tía Blanquita, Papi's older sister, takes care of my baby brother, and sometimes I do too. Our whole extended family rallies to create a schedule with different shifts to make sure my sister is never alone at the hospital and so that my parents can get some support. Every time Mami comes home, she looks exhausted and weaker by the day. She is less talkative, and that positive attitude she brought to keeping our apartment spotless shifts as she breaks down into tears constantly while cooking and cleaning. Before going to bed, she asks me to join her in prayer. We pray together for what feels like an eternity.

One day I arrive home from school to find Estefania waiting

for me by the windows. Her thick black hair that Mami used to tie back with colorful clips is gone, and her vibrant brown skin looks almost ashen and very pale. I'm shocked by the sight, but she is just so happy to be home and she waves at me, smiling from ear to ear. I can see her sweet dimples. "I'm so happy to see you! Welcome home!" I'm only ten, but I try my best to project love and happiness as I hold back my tears, gently embracing her fragile body in my arms. For the following thirteen months, my brave little sister fights tooth and nail. But ultimately the cancer defeats her and rocks our family. Estefania passes away at home in May 1996. Before she leaves us, I hold her little hand tightly. She has an oxygen mask on and can't talk anymore. "I will miss you, hermanita. I love you," I tell her, sobbing. She looks right into my eyes and a tear comes down her right cheek. I know that is her way of saying, "I love you too," as our relationship transcends into the eternal spiritual connection that I still hold with me today.

Mami tells me that when our loved ones pass away, they are relieved of the pain and suffering they experienced on this earth. She cries every morning while praying aloud. I grieve in silence, crying in hiding. As the oldest child in the family, I take on some unspoken responsibility to avoid making things harder for Mami and everyone else around us. I am tormented by a deep feeling of shame and guilt. I regret all the times that I didn't let my sister hold or sleep with my favorite stuffed animal, a medium-size husky dog. During the wake, I stand by her casket and ask her to forgive me. Before we head to the cemetery, I ask Mami to place the stuffed husky dog inside the casket. It's my last gift to her.

We are barely surviving the loss of my sister when a public crisis collides with our private one. In August 1996, three months after my sister's passing, the newly elected president, Abdalá Bucaram, enacts new policies that send the already-hard economic situation for most Ecuadorians into a tailspin. Bucaram, whose nickname is El Loco (The Madman), is a businessman and politician from a populist political party. He promises a government for the people, not the wealthy, but he does exactly the opposite. In the first six months of his administration, he enacts neoliberal policies, which governments all across Central and South America are being pressured into by the US. The Bucaram administration moves to privatize social security and telecommunications, puts a freeze on the minimum wage, and eliminates government subsidies for public utilities. The moves make a giant shift in the economy, resulting in massive profits for tycoons and American multinational companies and cuts to services for the poor, which seem to be hitting us from all sides. Families like us are unable to pay rent and utilities or afford basic needs like food, water, and public transportation. Mami doesn't have money for eggs, cooking oil, and other basic groceries. I hear my parents talking. "I feel helpless," Mami says.

The country had been struggling politically and economically before Bucaram's election. In the 1960s, the US supported military coups across Latin America to put a stop to the growing power of Indigenous and peasant movements seeking workers' rights and land reforms. In Ecuador, the US backed a military coup to oust democratically elected president Carlos Julio Arosemena in 1963. The military regimes that ruled the country for the next sixteen years enacted "free market" economic policies demanded by their American backers that further exacerbated economic inequality. US involvement continued in subsequent governments in the '80s and '90s, influencing policies that favored privatization of social infrastructure and advanced corporate and US interests to squeeze profits out of Ecuador's oil production and exports. By the late 1990s, almost half of the population lived below the poverty line.

In response to Bucaram's policies, there are mass protests and a national strike demanding he leave office. Over two million Ecuadorians take to the streets, mostly in the largest cities. The country is in chaos. In Quito, violent confrontations break out between police and protestors outside of government buildings. Schools close and martial law is declared so people can't go to work or leave their homes. The images on TV of protestors pepper sprayed by police, tires on fire, and smoke blocking traffic in the streets will never leave my memory. We watch the news in fear. My parents assure us that we are safe, but I can see the uncertainty in their eyes. The people prevail and Bucaram gets ousted. Political parties and the military fight for control of the government, and in a matter of seven days, Ecuador has three different presidents. Our family's life will never be the same. The economic and political instability leads to mass layoffs. Thousands of people lose their jobs, including Papi. Desperate, he takes on a job as a truck driver transporting roses for less than half the money he was making before. Mami makes linen tablecloths and napkins and walks around the neighborhood, stopping at every restaurant to sell them. Soon we can't afford rent or my school tuition. Our food portions get smaller.

My schooling has always been my parents' top priority, and they do whatever they can to pay that tuition bill. But as the economic situation around us grows tighter, even that becomes impossible. At school, I am shamed for not being able to pay tuition. One day a nun from the financial office wearing a long white robe and a black veil comes into my classroom. She calls out my name along with a few other students' and loudly declares that we can't return to school until our parents pay tuition. All of the other girls watch us get up in silence as this person who was supposed to represent Jesus Christ unapologetically shames a group of children for being poor and threatens to kick us out. I don't know until that moment that my parents are late with tuition payments. As I walk out of the classroom, Mami's words about education being the only path to having a better life haunt me. I feel the walls of my parents' greatest nightmare close in around me and the little light of hope from education being snuffed out.

After the heartbreaking loss of my sister, and the crushing reality that they can no longer provide for their children in Ecuador, my parents grow hopeless and desperate. For their whole lives, they've seen things on TV and have heard that the United States is a country where everyone, regardless of where they came from, can provide for their families and accomplish their dreams. But leaving Ecuador to seek a better life in another country isn't a choice my parents consider. They resist the idea of parting with their home, families, and loved ones. As a child, I imagine that when people live in a place where things are so hard, it's not too difficult to believe that things may be better somewhere else. The grief and unknown danger of leaving become less bad than the guaranteed misery of staying home.

2

THE JOURNEY

(Left to right) Esther (maternal grandmother), Jonathan, Ligia, Cristina, and Fausto (dad) in the classic immigrant picture in front of a luxury car in Manhattan, days after their arrival in New York, 1998
(courtesy of the author, edited by AC Studio)

Love knows no borders.

—Unknown

Papi had visited the US in 1980. He was twenty-five years old, unmarried, and working full-time at a car manufacturing plant. He had always dreamed of visiting New York City. His friends who lived in Brooklyn encouraged him to visit and offered to host him. To get a tourist visa, applicants must provide evidence for the purpose of the trip, the ability to pay all costs, and the intent to leave the US after the visit. Most people who are able to get tourist visas are middle-class or rich. Papi knew it would be hard for someone like him to get a visa, but he gave it a try. He did his best to present himself as worthy of visiting the US. In his application, he included records of his education, employment history, and financials, and the day of the interview at the US embassy, he even brought all the awards he had won at wrestling tournaments in Ecuador and other Latin American countries. Luckily, his visa was approved, and he traveled to New York for a few weeks over the Christmas holidays to experience the famous city he had only seen in movies.

He was captivated by the diversity and Black culture of Flatbush, where he stayed with his friends. The neighborhood was full of tasty foods, loud music in languages he didn't understand, and immigrants from the Caribbean, Latin America, and various African countries. He was amazed by the city—the subway, Central Park, Times Square, the megastores, and the skyscrapers. He proudly talks about the city's abundance, bragging about buying jeans for everyone in his family by the pound and getting Mami, who at the time was his girlfriend, her first puffy jacket. He returned to Ecuador with the dream that one day he would take his family to visit vibrant New York City.

During his visit, he learned about the stories of many immigrants who had left home seeking a better life in the US. He realized not everyone was lucky enough to get on a flight to get to the US. The immigrants he met had fled violence, political unrest, and poverty, or even worse situations, risking their lives crossing multiple borders unlawfully to get to the US; many of them endured rape, drug-cartel violence, and kidnappings. Some of them lost their loved ones on the journey. But it wasn't always this hard to migrate to the US. The US first established visa requirements in 1924 through the racist Johnson-Reed Act. It prioritized visas for people from northern and western Europe, considered the "best" race based on eugenics. To ensure that the demographics of the US remained majority white, the act limited the number of "undesirable" immigrants entering the country—setting up, for the first time, a quota of 150,000 admissions per year for immigrants from southern and eastern Europe, Africa, and the Middle East and banning all Asian immigrants. Basically, if you were Jewish, Catholic, or a person of color, your road to the United States was made more difficult. Chinese immigrants were initially barred when Congress passed the Chinese Exclusion Act of 1882. The Johnson-Reed Act also created the US Border Patrol, as people catchers modeled after the Texas Rangers and "Slave Patrols" that terrorized and dragged Black people back into enslavement, to patrol the US-Mexico border.

Before 1924, people didn't even need a passport, a visa, or a green card to enter the US. There were no limits or quotas. In fact, it was quite easy. The majority of immigrants who arrived at Ellis Island and other major ports of entry were briefly screened, their names were recorded, and that was it. For decades, the US maintained what today would be considered an "open borders" approach to immigration.[1] The adoption of the Johnson-Reed Act was the result of backlash to mass migration from some Asian countries but mostly from Italy, Greece, Russia, and Hungary (some of whose descendants are today waving MAKE AMERICA GREAT AGAIN flags and holding MASS DEPORTATION NOW signs).

Between 1890 and 1924, the country's immigration debate centered on two key points: job competition and eugenic theories. The arguments against newcomers were led by mainstream political and labor leaders like Republican senator Henry Cabot Lodge from Massachusetts, Representative Albert Johnson from Washington, who was an active Ku Klux Klan member, and Samuel Gompers, president of the American Federation of Labor (AFL), as well as scientists and eugenicists who argued that Anglo-Saxons from England were superior.[2] Building on racism and the rise of nativism, the 1924 policy targeted immigrants who were considered "less white," including Jewish immigrants seeking refuge from the Nazis, and Catholic immigrants.

People migrating to the US before World War I would have simply shown up at a US port of entry and walked in. But nearly seventy-five years after the Johnson-Reed Act, immigrants must meet the requirements for one of the following pathways: (a) employment sponsorship based on specific conditions and labor skills; (b) family sponsorships, which, depending on the country of origin and family category, can take more than twenty years; (c) temporary visas, for time-limited purposes, like student or tourist visas; or (d) humanitarian need, like a request for refugee status or asylum. This new approach to immigration was established by the Hart-Celler Act of 1965, which eliminated the racist quotas of the past and instead restricted immigration on the basis of family relationships and labor skills. It was championed by second-generation immigrants from eastern and southern Europe, especially those from Jewish and Catholic backgrounds, who advocated for an end to the discriminatory quotas and for their own families to have an easier way in. The law was regarded as a major progressive victory, but with the Hart-Celler Act, the immigration system now had, for the first time, limits to the number of people who could migrate from Mexico, the Caribbean, and Latin America, as well as overall caps on migration numbers. I sometimes wonder what the legislation would have looked like if there had been people like me in the room where the deals were cut. The policy caps entry at 290,000 people per year, with no more than 20,000 people arriving from any single country. The quotas, of course, have nothing to do with the reality of life along the US-Mexico border or the realities of the deep ties between the US and countries to the south. In the 1960s, immigration from Mexico alone comprised approximately an average of 200,000 workers per year as part of the Bracero Program, so the new quota turned thousands of Mexican workers into "illegal immigrants." The law created long waiting periods for people from countries with a high number of immigrants to reunify with family members already in the US. Countries like Mexico and India reach their visa admissions cap quickly every year, making the wait time for families from these countries between ten and thirty years, even when the family sponsor is a US citizen. Meanwhile, immigrants from many European countries generally have no waiting period for family reunification. It's the legislative version of "we got ours; now, you stay out."

When immigrants or refugees can't enter the country through family ties, employment, or on humanitarian grounds, realistically, the only other alternative to enter and stay in the US is unlawfully. Most people who are fleeing poverty, persecution, climate disaster, and violence have no option but to make the long and dangerous journey across land and seas to reach the US-Mexico border. In 2021, in response to the increasing number of people from Central America, Haiti, and other Caribbean countries seeking asylum, Vice President Kamala Harris, the first Black woman and child of immigrants to become vice president of the United States, hosted a press conference in Guatemala and told people, "Do not come. Do not come."[3] As if the people fleeing cartel violence and deep poverty have a choice. Her message couldn't be more out of touch from the human reality and the factors that force people to flee their homes. This rhetoric shames and criminalizes people for seeking refuge, while papering over the role of the US in creating the conditions that force people to migrate in the first place.

US intervention and economic and trade policies are common

causes of migration in Latin America and the Caribbean. To take just one example, the US invaded Haiti in 1915 and occupied the country for nineteen years, executing Haitians opposed to the occupation, taking natural resources for US interests, and rewriting the country's laws to allow foreigners to purchase land.[4] Smedley Butler, a former general in the US Marine Corps and leader of the American force in Haiti, wrote in 1935, "I helped make Haiti and Cuba a decent place for the National City Bank boys to collect revenues in. I helped in the raping of half a dozen Central American republics for the benefits of Wall Street."[5] The US occupation of Haiti ended in 1934, but its legacy includes government corruption, political instability, crumbling infrastructure, and poverty, all of which have worsened with the impact of natural disasters.

Increasingly, climate change has also become a dominant factor, domestically and globally, in forcing people to leave their homes. And the US bears significant responsibility as one of the world's largest contributors to global climate change. In 2020 alone, Central America was hit by thirty cyclones that destroyed entire parts of the region. In Honduras, Hurricanes Eta and Iota left more than 250,000 people without access to water, electricity, or healthcare. Entire villages were destroyed.[6] In Guatemala, the hurricanes forced Indigenous families whose farmlands were devasted to flee. Alba Juárez Méndez left her village of Sóchel in the province of San Marcos where she grew potatoes, beans, and corn for a living. The village no longer had access to fresh water after the hurricanes. She took the risk of walking and hitchhiking with her two-year-old daughter, Yareli, to seek asylum in the US and reunite with her uncle in Tennessee. When they reached Ciudad Juárez, Mexico, authorities didn't let them pass to the US side of the border and told her they didn't have space for her and her daughter in any of the eighteen shelters in the area.[7]

Throughout our country's history, immigrants in desperate situations have found alternative ways to enter the US. Immigrants like Jewish composer Irving Berlin and his family—escaping tsarist Russia and a pogrom that destroyed his village—used false passports to enter the US.[8] Donald Trump's son-in-law Jared Kushner comes from a family that crossed multiple European borders unlawfully, lied about their country of origin, and falsely listed a sponsor in the US to get around visa limits in the 1930s.[9] Post–World War II, the parents of Allan Gerson, an international lawyer widely recognized as the first American attorney to successfully sue a foreign government for complicity in acts of terrorism, bought another family's last name in the underground market and made it to New York in December of 1950, desperately fleeing refugee-camp conditions and anti-Semitism after surviving the Holocaust.[10] There are millions of stories of Americans whose families entered the country unlawfully. On the PBS series *Finding Your Roots*, celebrities often discover shocking truths about their family's immigration stories. In one episode, former *CBS Evening News* anchor Norah O'Donnell finds out that her Irish grandfather was undocumented and entered the country by crossing the Canadian border unlawfully in 1924.

The big difference between then and now is that our current immigration laws criminalize immigrants who are fleeing poverty, climate crises, state violence, and persecution. Today, immigrants and refugees who are mostly people of color arriving at our borders are arrested, incarcerated, separated from their families, and deported, or even die, in detention facilities. In 2018, Trump heartlessly separated more than five thousand refugee children from their parents at the US-Mexico border and put children in actual cages. And under Joe Biden's administration in 2021, US Border Patrol agents on horseback violently blocked Haitian refugees from entering the US, forcing them back into Mexico and denying them the right to seek asylum.

In stark contrast, European immigrants who entered the country unlawfully or were undocumented in the nineteenth and early years of the twentieth century were protected from deportation and given amnesty. These immigrants, predominantly white, were permitted to work and faced no restrictions to access public benefits like unemployment and cash assistance. In fact, hiring an undocumented worker only became unlawful in 1986, while policies to allow the deportations of parents of US citizen children and restrictions on public benefits were established in the 1970s. Yet, hypocritically, many white politicians have argued that their ancestors came to the US "legally" or the "right way" while changing the rules to make it more and more difficult for subsequent generations of immigrants to do the same.

Against all odds and despite dangerous risks, migrants and refugees do what I and anyone would do for love. Love for our families. Love for life. Leaving one's country, family, and home behind is often the last resort to protect and save the lives of loved ones. Migration is not a criminal act but an act of love and bravery. Migrants and refugees are true heroes. My parents' love for my brother and me knows no bounds, and they join the millions of migrants and refugee heroes that take great risks for their children and families to have a chance at a better life.

We land in New York City's LaGuardia Airport in the summer of 1998. Our bodies can feel the big difference in elevation, from 9,350 feet in Quito to just 33 feet above sea level in New York City. The humidity is suffocating. My swollen feet are trapped in my brown booties. I can't wait to take them off! I am disappointed to see no skyscrapers—only houses and brick apartment buildings. I wonder if we are in the right place. Is this the same city I had seen in *King Kong*? The walk between the gate and baggage claim feels like it takes forever. People are rushing through the corridor, almost stepping over me. *Are Americans always rushing?* I wonder. I can see Mami's eyes filling up with tears in anticipation of reuniting with her sisters. Tía Rosita has been living in the US for about a decade and Tía Sarita for nearly two years. Our family waits for us in the baggage claim area, and as we round the corner, we hear them: "Hermana!" my tías shout, waving. The three sisters embrace, shedding tears of joy and grief for their reunion and the time that has been lost. I'm excited to see my cousins again and join our family to celebrate my cousin Anita's quinceañera. I didn't know that this humid summer afternoon would mark the beginning of our new life.

3

HOW TO BE A "GOOD" IMMIGRANT

(Left to right) Cristina, Jonathan (Cristina's brother), and her cousins Jorgito (back row), Henry (front row), and Anita in front of South Street Seaport, New York, 2000 (courtesy of the author, edited by AC Studio)

You broke the ocean in half to be here. Only to meet nothing that wants you.

—Nayyirah Waheed

We have our first meal in the US at my aunt's one-bedroom apartment a few miles away from LaGuardia Airport. My tías live in Elmhurst, Queens, a neighborhood of Italian and Jewish immigrants in the first two-thirds of the twentieth century that became predominantly the home of people from China and Latin America after quotas were removed in 1965, opening the door to non-European migration. The neighborhood is multiracial and multiethnic. The streets bustle with people from all backgrounds, some wearing turbans and veils, coming in and out of shops with signs in Spanish and languages I don't recognize, like Bengali. My aunts' neighbors are immigrants from India, Pakistan, China, Colombia, the Dominican Republic, and other parts of Latin America. The thirteen-year-old in me is surprised to realize that there are no "Americans" where my tías live. The people in Elmhurst look nothing like the white, tall, blond Americans I had seen on dubbed sitcoms like *The Golden Girls* and *Full House*.

For our welcoming dinner, Tía Sarita makes cariucho, an Ecuadorian dish commonly made for fiestas. The dish includes potatoes, lettuce leaves, a peanut sauce, sautéed chicken, avocado, and sliced tomatoes. But Tía's apartment doesn't smell anything like Ecuadorian food. Instead, the smell of curry and spices from her neighbors envelops the whole place. "We've gotten used to it! This is what it's like to live in New York City," Tía says with a smile on her face.

Eleven of us—Tía Sarita; her husband, Tío Francisco; their two children, Anita and Jorgito; Tío's mother, Polita; Tía Rosita and her son, Henry; and my brother, parents, and I—cram around a table meant for six. Standing, we hold hands tightly to say grace before our welcoming meal. Tía Rosita, who has become a devout evangelical Christian in the US, leads us in prayer. She praises God for our safe arrival and gives thanks for our food and the blessing of being together as a family after so many years. "El pueblo de Dios dice, 'A comer!'" she says joyfully, clapping her hands together. While we eat, the adults share stories of how they have survived in this country.

Tía Sarita shows us her hands covered with rashes and cracks caused by the chemicals she is exposed to at the jewelry factory where she works in New York City's diamond district in Midtown Manhattan. The skin from her fingers peels off as if she had spent hours under the sun. "My hands are itchy and in pain all the time, but at least I have a job," Tía says. She proudly talks about how her factory job enables her to pay bills and support her siblings and abuelita back home. In Ecuador, Tía Sarita was a stay-at-home mom. Her work raising her children and keeping up the house was not culturally valued or recognized. Having a job, despite the working conditions, makes her feel seen and empowered. After paying bills and sending money to support family in Ecuador, she spends the bit of cash left shopping for clothes for everyone in the family at the Queens Center mall, which is two blocks away from her building. When she is not working, cooking, or cleaning, she is at the mall. She becomes a master at getting the best deals and sales. With joy, she shows us her recent find from JCPenney—black dressy pants for ten dollars!

Polita, Tío Francisco's mom and the matriarch of the family, is a domestic worker. She has a green card and works for a well-off family in Manhattan. Polita came to the US in the '80s seeking a better life after struggling to make a living as a single mother in Ecuador. She left behind her only child, Tío Francisco, and sent money for his education. Polita lived in the country undocumented, in constant fear of deportation, only leaving her home for work. She didn't trust anyone. She avoided making friends and letting anyone know where she worked or where she lived. She tells us of a day when she and her sister, Maria, who was also undocumented at the time, were walking to work and heard immigrants shouting, "La migra! La migra!" while running to hide. They ran as fast as they could, reaching the apartment building where they worked and hiding in a closet. They dodged la migra that day. "Gracias a Diosito," she says, looking up to the ceiling.

Those years of living in fear and in the shadows came to an

end when President Ronald Reagan and Congress passed the Immigration Reform and Control Act (IRCA) in 1986. IRCA expanded the criminalization of immigrants in exchange for a pathway to citizenship for some undocumented workers and longtime residents. The law called for a 50 percent increase in Border Patrol staffing and imposed sanctions on employers that hired undocumented people, while legalizing some agricultural workers who had worked in the country for at least ninety days, and immigrants without lawful immigration status living in the United States since 1982. IRCA also changed the registry date from the Registry Act of 1929 from June 30, 1948, to January 1, 1972, allowing people that entered the country before 1972 to adjust their immigration status as well. Polita became one of 2.7 million immigrants who got lawful immigration status under IRCA.

Polita is sixty-nine years old when we arrive. She has difficulty walking due to arthritis. Yet she is on her feet more than eight hours a day cooking and cleaning. Retirement is not even on her mind. This country has taken her health, physical strength, and the best of her working years, but she feels deep gratitude. "I'm thankful for all that this country has given me," she tells us. She talks about how working in the US allowed her to help her only child, Tío Francisco, to attend school in Ecuador. Under immigration law, Polita is not eligible to petition for her son. Green card holders cannot petition children who are over twenty-one years of age and married. If she becomes a US citizen, she could petition for Tío. But because Tío Francisco and his family have been undocumented in the country for more than a year, petitioning for him means he and his family would be subject to a penalty ten-year bar from entering the US established by the

Illegal Immigration Reform and Immigrant Responsibility Act (IIRIRA) passed by President Bill Clinton in 1996, which exponentially increased the criminalization of immigrants, this time without new pathways for longtime residents.

A ten-year bar applies to immigrants who have been in the country unlawfully for one year or more, making them ineligible to adjust their immigration status. To become eligible to be petitioned by Polita when she becomes a US citizen, they would have to leave the country and face a bar from returning for ten years. The only way to avoid a ten-year immigration bar is through a separate waiver or pardon, which, at the time, a lawyer tells them they are not eligible for. Even if the waiver was an option for Tío Francisco's family, a decision to approve or deny it would only be made after an interview at a US consulate abroad, without any guarantee that they would be approved and allowed back in the US. Plus, the approval process for a US citizen parent petitioning for a married child can take between twelve and fourteen years due to the annual cap on visas. The immigration system leaves them with no real option but to remain undocumented to keep their family together in the US.

"Es duro. No es fácil," Tía Rosita says.

"Así es este país," Tía Sarita agrees.

Polita wants to apply for naturalization but hasn't yet. She is afraid of failing the English and civics tests required to be granted US citizenship. But she is enthusiastic about studying, charging her grandchildren, my cousins Anita and Jorgito, with helping her. "You will help me, right?" she asks them. They nod in agreement with the reverence we are taught to give to our elders. I'm in awe of Polita's courage, perseverance, and resilience.

I am devastated to learn about how difficult it is for Tío Francisco and his family to get immigration papers. I never thought US immigration laws would be this difficult, arbitrary, and unjust. I worry about the future of my family in this country. Without a US citizen family member who can petition for my parents, I feel pessimistic and overwhelmed at the outlook for my family to one day have a green card. When I'm in college and become an organizer, I will learn that IIRIRA also enacted immigration bars for people who entered the country unlawfully. If not for IIRIRA, 5.3 million undocumented immigrants, nearly half of the total undocumented population, would have authorization to live here.[11] Our immigration system, by design, has created millions of undocumented immigrants. Today there are 11.2 million undocumented people in the country, most of whom have lived here at least ten years.[12]

Tía Rosita shares a heartbreaking story of the night she and her husband, Tío Henry, were forced out of the apartment with their newborn, my cousin Henry, the only member of our family born in the US. They were renting a room in Elmhurst, in a building near the hospital, from another immigrant who had lived in the apartment for a long time. They didn't know that the man they sublet from had been in a back-and-forth with the landlord in the courts and received a court notice of eviction. On a rainy night, they were shocked by a marshal who showed up at the door and forced them and their newborn out of the apartment. They couldn't even grab their belongings. They reached out to a friend for help and were able to share a one-bedroom apartment with their friend's family for a while until they could save enough money to rent a place of their own. This country is tough—that's the way it is. But my family doesn't lose hope. They have faith in God and the promise of this country. "We are good people. We have come here to work and provide our families with a better life. God will guide those in government to do what's right," they say.

In the months to come, my tías and tíos would also share

practical advice about how to navigate this country: Work hard. Don't bring attention to yourself. Keep your head down and don't make any demands. Be thankful for what you get. Follow the law and stay out of trouble. Avoid encounters with the police because they can lead to deportation. Learn English and pay taxes. They tell us that even if you are undocumented, you can pay taxes. All you have to do is apply for a tax identification number with the Internal Revenue Service (IRS). Paying taxes is the law, and if you are ever caught by immigration authorities, it will help you show that you are a "good" immigrant. Not like one of the immigrants featured in the news. Those who Lou Dobbs talks about on CNN while repeatedly playing the same footage of brown men running across the US-Mexico border.

I am confused. I don't understand how undocumented immigrants are supposed to hide from the government but, at the same time, present ourselves to a government agency to get a tax identification number to pay taxes. *It must be how this country works*, I think. In my teenage mind, my takeaway from the many conversations we have with our family is that we must strive to do all we can to prove to this country and its institutions that we are worthy of living here. As the oldest daughter, I feel the weight of the responsibility to help my parents follow all this advice. We will do everything to show that we are "good" immigrants. For my part, I'm eager to learn English and do well in school. I will learn, however, from painful experience, that no matter how hard we work or how "good" we are, this country considers all of us immigrants of color "bad."

We live with Tía Sarita and her family. The one-bedroom apartment is tight for nine people, but we make it work. The living room is divided in half by a tall china closet, creating a sleeping area for my tía and tío, and a small space with a TV and two couches. The rest of us sleep in the bedroom on twin-size beds and foldable mattresses. I share one of the two twin-size beds by the window with my cousin Anita. Polita sleeps in the other twin-size bed opposite to ours. My parents, brother, and my cousin Jorgito sleep on foldable mattresses on the floor. We all share one bathroom. My cousins and I usually have to hold our pee for a while; often competing for the bathroom, running as if we were running for our lives. I start learning English with my cousins, watching TV and listening to that summer's top hits. We watch *Armageddon*, singing along to "I Don't Want to Miss a Thing." We get the song's lyrics, and I begin looking up the words' pronunciations and meanings in an English-Spanish dictionary. I do the same with "The Boy Is Mine" by Brandy and Monica, "Doo Wop (That Thing)" by Lauryn Hill, "Everybody" by the Backstreet Boys, and "Hypnotize" by the Notorious B.I.G.

At night, Jorgito and I bond playing the *Mortal Kombat* video series with the lights off and no sound while everyone is sleeping. We turn the TV slightly toward the kitchen so the light won't disturb Tío's and Tía's sleep. When one of us reaches a fatality, a deadly move that finishes our opponent, we celebrate in silence, jumping up and down with our eyes wide open and our mouths shut. We barely get any sleep. Tía Sarita is usually up before six in the morning and uses the bathroom first. She then turns on the TV to watch *Despierta América*—the Spanish equivalent of ABC's *Good Morning America*—on Univision while she gets ready to go to work. The show's theme song becomes our morning alarm.

We feel lucky and blessed for what we have. We hope to one day rent our own place, but as newly arrived immigrants who are also undocumented, it is difficult, if not impossible. To rent an apartment, my parents need to first find a job, save money for several months for rent and a deposit, which is two months' rent, and find someone with immigration papers who would have a good credit history to apply and be listed on the lease. As undocumented immigrants, my parents don't have immigration papers or a credit history. But there is a way that other undocumented immigrants rent apartments in my tías' building. The superintendent is known for figuring out ways to rent apartments to families like mine. He charges families based on the number of people and the size of the apartment. An immigrant from Eastern Europe in his fifties, the super tells my parents he can help them for $700. At the time, a studio apartment in the building rents for about $800 per month. This means that in addition to continuing to cover daily living expenses, my parents need to save for three months of rent, two of which are for the deposit, plus the fee from the super to help us—a total of $3,100. Saving that much money feels like an impossible task, but my parents don't lose hope.

For weeks Papi walks along commercial streets in Midtown Manhattan and Queens looking for jobs. One day, after walking for a few hours and drenched in sweat from the heat, he approaches Latine immigrant workers at a car wash on Queens Boulevard and asks them if they need help. One of the workers tells him his boss is looking for help and takes him inside the shop. The owner of the car wash is an Italian American man in his forties. He tells Papi he needs him to start right away—he would get paid five dollars an hour, work Wednesday to Sunday, and get to keep the tips of the day, which are equally divided among all the workers on his shift. He would be paid every week in cash. No benefits. Papi returns home with a big smile on his face—he has gotten his first job in the US! We welcome the news with joy and hope this job will be the beginning of a better life in this country. Papi has never worked at a car wash before but is eager to perform above and beyond to show his worth.

Washing and drying cars under the burning sun and in the

humidity of the summer requires a great deal of physical stamina and effort. Papi comes home exhausted, with sunburns on his arms, face, and neck. A few weeks after he starts, his employer stops paying him and other undocumented workers without explanation. Papi asks me to speak to the car wash owner about his wages because his English isn't fluid. As a fourteen-year-old, I am terrified to talk to Papi's boss. We practice my speech. But practicing doesn't take away the fear of what could happen to us. Will the car wash owner call the police? Will he call immigration on us and the other workers? Will he fire Papi? My mind is racing with the potential scenarios. My hands shake as I hold the phone close to my ear. With a trembling voice, I ask his boss when he will pay Papi and the other workers. I anxiously wait for his response. Papi is pacing fearfully across the room. The owner says he won't pay them. "They're illegals. If they don't like it, they can leave," he says without remorse. I hang up crying, feeling powerless and in despair. I can't do anything to get Papi paid and hold his boss accountable. Reaching out to any government institution to file a complaint or ask for help could bring attention to us and get us deported. "I must find another job," Papi says.

I will learn that Papi's experience is not an isolated incident. Our country's laws, institutions, and systems enable the exploitation and criminalization of undocumented workers. In 2008, Josue Diaz, along with other undocumented workers in Texas, was part of the cleanup and rebuilding efforts after Hurricanes Gustav and Ike. Josue and his coworkers filed a complaint against their employer for discriminatory pay and hazardous working conditions. In retaliation, the employer reported them to local police and Immigration and Customs Enforcement (ICE). ICE arrested Josue and his coworkers and ordered their deportation.[13] Undocumented workers like Josue make up 5 percent of the country's workforce—about eight million workers—but they are overrepresented in certain industries, making up half of the country's farmworkers, 15 percent of workers in the construction industry, and 9 percent of workers in the food and services industry.[14] Abuse and retaliation against these workers are the norm. A landmark study of 4,387 workers by the National Employment Law Project found that 60 percent of undocumented workers do not get paid minimum wage, 76 percent are not paid overtime wages they are legally entitled to, and 43 percent experience one or more forms of illegal retaliation from their employer, like the threat of getting their hours or pay cut and being reported to immigration authorities.[15]

While Papi looks for another job, Mami and I prepare to register me in school. We fear the school may ask about our immigration status, but Tía Sarita walks us through how she registered my cousins and tells us that disclosing one's immigration status is not required to attend school. Relieved, we put together all the paperwork needed for the registration: my birth certificate translated into English, passport, vaccination record, the last report card from my school in Ecuador, and our home address. Although Tía tells us it is safe to show up to school for registration, we are still anxious and intimidated. This is our first interaction with a government institution in the US. We are afraid of not understanding what the school staff may tell us in English. Will we be looked down upon for not speaking the language? To our relief, Tío Henry, the only adult in the family who speaks English fluently, offers to come with Mami and me to the school.

The beige brick school is huge, occupying the entire block between Forty-Eighth and Fiftieth Avenues on Ninetieth Street. The top of the building resembles a church with stepped gables and a green tower. Big letters on the front entrance proclaim NEWTOWN HIGH SCHOOL. As we get closer to the entrance, I realize the building looks like a jail, with a run-down facade and bars on the windows. There are no green spaces or recreational areas. In Ecuador, our school had a playground, basketball courts, and green spaces for students to play during lunchtime. I wonder where students in Newtown have a place to play.

I'm shocked to be met by two security officers in police uniform at the entrance of the building. But Tío does not seem afraid. As if he is used to seeing security officers in schools, he approaches one of them and asks him in English about where we need to go for registration. Mami and I stand behind him. The officer directs us to the school's library on the second floor. My heart is racing as we walk up the stairs; I wonder why there are security officers in the school and worry about something going wrong and being denied registration. This is part of the immigrant journey and trauma—you are never fully certain of something until it happens.

We receive a warm welcome from two teachers who are guiding families through the process. One is a white woman in her forties with long blond hair, and the other is a young Asian American woman with short black hair. I am surprised and relieved that they speak fluent Spanish. They patiently walk us through the forms we need to fill out. Their kindness makes me feel more at ease. I begin to pay more attention to my surroundings, and with curiosity I examine the bookcases and library sections around us. The smell of old books calms me. I begin envisioning myself as a student spending time in this library.

Part of the registration process includes taking math and English tests to assess my proficiency level. I am placed in the entry level for the school's English as a second language (ESL) program and in tenth- instead of ninth-grade-level math because I can solve equations. The white teacher compliments Mami: "Your daughter is so good with math," she says. Mami smiles with confusion. She doesn't understand what the teacher says.

Tío Henry interprets for Mami, and both say thank you with pride. I am astonished to be placed at a higher level of math. I had always struggled with math in Ecuador, especially with division, and over the years had grown to dislike the subject and feel deeply insecure about my math skills. I am far better at history than math, but in that moment, I am cheered by the teacher's compliment and overjoyed that I made Mami proud. The only step of the process we can't complete that day is the verification of my vaccines. The teachers tell us we need to go to a government-run clinic located in Jackson Heights. New York's health department must verify my vaccination record and provide any additional vaccines before we complete the registration process. We leave the school feeling accomplished. I am one step away from becoming a registered student at Newtown High School.

A few days later, Mami and I go to the clinic in Jackson Heights. This time, Tío Henry can't come with us, so we are on our own. I struggle with the same fears and anxieties I felt when we went to Newtown. But Mami looks at me with fierce determination and confidence. She reminds me that just like in the school, we may find people that speak Spanish. "I'll figure out a way for the staff at the clinic to understand what we need," Mami says. Her courage and determination constantly help me ease into these intimidating situations.

The clinic is in an old building at the intersection of Thirty-Fourth Avenue and Junction Boulevard. Jackson Heights looks a lot like Elmhurst. The neighborhood is busy, with all kinds of immigrants in the streets. Junction Boulevard is a vibrant commercial area, with many shops, immigrant food street vendors, and hair salons blasting merengue and salsa in the background. When we enter the building, we are struck by how deteriorated it looks. The paint on the stairs and walls is fading, the elevator is out of service, and some of the doors have no knobs. In the lobby, there are signs in English and Spanish directing people to the second floor for vaccinations. There, a nurse welcomes us in Spanish and brings us to a smaller room, where a doctor asks us to take a seat. The doctor speaks Spanish too! She tells us she is from Puerto Rico. Mami and I heave a sigh of relief. The doctor carefully reviews my vaccination record from Ecuador. She tells us I need a few boosters and a tuberculosis test. She warns us that most people from Latin America test positive for tuberculosis because the vaccine, which is administered to all children in Latin America, contains bacteria closely related to tuberculosis. If I test positive, which I do, I will need to take medication for a couple of months provided by the clinic and show the school a blue card signed by the doctor confirming this.

The last step of the registration process is completed! Mami and I walk out of the building feeling accomplished and a little more confident in our ability to navigate our new home. My new vaccination record is a small foldable yellow card with stamps from New York State's health department. This is my first official document issued by a government agency in the US. I hold it with pride. Despite knowing we aren't allowed to live in this country, the fourteen-year-old in me feels officially recognized by my new home's government. And it feels good.

After a few months of living in the US, I'm getting ready to start high school. I am nervous about what awaits me. Will all my teachers be like the ones I met during registration? Will I make friends easily? Will I be made fun of for not speaking English? I'm anxious, but I remind myself that my cousin Anita attends the same school, and if I need anything, I can reach out to her. I also struggle with feelings of inferiority. I feel ashamed for not looking "American," not speaking English, and not having immigration papers. Growing up in Ecuador, I was taught that white skin and European features like blond hair and blue eyes are better—and more beautiful. My darker skin, straight black hair, and slanted eyes are undesirable. As a child, I heard adults around me say that marrying a white person would "better our race," as if we were flawed. The idea that Europeans, who violently colonized Ecuador and Latin America, are better than us is part of the legacy of colonialism. This idea is embedded in the country's culture and legitimized by its laws, systems, and institutions. In a country where Indigenous people make up close to 30 percent of the population and Afro-Ecuadorians constitute 7.2 percent, I experienced and witnessed how the social hierarchy favors white and light-skinned people and treats Indigenous and Black people as inferior.

I don't believe the adults around me understood they were teaching us to feel less than. They simply passed on what they had learned from their parents and their parents' parents. I hold compassion for them and for us. Because what spaces and support do they have to process and heal the generational pain and trauma of Indigenous ancestors who were killed and raped? In Ecuador, I learned in school that Christopher Columbus is a hero, deserving of celebration and praise for discovering the Americas and opening the way for the Spanish to colonize the region and Indigenous people. That the Spanish committed genocide and stole Indigenous people's land wasn't the focus of history lessons. The underlying message was that we were better off as a colonized people. I internalized the lie that I'm inferior. Now in the US, feeling like an unwanted guest, I come to believe that we must be exemplary immigrants to protect ourselves and survive in this country. For some immigrants this survival mechanism often means assimilation—getting as close as possible to whiteness and shedding one's culture, identity, and language.

To say that starting high school in the US is a culture shock for me is an understatement. In Ecuador, my Catholic girls' school taught me to fear God, teachers, and nuns. Teachers and nuns followed our every move and were strict about everything: the way we wore our uniforms, the way we walked, and the way we talked. Every day my uniform—a blue pleated skirt and white blouse—needed to be well ironed and impeccable. The skirt had to sit four fingers below my knee to not bring attention to my legs, and my black leather shoes needed to shine in the light and in the dark. We were punished for asking a "wrong question." I had a hard time learning math. During one lesson, I asked my teacher for help solving a division problem. Instead of helping me, she called me dumb while hitting me on the head with a piece of white chalk. Breaking the rules is considered an offense to God—a sin. I am shy, self-conscious, and very fearful of committing sins.

The first day of school I wait for what feels like an eternity to take a shower. Polita takes longer than usual in the bathroom, and I'm late. I rush out of my aunt's apartment with my hair still wet. I imagine high school to be like the sitcom *Saved by the Bell*, which I watched religiously in Ecuador. In the sitcom, students, who are mostly white, have the freedom to wear whatever they like instead of uniforms, have fun in school dance contests, and enjoy spacious red lockers where they keep their books, supplies, and even a change of clothes. But Newtown High School has little in common with *Saved by the Bell*'s Bayside High School. At the time, Newtown is one of New York City's most ethnically diverse schools, with immigrant students from more than seventy countries. It is also one of the most overcrowded in the city, with more than 4,000 students in a building intended to serve 2,600. In 1994, four years before I attended Newtown, the *New York Times* reported that the school's level of violence was about average, with over twenty serious incidents during the 1992–1993 school year, including robberies, assaults, and weapon confiscations.[16]

Many of the students come from LeFrak City, a large apartment complex sprawling across the neighborhoods of Elmhurst, Corona, and Rego Park. Built in the 1960s, LeFrak City was initially home to predominantly middle-class white families, but in the 1970s, white families fled the complex when more Black people and immigrants moved in after a federal housing-discrimination suit forced LeFrak's owner and management to stop denying housing to African Americans. In the late '90s when we come to the US, LeFrak is home to predominantly poor and working-class Jewish immigrants from the former Soviet Union and African and Muslim immigrants. We live a few blocks from LeFrak, where there are always police cars driving around and officers patrolling the streets. We stay away to avoid any encounters with the cops.

My parents, tías, and tíos have no idea that my cousins and I, along with hundreds of other immigrant students of color, are zoned to an overcrowded school where police presence, metal detectors, violence, drugs, and gangs are the norm. They believe US schools are the best in the world and have high hopes of their children having access to an American education. But as newly arrived immigrants, we don't know that the neighborhood we can afford to live in determines the safety, funding, and quality of the public schools we have access to. Nationally, the poorest school districts in the country are those serving Black, brown, immigrant, and other students of color. Nonwhite school districts get $23 billion less in funding every year compared to majority-white school districts.[17] In an immigrant neighborhood like Elmhurst, the schools are poorly funded, all struggling to manage more students than they have the capacity to serve, with few parks or green spaces for children and young people to play in.

I run to school as fast as I can but I am still twenty minutes late. My first class is gym, which is held in a field six blocks away from school by the Queens Center mall. I'm drenched in sweat. I don't know that students change into their gym clothes in front of one another in the locker room. I can't imagine doing that. For the nuns, this would be a sin, I think. It feels terrifying for parts of my body to be exposed to complete strangers. I look for a bathroom to change into my gym clothes and an old pair of sneakers I'd use for gym class. I leave my belongings in one of the lockers. I'm comforted to see that most of the students look just like me. Students at Newtown come from all over the world, mostly from Latin America, the Caribbean, and Asia. They speak multiple languages—Urdu, Cantonese, Spanish, English, and what I come to know later as Spanglish. The gym teacher checks my name on a list and gives me the option to walk or run around the track. Is that it? I expect a gym class with more instruction, but this is easy, I think.

I walk by myself for the remaining thirty minutes of class. Back in the locker room, I find my locker swung open and the new sneakers that my parents bought me for school gone. I'm in disbelief. A girl with dark-brown lipstick approaches me and whispers in my ear, "Esto le pasa a las 'freshman.'"

"What's a freshman?" I ask.

She rolls her eyes. I ask her to help me speak to the teacher, a short white woman. At first, the teacher is dismissive, but then she makes an announcement asking students if they've seen my shoes. Most of them ignore her, pack their bags, and start heading out of the locker room. The teacher explains this happens often and advises me to use a combination lock moving forward. I've never seen a combination lock, but I take note. I feel powerless and heartbroken. All I keep thinking about is how hard my parents worked to get me those sneakers at Payless. Getting my sneakers stolen is the first of many experiences at Newtown that make me feel unsafe and marks the beginning of building my New York City tough skin and street smarts.

As I walk to the school building for my next class, I am shocked to see lots of cops patrolling the school and its surroundings. I don't remember any cops on *Saved by the Bell*. The cops look at us, the students, as if we are doing something wrong simply by walking along. They treat us all as suspects. Over time, I witness cops stopping young Black and brown students for no reason and searching them while their hands are up. I don't feel safe around school security officers or the cops. I avoid any interaction with them because I'm afraid that they may ask me about my immigration status. I try not to call any attention to myself. I'm shy, and stay low. I fear deportation and students making fun of my accent.

I'm also afraid of the gangs. Every time I go to the bathroom on the second floor, I find girls with big hoop earrings, thick black eyeliner, and dark lipstick doing their makeup. While I'm in the stall, they try to recruit me to join their gang. I beg them to leave me alone. They are persistent, so I start avoiding the bathrooms on the second floor, opting for the bathrooms in the basement. The gangs in the bathroom try to recruit my cousin Anita too. One of the girls tells my cousin that a gang leader likes her. She proposes setting up a time for Anita to meet him and promises her the gang will protect her and be like her family. Anita is afraid and refuses, but the girl threatens her. "You will be jumped by the gang in the morning if you don't meet him," she tells Anita. For the rest of the week, Tía Sarita walks Anita to school. They both fear the worst, but Tía is determined to protect her daughter. Reaching out to the police for help is not really an option. They could report our whole family to immigration and all of us could be deported. The police are not here to protect people like us. We never find out what happened, but the gang members never attack Anita that week and the girls stop talking to her. In a school where there is more police presence than social workers, we don't have access to support or mental health resources. Tía Sarita and Anita don't have anyone to talk to about what happened. We don't talk about it among ourselves either. We accept that this is how school must be in the US.

Over time, Anita and I get to know some of the girls from the gangs. We realize they are young women like us, immigrants or children of immigrants, looking for friends, seeking belonging and love, and holding on to dreams of a better life. In the absence of loving blood family members, some of them are looking for chosen family. The gangs become their community and family, and where they find belonging. One of the girls shares her dream of making enough money one day to stay at least one night at the famous Plaza Hotel. I haven't seen the hotel in person, but I remember seeing it in the movie *Home Alone 2*. Years later, when we are in our thirties, Anita and I will remember the bathrooms and the gangs and laugh. Laughter is our coping mechanism.

"How did we make it?" I ask her.

"I don't know, man, but we did," she says. We are both in awe of our resilience and the courage of our parents.

During lunchtime, fights frequently break out. Sometimes students end up stabbed. One day, I walk to earth science class and pass a puddle of blood in the hallway while security officers are closing off the area with yellow caution tape. One of them stares at me. I look down at my shoes, avoiding eye contact. School security officers are dressed in navy blue uniforms with gold-plated badges bearing their last name, just like the cops outside of school. For me, they are the same. After the 1999 Columbine school shooting, Congress approved the funding of full-time police officers in schools, known as school resource officers. They are present in 80 percent of high schools with more than a thousand students.[18]

Despite their title, the job of school resource officers is to charge students with crimes, not to provide resources and support. High schools with large numbers of Black and Latine students are more likely to have these officers than schools where most of the student population is white. More than twenty years after the Columbine shooting, police presence in high schools has not prevented shootings.

I avoid the lunchroom for fear of being in the middle of fights, and instead I go to the library for lunch. The library becomes my shelter. I also stay away from students who smoke pot because the simple act of smoking weed or getting caught with people who have it could lead to interactions with the police and therefore deportation. This, of course, is after I learn what pot is and how it looks. The first time I see it, I don't even know what it is. I'm walking to class and a short, skinny Dominican student whose nickname is Shorty approaches me in the hallway. Students make fun of him because he looks more like a kid from middle school than a high schooler, but he is unbothered by the bullying. I never get to find out his real name, but I like Shorty. He is friendly and funny, always cracking jokes in Spanglish with a big smile on his face. I also like the way he dresses. He looks straight out of a '90s hip-hop music video, wearing a black North Face puffy jacket, baggy jeans, and Timbs that look brand-new. Shorty tells me that he has something special for me, showing me a small plastic bag with what I think looks like oregano—the oregano that Mami uses for soups and salads at home. I give him a strange look and ask him why he brings oregano to school. He looks at me in disbelief and walks away. I am confused. When I share this story with my cousins, they explain that he was offering me weed. We all just crack up.

Later, when I am in my early twenties, police violence will hit home. In 2006, when my brother, Jonathan, is just twelve years old, a police officer assaults him on the street as he walks home from school because he is a young brown man and therefore suspicious. Jonathan's transition to this country isn't easy either. When we arrive, he is a talkative and playful four-year-old. He asks why about all things. Once, he almost approaches a Sikh Indian man wearing a turban in the street because he thinks he is a genie—like the one from the Disney movie *Aladdin*. His first few months in school are challenging because he doesn't speak English. He feels self-conscious and intimidated. Jonathan becomes a very shy boy. After the cop shoves him against the wall of an apartment building while violently searching him and pressing on his neck, suffocating him, Jonathan comes home in tears, distraught and traumatized. Mami is outraged. Like many people, she believes that the police are supposed to keep communities safe. But that day she is confronted with the reality that the police do not keep us safe and that her son is a target because he is young and brown.

As his older sister, I am devastated and angry. But I don't feel powerless. By this time, I'm beginning to learn from organizers and advocates about our rights and the power of everyday people coming together to fight deportations and racial profiling. Mami and I are determined to not let this police officer off the hook. We head to police precinct 115 in Jackson Heights, a few blocks away. A white police officer is behind the desk right at the entrance of the precinct. I tell him I want to file a complaint against one of the officers who physically assaulted my brother. He laughs at me and tells me to call the Civilian Complaint Review Board (CCRB), an independent agency created to receive and investigate complaints of police violence and misconduct. The officer's laughter and dismissiveness send the message that people who look like us don't have the right to speak up and demand accountability. We are supposed to accept that police have the power to do whatever they want with our bodies and our lives. Mami and I walk back home feeling agitated but not defeated. I will go online and begin the process of filing a complaint with the CCRB. For years afterward, we receive notifications that they are still reviewing the case, until we stop hearing from them. The cop that physically assaulted my brother still works in the same precinct.

My brother feels violated. We all do. But we don't know yet about resources we can access to address the mental and emotional impact of the assault, or racial-justice organizations fighting against police violence. I don't know of the work of young people of color from community organizations like Sistas & Brothas United in the Bronx fighting the criminalization of youth and their campaign for #PoliceFreeSchools. Although I know about Amadou Diallo, a young Black immigrant who was killed by police in the Bronx in 1999 (one year after we arrived in the US), my young mind does not make the connection between his killing and the systematic racial profiling and police violence experienced by Black and brown youth like my brother. Four police officers shot forty-one rounds at Diallo. A panel of four Black and eight white jurors found the officers not guilty of any charges. The officers who took Diallo's life continued working for the police department without any accountability. Diallo's case feels distant to us, partly due to the anti-Black racism within Latine and non-Black immigrant communities. We buy into the narrative that he must have done something wrong. We think that won't happen to us because we are "good" immigrants.

But I will realize as a college student and community organizer that the police profiling and violence we experience is intentional and systematic. In schools, law enforcement and harsh school discipline policies are used to funnel young people into the criminal punishment system in what advocates and organizers have coined "the school-to-prison-to-deportation pipeline." A 2011 report from the Justice Policy Institute found that "when schools have law enforcement on site, students are more likely to be arrested by police instead of discipline being handled by school officials."[19] Arrests disproportionally impact Black and brown students. This doesn't mean that students of color misbehave more than white students. Joshua Rovner from the Sentencing Project put it this way: "Black and white youth are roughly as likely to get into fights, carry weapons, steal property, use and sell illicit substances, and skip school."[20] In NYC, most youth who are arrested every year are Black and Latine. Young people of color live with the constant fear of being targeted by police and law enforcement.

As I learn about the policies targeting young people of color, I follow the case of New York's racist stop-and-frisk policy, implemented and expanded in the '90s by Republican mayor Rudy W. Giuliani. This policy enables the police to use "reasonable suspicion" to stop, interrogate, and search people on the streets, leading to thousands of Black and Latine New Yorkers being stopped without cause while walking on the street, going to work, or heading to school. I realize that what happened to my brother was NYPD policy. Between 2004 and 2012, the NYPD makes 4.4 million stops; more than 80 percent of those stopped are Black and Latine people, and nearly all are innocent.[21] People impacted by police brutality, their families, along with racial justice community organizers and allies, launch a campaign—Communities United for Police Reform—to expose the racist practices of police, many courageously sharing their stories and demanding accountability. In a historic ruling in 2013, a federal judge finds NYPD's stop-and-frisk practice illegal. Despite this legal victory, more than a decade later, the NYPD is still unlawfully stopping, questioning, searching, arresting, and intimidating Black and Latine New Yorkers.

The police not only have the power to stop people for "reasonable suspicion." They also have the power to label young people as gang members without evidence. Investigative reporting and community organizing have exposed school resource officers collaborating with ICE to share information to target students of color, predominantly Latine, with alleged "gang affiliation." The label "gang affiliation" is disproportionally used to arrest, incarcerate, and deport Latine youth. In 2017 in Long Island, Alex, an undocumented immigrant student who fled Honduras because of gang violence, is accused of "gang affiliation" for drawing Huntington High School's mascot on a school's calculator. The mascot, a blue devil with horns, is interpreted by a school resource officer as a gang symbol, and he records the incident in a report accusing Alex of possessing "gang paraphernalia" and "defacing school property with gang signs."[22] The report is shared with ICE under New York's Operation Matador, a partnership between ICE, local police departments, and officers in schools to target and detain Latine immigrants suspected of affiliation with gangs. Under Operation Matador, ICE arrests 816 people, about 170 of whom are young people like Alex who fled Central American countries because of gang violence and are in the process of seeking asylum. Many of them are minors. Although there is documented evidence of the existence of white gangs, we don't see operations of this kind targeting white people.

In my time at Newtown, I focus on learning English and doing well in my classes. Getting good grades is not only about going to college but also about making my parents proud and honoring their sacrifices. By sophomore year, I become an honors student and I work as hard as I can to become a strong college candidate. I do everything my teachers tell me to do to support my college application—take AP classes, do community service, join student government and student clubs. I start getting the sense that I just might make it to college and fulfill our family's dream. When I reach eleventh grade, my friends and classmates from the honors program talk about preparing for the Scholastic Aptitude Test (SAT). Some of them spend time together in the library taking practice tests. I find out that the test is a requirement to apply for college, but I don't know if, as an undocumented student, I can even register for it. I'm too fearful and embarrassed to ask for help. Most of my friends also take an SAT prep course together and constantly chat about their dream schools. My best friend, Rosa, an immigrant from the Dominican Republic who arrived in NYC when she was twelve and is a permanent US resident, dreams of becoming a doctor and tells me she is applying to Columbia University, Harvard, and Cornell. She asks me about my dream schools. I briefly say I dream of applying to the same schools and abruptly change the conversation. Inside, I feel ashamed and heartbroken. I'm uncertain that a college education is even a possibility for me, much less applying to Ivy League universities.

For a while, I pretend to be like everyone else in the honors society, preparing for the SAT and doing research about colleges, financial aid, and scholarships. I don't share that I'm undocumented, but having to hide a part of yourself can make you feel alone and isolated. What I don't know at the time is that there are thousands of students like me in New York and across the country. In the early 2000s, the Migration Policy Institute estimates that there are sixty-five thousand undocumented students graduating from high school every year. Currently, that number is close to one hundred thousand.[23] Undocumented students have had the right to a K–12 public education since 1982, when the Supreme Court found it unconstitutional to discriminate against students based on immigration status. But higher education isn't protected by this decision, leading millions of young people of color like me to be denied college access.

When I finally get a registration form for the SAT, it requires my Social Security number. I don't have a Social Security number and fear that filling out this form could get me deported. I struggle in silence about what to do next. Even though I'm incapacitated by fear, I cannot ignore that the test date is getting closer, and all my friends are preparing for it. I decide to talk to Ms. B, as we call her, who is an ESL teacher and the Key Club advisor. Ms. B is friendly and speaks Spanish with a funny accent. She checks on me frequently. She asks about my family and how I'm doing in my classes. I feel safe with her. I reveal to Ms. B that I'm undocumented and ask her if I can take the SAT despite my immigration status. Ms. B looks at me with a gentle smile and tells me she will keep our conversation confidential. She advises me to register for the SAT and to leave the Social Security number question blank. Ms. B explains that the information provided to the SAT is confidential. Yet, there is another question I worry about. The form also asks whether the student is a lawful permanent resident or a US citizen. I'm neither. I check the box that says, "Not a green card holder." My heart is racing with fear and questions about whether my information will be shared. The future I had spent years planning for is suddenly uncertain.

I wait for what feels like an eternity to receive a response to my registration form. A letter finally arrives, and when I open it, I cry with relief and joy. I am not denied SAT registration for being undocumented, and I'm one step closer to college. The next challenge is preparing for the test itself—a time-limited, multiple-choice, standardized exam that is 50 percent math and 50 percent reading and writing. As an English language learner, it feels impossible for me to catch up. I feel like I am swimming against the current in a sea of thousands of unknown English words. Our family does not have money to pay for a prep course. Instead, I borrow SAT books from the library and save money to buy one practice exam book, which feels like a luxury. I study every day and most weekends, but I constantly feel I'm behind, and my score in practice exams is often less than average. A voice inside of me tells me I am not smart enough for this test or college. The voice gets louder and louder.

Later in life, I get to unmask the idea that my performance on the SAT is a measure of my intelligence when I learn that standardized tests have a long history of racism, classism, and nativism that disproportionately benefit white, middle-class students. National admissions-test expert Jay Rosner explains in "How the SAT Creates Built-in-Headwinds" that questions answered correctly by more Black than white students are deemed not "good questions" and therefore discarded.[24] In fact, the test was created by a group of psychologists who believed Black people are inferior. Carl Brigham, a eugenicist and one of the psychologists who developed the test for the College Board, wrote, "The decline of American intelligence will be more rapid than the decline of the intelligence of European national groups, owing to the presence here of the negro."[25] The SAT was developed to "scientifically" label nonwhites as mentally and intellectually inferior.

I take the SAT twice and end up with a score slightly above average. I don't meet my score goal, but I hope colleges look at my grades, AP courses, and extracurriculars too. When the time comes to fill out college applications, I seek help from my school's college advisor. In an underresourced and overcrowded high school of more than seven hundred seniors, I wait for forty minutes in a long line to meet one of our only two college advisors. My hands are cold and sweaty. Finally, it's my turn; I clasp my hands tightly together to stop them from shaking. I sit down in front of the advisor, an Italian American teacher in her forties who also teaches AP calculus. As she looks at my transcripts, I feel that she holds the dreams of my whole family in her hands. She asks me if I have a Social Security number. I nervously say, "No." Then she asks me if my parents have Social Security numbers. I say, "No, they don't have one either." She just sits there, looking straight at me, and I know she knows I am undocumented. Then she tells me I can't go to college because of my immigration status. She doesn't even offer to help me. She looks over my head and shouts, "NEXT!" to the next student in line.

I sit there stunned. Then I walk out of the office crying. At home, I drop my bookbag on the floor and throw myself on the bed. Sobbing, I tell Mami that I can't go to college, and we must give up on our family's dream. She looks at me with the same fierce determination she had when we went to get my vaccination record for the school registration. I half expect her to cry with me, but instead she says, "We won't give up, mija. We've sacrificed too much for us to give up. We came here for you to have what we didn't have. You will go to college!" I repeat what the college advisor had told me, but Mami is not taking no for an answer. She tells me to go back to school to find someone who will help me. And then brings up every teenager's worst nightmare: "If you don't go back and do it, I will go to school and do it myself." I am now faced with an even greater fear—being embarrassed by Mami at school.

I go back to school the next day and ask Ms. B for help. She tells me she is not sure how to support students in my situation, but she will figure something out. When we talk again, she tells me that although I can't access financial aid, I can apply to the City University of New York (CUNY) regardless of my immigration status. Had Mami accepted the counselor's word, I probably would have given up on the dream of a college education. I learn that being a "good" immigrant and a good student doesn't protect me from biases and systemic racism. To this day, I wonder how many students of color encounter educators like my college advisor who uphold and enable systemic discrimination and racism in schools, educators who don't believe we are smart enough or worthy of an education and a better life. It shouldn't be that only some of us, by pure luck, get to have a teacher like Ms. B.

Here's what she wrote in my yearbook:

> *Dear Cristina, don't forget about all the fun we had! You're a wonderful girl and friend. Keep working hard and you'll be a success in whatever you do! Call/Write/Visit! Love, Ms. B*

4

THE WAR ON US

Flowers, handmade cards and drawings, American flags, and other mementos left in the area near the World Trade Center in the months after the 9/11 attacks (courtesy of Walter Barrientos)

> *Unresolved grief inside a person is tragic; unresolved grief inside a nation is catastrophic. It releases enormous aggression.*
>
> —Valarie Kaur

In my sophomore year, I join the Key Club—a multiracial, multiethnic, and multicultural community of mostly Asian, Latin American, and Caribbean students. We are immigrants or children of immigrants. They teach me about different cultures, languages, and holidays: Chinese New Year, Diwali, Ramadan, and Hanukkah. We have a few things in common: our families came to this country seeking a better life, we dream of going to college, we join the Key Club because our teachers tell us community service will help our college applications, we enjoy helping others in the community, and we all have an accent. We volunteer to clean parks in the community, support elementary school teachers in after-school programs, distribute holiday baskets at the Elmhurst hospital, and raise funds for the March of Dimes. We also host school events to celebrate each other's cultures. In this community, being an immigrant and an English language learner with an accent is welcomed and embraced. Here I find joy and belonging.

I find out Ms. B is looking for volunteers to help plan a Key Club food festival. I've never volunteered to put an event together, but I'm encouraged by Ms. B. She makes learning new things easy and fun, so I decide to give it a try. We make flyers for the event, post them around school, and recruit students to bring food. The day of the event, we transform the cafeteria into a multicultural food hall, setting up booths where students can share a popular food from their country of origin or their heritage. Students from India, Mexico, Colombia, Ecuador, Thailand, Bangladesh, the Dominican Republic, China, Venezuela, Peru, the Philippines, and Pakistan bring food and flyers with information about their typical dish and its ingredients. This is the first time that I try one of India's most popular snacks—samosas. My friends from India have the best booth. If this were a competition, they would get first place. They are wearing beautiful golden-and-green saris, they have Indian music playing in the background, and their makeup is on point. I exchange Ecuadorian empanadas for some samosas, and we talk about how both are basically stuffed dough. Our countries are far from each other, but the similarities in our food make us feel closer.

Although my Key Club friends and I share similar stories and dreams, my immigration status sets me on a different path. In our senior year, many of them begin to hear back from universities they applied to. Rosa receives a request for an interview from her top school: Columbia University. She is intimidated and nervous. As her best friend, I offer to go with her to support her. I'm intimidated as well, but I play it cool. "No worries—you will kill this interview," I tell her.

The day of the interview arrives, and we head to Columbia University. It's our first time taking the train from Queens to Manhattan's Upper West Side. We are so immigrant that we almost never leave Queens. I fear we may get lost, so I bring a foldable MTA subway map. We take the 7 train to the Times Square–Forty-Second Street station to transfer to an uptown train. We decide to hop on the uptown 2 express train to get there early. You know the saying—"Be early to be on time." But we don't know that the 2 train doesn't stop at Columbia University's 116th Street. The train passes 116th Street and Lenox Avenue, and it dawns on us that we are on the wrong train. We start nervously cracking up. Of course, this is before our anxiety kicks in, and we rush out of the train on 125th Street. Rosa is worried she will be late. We run to the other side of the platform to catch the southbound 2 train. We finally get to 116th Street with minutes to spare.

Passing the main black gate on to Columbia's campus, I feel as if we've entered a Roman city. Our eyes are immediately drawn to a building with a grand staircase that leads to an entrance with imposing round pillars. We are both completely starstruck. In awe we look around and notice that nobody looks like us. The students with their fancy bookbags and shoes make us feel self-conscious about our outfits. I'm wearing boot-cut jeans from Conway, a red T-shirt, and black chunky loafers from Payless. Rosa is wearing a white button-down shirt and black pants. She worries about her look impacting first impressions. I remind her, "Rosa, you got this."

While Rosa is in the interview, I wait on the steps of Low Memorial Library, the building that first captured our attention. The staircase is like the entrance to the famous Metropolitan Museum of Art that I have heard so much about but only seen on TV. I sit there imagining what it would be like to live without fear of being undocumented and to have the chance to apply to the same schools as Rosa so we could go to school together. When Rosa comes out of the interview, she is smiling. I'm anxious to know how it went. The interviewer was warm and welcoming, making her feel that if she was accepted, she would have a community of support, including help looking for all the options for financial assistance. She'll find out in a few months if she was accepted. We head back to Queens feeling hopeful she will make it into Columbia.

I am uncertain about applying to CUNY because I don't know if we will be able to afford tuition. My undocumented status makes me ineligible for financial aid and scholarships. And although Mami assures me we will figure it out, I wonder if I should just give up. My heart breaks at the thought that my parents would have to work even more. Mami keeps the faith. She believes in miracles. "Ten fe, mija," Mami tells me. Like Mami, Ms. B keeps encouraging me to prepare my application for CUNY. She walks me through the application form and explains that I must rank my school choices. I have no idea where to start. I don't know anything about the four-year colleges. Ms. B helps me get started by first asking me about my college major. I tell her I want to be a lawyer and that I had read in a book about college majors that a political science major prepares college students for law school. The idea of becoming a lawyer doesn't come from me. It is Papi's dream. When Papi was young, he dreamed of becoming a lawyer, but he had no money or family support to go to school. Ever since the eight-year-old me heard him share about his unfilled dream, the dream became mine. If Papi can't become a lawyer, I will. I don't know why Papi dreamed of becoming a lawyer, but I do know that my parents believe legal and medical careers guarantee financial stability. I don't feel free to explore other careers or interests. As children of immigrants, we often carry the responsibility of fulfilling our parents' dreams. It is both a heavy burden and a source of motivation.

Ms. B suggests that I visit the CUNY colleges that offer political science as a major. I sign up for in-person tours at Queens College and Brooklyn College. Queens College is easier to get to for me—it's close to Elmhurst, where we live, and right by Flushing, Queens' Chinatown, with a transit hub of multiple buses and trains on Main Street. I hop on the Q88 via Horace Harding Expressway, and I'm there in twenty minutes. I enter the campus and immediately fall in love. The quad mirrors Columbia's and has a view of the Manhattan skyline. There's plenty of space to hang out in green areas and read under the trees. The nerd in me is in awe of the Rosenthal Library—six floors of books! I check out the tennis courts and the music building. Entering the Copland School of Music feels like going into a relaxation retreat. The building has a majestic atrium with a full glass ceiling. I sit by a garden in the atrium, listening to students playing classical music. I can see myself walking around the quad, reading in the Rosenthal Library until dawn, stopping by the music building during a break, and getting bubble tea after class in Flushing. I don't need to visit Brooklyn College. No shade or anything, but after the tour, I just know that Queens College is my number-one choice. Brooklyn is second. I'm a Queens girl through and through. I send my application, hoping to make it into my number-one college choice.

We are about a week into our senior year in high school, and on the morning of September 11, we are told via the intercom that due to safety concerns, we will be dismissed early. I'm sitting in my AP statistics class in the front row by the window. The sun is hitting the left side of my face, and I look out the window to check if something is going on outside the building. I see nothing. Our teacher looks frightened and shocked. She tells us planes crashed into the twin towers and urges us to pack our stuff and head home to our parents. I have a vague memory of how the twin towers look. I have walked by the towers only once and got dizzy when I looked up to the top floors. In a world without smartphones and social media platforms, we have no idea that this is part of four coordinated terrorist attacks with two more planes that crashed into the Pentagon and in a field in Pennsylvania. I pack my notebook and scientific calculator and head home.

Mami is at home doing laundry when she hears about the attacks on Univision. She runs out to Jonathan's school to pick him up and waits for me outside of our building, crying and in despair. At home, we stay glued to the TV. In horror we watch the towers in flames and people jumping out of the windows. I can't even fathom the despair people inside the towers are feeling. In less than two hours, both towers collapse. I don't know anyone who was in the World Trade Center that day or their families, but I shed tears of pain as if I had known and loved every single one of them. My young mind and heart cannot comprehend this act of violence.

We try calling our family members and friends to make sure they are safe, but phone lines are jammed, and calls can't get through. The uncertainty and anxiety are high. Police and the military are deployed throughout the city. There is a constant stream of sirens on the street. The subway system is suspended. The bridges are shut down. Everyone is scrambling to make it back to their loved ones. On TV we watch thousands of New Yorkers walking on the Queensboro and Brooklyn Bridges. Those who had been near the World Trade Center are covered in ash. Tío Francisco gets in his gray Ford minivan and drives to the Queensboro Bridge to look for Polita and her sister, who had taken the train into Manhattan earlier in the morning for work. We are worried because they are in their late sixties and don't speak English very well. As Tío Francisco looks for them, he also offers rides to people who are desperate to get to their children and families deeper into Queens. He takes people to Jackson Heights and Corona. It doesn't matter that they are complete strangers. Tío Francisco and many other New Yorkers come together to help and support each other in this moment of crisis.

We fear other parts of NYC could be targets of attacks. My mind is racing: What do we do if our neighborhood gets bombed or attacked? Where can we seek shelter? Will they allow undocumented people into shelters? Are we on our own? We stay tuned in to the news. Government officials announce that all schools will be closed the following day. At 8:30 p.m., President George W. Bush addresses the nation. "America was targeted for attack because we're the brightest beacon for freedom and opportunity in the world," he says. He closes by saying, "None of us will ever forget this day."[26] His message does not entirely resonate with me. My family and I don't experience the freedom he speaks of, but he is right about one thing: I'll never forget this day. Our lives as immigrants and the politics of immigration policy will never be the same after the attacks.

It's early evening and my eyes are burning from crying all day. We are all together, my cousins and aunts, and we are paralyzed by the terror and the pain. My cousins and I find out that our neighbors are spontaneously congregating in the lobby of our building to hold an impromptu vigil. We quickly look for candles and join our neighbors. Everyone looks exhausted and shocked. Across New York City and the country, people come together to hold vigils in honor of the victims. It's comforting to be in community with our neighbors. Many of us are still waiting for our family members to get home. As we pray, more and more neighbors start trickling in. Many of them are covered in ash and dust. They work in Manhattan's restaurants, coffee shops, and office buildings. They are nannies, domestic workers, construction workers, and building maintenance and service workers. They are the backbone of the city's economy. We celebrate their arrival. We hear that Polita and her sister are safe and will stay at their bosses' homes for the night. Embracing each other, we are relieved to know that all of us are well and safe.

Back in our apartment, I can't go to sleep. I'm tossing and turning in bed, thinking of the images of people jumping off the towers and those who couldn't escape. I'm devasted for all the lives lost. I pray for them and their families, holding their pain and loss as my own. I feel this attack is against me. Against my family. Against my community. Against my home. For the first time, I recognize feeling a sense of attachment to this country that I had not felt before, even though this country doesn't accept me or want me here.

In the days and weeks that follow, more details become known about the terrorists. It's reported they came in with business, tourist, and student visas. It quickly hits me that immigrants like us are now suspects too. Muslims and immigrants of color, US citizens and noncitizens alike, become the target of increased police surveillance, racial profiling, violence, and hate. Police and army officers are everywhere in the city. We see them at subway stations, bridges, and major transportation hubs. As part of the country's increased security measures, law enforcement has the power to stop anyone who "looks" suspicious. They have the authority to perform body searches using metal detectors and to request forms of identification. When I walk by the subway station, I see soldiers in combat gear carrying rifles across their chest racially profiling Muslim immigrants and searching their bags. I avoid eye contact with law enforcement. For Muslim and immigrant communities, there is no space to grieve this tragedy and the loved ones whose lives have been lost because of the attacks. In our pain, trauma, and grief, we are faced with becoming the enemy, the "other"—the suspects of terrorism.

When we return to school, the mood is somber, but our teachers try their best to help us process the moment and make us feel safe. They create spaces for conversation and writing assignments where we can explore our feelings. Students write poems about the fear and grief we are all feeling; they read them during assemblies and get them published in the school's newspaper. Over the course of the next several weeks, I hear some students teasing Muslim classmates. Jokingly, they ask if they have bombs in their bookbags. "Don't blow us up," they shout. On the news, we hear about Muslim youth being bullied and physically attacked in schools. Acts of violence and hate against people that "look" Arab or Muslim, predominantly from the Sikh community, are reported frequently. On September 15, 2001, Balbir Singh, a Sikh American father, is killed by a man in Arizona while he is planting flowers in front of his gas station. The murderer, calling himself a patriot, says he wanted to "go out and shoot some towel heads" in retaliation for Osama bin Laden's leadership role in plotting the attack.[27]

Muslim and immigrant communities are increasingly targeted for deportation. In the immigrant neighborhoods of Elmhurst and Jackson Heights, we hear about white ICE vans showing up and neighbors disappearing from one day to the next. As a college student and organizer in my early twenties, I will learn that after 9/11, the federal government conflates immigration and terrorism. In 2002, President Bush works with Congress to pass the Homeland Security Act, which moves all government immigration functions from the Immigration and Naturalization Service agency, under the Department of Justice, to a newly created Department of Homeland Security (DHS). The DHS creates three entities: US Citizenship and Immigration Services (USCIS), US Immigration and Customs Enforcement (ICE), and US Customs and Border Protection (CBP). The goal of these agencies is to dramatically increase immigrant detention and deportation and to expand border security and the border wall. The Bush administration launches a special registration program to collect personal data and travel details from noncitizens, particularly targeting Muslim men. Under this program, Muslim men, regardless of immigration status, are required to come forward and register with the government. Nearly thirteen thousand Muslim men are placed into deportation proceedings. Under the Bush administration, the average daily population of detained immigrants goes from twenty thousand to thirty-two thousand.[28]

In the name of national security, Congress and the White House build on the Illegal Immigration Reform and Immigrant Responsibility Act (IIRIRA) of 1996 to create the massive detention and deportation machine we have today. DHS begins implementing the 287(g) program, included in the IIRIRA reforms, by increasing the number of sheriffs and county commissioners and formalizing agreements with the DHS to deputize local police to enforce immigration and collaborate with ICE to detain and deport immigrants. The deportation force will grow over the years, with CBP's budget more than doubling to $11.5 billion by 2010, with a 43 percent increase in staff. ICE's budget will more than double to $5.74 billion by 2010, with its staff growing by just under 40 percent. Today, the US government spends over $18 billion annually on its immigration enforcement agencies, more than on all its other principal criminal federal law enforcement agencies combined, including the FBI, Secret Service, and the Drug Enforcement Administration (DEA).[29] Decades after 9/11, Muslim communities continue to be at the center of racist attacks. Fifty-one percent of American Muslim families report their children are the targets of bullying, hate, and violence in schools.[30] In 2017, President Donald Trump's administration institutes a Muslim ban, barring travelers from several Muslim-majority countries from entering the US. In response, the country erupts in mass protests at airports, condemning the policy. Racial justice leaders and organizers from Muslim and ally communities challenge the ban in the courts, halting its implementation. But the Trump administration does not back down, moving to issue three more versions of the ban, one of which is backed by the Supreme Court, impacting Muslim immigrants from Iran, Libya, North Korea, Somalia, Syria, Venezuela, and Yemen. In his 2024 presidential campaign, he commits to expanding this ban and barring refugees from Gaza from entering the US if he is elected president.

I learn from longtime immigrant rights advocates that in those early days of September 2001, a series of meetings between Mexican president Vicente Fox and US president George W. Bush took place, including a private cabinet meeting, a state dinner, and a meeting with a joint session of Congress, to discuss cross-border trade agreements and immigration policy. The conversations aimed to bring negotiations on a bipartisan, multinational immigration reform proposal to a close, which included a pathway to citizenship for millions of undocumented people, including my family. On September 6, the two countries agreed on a framework for reform, stating that "U.S.-Mexican relations have entered their most promising moment in history."[31] Five days later, the terrorist attacks end the chances of these conversations moving forward and hurt any effort to advance immigration policy reforms that sought to create a pathway to citizenship for undocumented immigrants.

In New York, Republican politicians start a debate about denying identification cards and driver's licenses to undocumented immigrants such as my dad. Months later, Papi receives a letter from the Department of Motor Vehicles (DMV) asking him to mail proof of his legal residency and/or US citizenship or his driver's license will be revoked. Papi works in construction and drives to New Jersey for his job. He is the breadwinner of our family. The possibility of Papi getting caught driving without a license and then deported is present in our minds and hearts every day. It is torture.

The wave of backlash against immigrants is relentless. CUNY also announces that it will comply with a provision from IIRIRA that prohibits public state universities from offering in-state tuition for undocumented students unless US citizen students are eligible for in-state tuition regardless of state residency. This means students without lawful immigration status like me are no longer eligible for in-state tuition. We are now considered "international students" and must pay international tuition fees, which are over double the cost: $3,400 in comparison to $1,600 per semester for four-year colleges. My parents and I are devastated at the news. My good grades and hard work don't really matter. The cost of tuition essentially denies undocumented students access to a college education. Across the country, thousands of youth face the same obstacle. In the years to come, courageous immigrant youth will go on to build organizations to empower undocumented youth and start a movement that will push educational institutions to welcome and support undocumented students and force changes in policy to provide in-state tuition to undocumented students in over twenty states.

The first states to adopt in-state tuition for undocumented students are Texas and California. Student-led organizing wins access to in-state tuition and state financial aid for undocumented students in Texas, the state with the second-largest undocumented population, in June 2001. The bill garners bipartisan support and is signed into law by Republican governor Rick Perry. Julieta Garibay, an undocumented young woman from Mexico, can now pursue her nursing degree at the University of Texas at Austin. With other undocumented students, she courageously founds the University Leadership Initiative (ULI) at UT Austin to empower undocumented students in the state. In September 2001, California adopts Assembly Bill 540 (AB 540). The law allows undocumented students to access in-state tuition but not state financial aid. Matias Ramos, an undocumented student from Argentina, pursues a degree in political science at the University of California, Los Angeles (UCLA), under AB 540. Matias, Cinthya Felix, and Tam Tran, all undocumented students at UCLA, create the first undocumented student organization at UCLA—Improving Dreams, Equality, Access, and Success (IDEAS)—to empower undocumented students. Both ULI and IDEAS will become anchor organizations of the immigrant youth movement and inspire undocumented students in New York and other states to push for similar policy changes.

As my chances of going to college seem to be moving further and further from reach, my high school friends celebrate acceptances to their dream schools. It's a sunny spring day, and Rosa and I head to my family's small studio apartment to check on the status of her application to Columbia University online. We are among the first generation of students to have internet access at home. But most families in our neighborhood can't afford to have computers, much less an America Online (AOL) subscription. Rosa doesn't own a computer. But Tío Francisco fixes computers as a side gig and gifts me a used one for my birthday. The computer is slow, but it works. We wait patiently for the dial-up connection to access the internet, reminding Mami not to use the landline phone until we check Rosa's email. When Rosa opens her inbox, she sees an email from the university. When we read the email, we scream, hug each other, and cry—Rosa is accepted to Columbia with financial aid and scholarships. I am deeply happy for her. I stand there, holding her in my arms, in awe of her and her family's journey. I think about her mom, a single immigrant mother from the Dominican Republic. I think of Rosa's journey to get to this moment—migrating to the US as a child, adjusting to a different culture and country and the cold winters of New York, and learning English. I think of all the times she stays at home doing homework instead of hanging out with friends at the park, and the times she helps me with my homework over the phone. All her hard work and that of her mother are recognized with this acceptance email. She's made it, and I'm proud of her. This feels like a huge victory, and although it is not about me, I feel this victory as my own. The moment is also bittersweet. I am sad that we will be separated. She is on her way to Columbia University. I'm uncertain that I will even go to college. In my heart, I'm holding joy for her and longing to have the same opportunity she has. She leaves our place to share the great news with her mom. I sit at our kitchen table, grappling with how our different immigration statuses define our futures and separate our paths.

5

AMERICAN DREAM

Cristina at her graduation from Newtown High School, Queens, 2002
(courtesy of the author, edited by AC Studio)

Education is borderless: It's your passport, your freedom. Nothing—and no one—should stop that.

—Jose Antonio Vargas

Every day after school, I check our mailbox, eager to find out if I got accepted to Queens College. I know we can't afford the tuition, but my heart longs for a miracle. A letter from CUNY finally arrives. The envelope is large and feels thick and textured. It's made of fancy paper with old charm to it. I've heard from my friends that rejection letters are usually sent in letter-size envelopes, whereas acceptance letters come in larger envelopes including a welcome packet. I'm anxious to find out what's in the letter, but I don't want to open the envelope by myself. I take the elevator up to the seventh floor and rush to our apartment. Mami is in the kitchen making chicken soup. I open the envelope, and I can't believe what I read. I reread it a few times. I have been accepted to my first choice, Queens College! I start to cry. I feel proud and excited.

I join Mami in the kitchen. She hugs me, and with tears in her eyes, she reminds me, "Te dije, ten fe, mija. Gracias a Dios!" For a moment, I let go of the daunting fear that I may not be able to afford college and join Mami in celebrating the good news and feeling the joy of overcoming so many odds. I feel immense gratitude for my parents' courage, sacrifices, and relentless will to fight for a better life for their children. I feel that perhaps the promise of this country may extend to people like me. In Mami's arms, I breathe in the smell of the soup's sofrito, a mix of sautéed garlic, onions, cilantro, salt, and cumin. The rich scent feels like having the arms of our ancestors around us. My parents, their parents, and their parents' parents couldn't go to college. I'm the first one in our family to graduate from high school and be this close to a college education. I feel our ancestors celebrating with us too.

Now sitting at our kitchen table, Mami is fiercely doing the math and thinking about all the ways we can collectively pay for my tuition. She has a plan. She will clean additional homes over the weekend, babysit another child, and sell Avon, and Papi could ask to work overtime at the construction company where he now works. "You are going to college," she declares with certainty. Mami's plan is to work four jobs in addition to caring for our family. Cooking, cleaning, keeping up with grocery lists, and doing laundry is a full-time job already. It breaks my heart that Mami's only choice is to compromise her health and her body so that I can go to college. I feel terribly guilty. I volunteer to help

Mami sell Avon and commit to finding a job. Mami disagrees. I must focus on school, she says, but I can't let my parents do all the heavy lifting by themselves. Against Mami's will, I begin helping her sell Avon and start looking for a job.

A couple of weeks later when Mami and I go grocery shopping, I see a CASHIERS WANTED sign at the local supermarket a block from our building. Met Foodmarket is at the corner of the LeFrak City complex. When you walk in, you feel like you are at a United Nations assembly. There are people from China, Bangladesh, India, Africa, Russia, Eastern Europe, and Latin America. They don't speak one another's languages, and some don't speak English, but grocery shopping brings them together. Families come in with their children and their abuelas and abuelos also. They chat in different languages, sounding like birds chirping in the morning. As Mami and I walk through the supermarket's aisles, I feel like I'm taking a multicultural master class, while Missy Elliott's "Get Ur Freak On" plays in the background. In the produce section, I learn about vegetables and fruits I've never seen before. I'm curious about nopales and dragon fruits but don't dare to touch them because they have scary-looking spikes. I overhear a Mexican woman talking to a neighbor about making tacos de nopal for lunch, but I'm too shy to ask how she removes the spikes before cooking them. In the Latin American section, we get lentils, rice, beans, and sazón. Next to the sazón, the overpowering smell of curry powder hits my nose. There is a whole section with Indian spices and products. Down the aisle, we hear two Chinese children loudly begging their mom for chen pi mei, Chinese candy. We don't get candy and sweets. Mami doesn't have a sweet tooth. She is more of a savory person. She raises us that way. I crave rice and lentils, salchipapas, breaded chicken, and fried plantains.

In line at the register, I'm in my head singing Britney Spears's "Oops! . . . I Did It Again," which is blasting in the background, but I have to tune back in to reality because Mami needs me to interpret for her. We have a produce bag full of green plantains for bolas de verde soup, an Ecuadorian specialty made of green plantain dumplings stuffed with beef and vegetables. The price of plátanos verdes that the cashier rings up is not the one on the sign. The cashier, who is from India, speaks in Hindi to another cashier, waving at her with the plátano in her hand. I don't understand Hindi, but I can tell she is asking her about the price of the plátanos. The other cashier shakes her head no. "I walk with you; show me sign," the cashier tells me kindly. I walk back to the produce aisle with her and show her the sign. She tells me it hasn't been changed from the weekend sales, but she will honor the price. Mami beams with pride for being on top of the grocery prices.

I know I have something my parents need and don't have—English. I feel a duty to help them with interpretation and translation. I take my duty seriously. I keep my Spanish fresh by reading Spanish newspapers and all the books from my AP Spanish class, and by watching the news and Mexican telenovelas on Univision. But every time I interpret for them, no matter how often I do it, I'm afraid of messing up, afraid of people making fun of Mami or me, or worse, of people shaming us for not speaking English. One day, at a bank, I see a Latine immigrant man being yelled at by a bank teller for not speaking English. "I don't speak Spanish. In this country, you must speak English," he tells the immigrant man, who, full of shame, walks out of the bank. I fear this could happen to me, to us.

At the supermarket, however, I feel less anxious. The cashiers and the workers are all immigrants, mostly from India, China, and Latin America. They are all friendly, kind, and patient with customers. Some of them step in to interpret when a customer needs help with a price, coupon, or a product. And sometimes, just like

I did, customers' immigrant children interpret for their families. I relate to those children. We are expert cultural navigators. We are our parents' agents, representing them to landlords, doctors, bank tellers, teachers, store cashiers, bus drivers, and police officers. It's a hefty responsibility for children who want and deserve to be just that—children. Immigrant parents leave everything behind to give their children a better life. Once in a new country, in a reversal of roles, they become dependent on their children to navigate a new culture and survive in a new world.

As an immigrant young person, I learn that language is power. Speaking English allows me to navigate the country more easily, to pursue jobs that my parents don't have access to, like the cashier job, and to defend myself when needed. Knowing the language is both empowering and a big responsibility. And although learning English shouldn't be a privilege, I feel I'm more privileged than my parents for being able to learn English at school. My parents want to learn English too, but this country is not set up for poor and working-class immigrants like them to learn the language. They work multiple jobs to sustain our family. They work at different times—early mornings, overnight shifts, and weekends. At what time exactly can they sign up for an English class? Free English classes are hard to find. The available schedules hardly align with their working hours. When Mami finally joins a free English class at a local church, she is so tired she can barely stay awake. But she tries and will continue trying to learn English over the years.

Before we leave the supermarket, I approach Cathy, the supermarket's manager, to speak with her about the cashier job. She is a tall, slim Korean immigrant who wears pearls to work every day. Cathy smiles at me and asks me to wait for her. She seems friendly and approachable. While I wait to talk to her, she yells in Korean at one of the Latine workers who is restocking cans of Campbell's chicken noodle soup in one of the aisles. I don't understand what she is saying, but she looks upset and frustrated. The worker just nods, puts his head down, and keeps working. I begin to fear she may not be friendly after all. But she returns to talk to me with a big smile. I have a hard time understanding her, both because I'm nervous and because of her accent. She tells me my English is "very good" and asks if I can work three days a week. I tell her I'm still in school and can only work during the weekends. I won't be considered for the job if I don't work three full days, she tells me. I am so desperate I plead with her to let me work Fridays after school and the weekends. Cathy agrees and gives me paperwork to fill out. She tells me I will get paid five dollars per hour and will have a fifteen-minute break per day. Fifteen minutes for a break feels short for an eight-hour day, but I have no other option. As an undocumented immigrant, I feel I have no right to ask why or for more. To me, this is the greatest work opportunity at a time when our family needs it the most.

Mami and I walk home feeling proud I had the courage to talk to Cathy, but I'm tormented by the uncertainty of whether I can work there without immigration papers. Papi tells me the supermarket hires undocumented workers.

"What? So . . . undocumented workers know that the supermarket's management knows?" I ask Papi.

He confirms. "Immigrants need the jobs, and the supermarket needs immigrants because Americans don't want those jobs," Papi tells me.

I begin wondering if all the cashiers at the supermarket are also undocumented. It would feel good to not be the only one.

But I feel conflicted about filling out the job application. This would be my first time submitting a job application, and I feel trapped. Filling it out could help me get a job and go to college, or it could raise questions about my immigration status and perhaps even lead to my deportation. This is the impossible situation that undocumented immigrants often face. I take a gamble, hoping for the same luck Papi and other undocumented workers have in landing in a place that would hire them. I fill out the form and drop it off. A few days later, I get a call from Cathy, asking me when I can start. I tell her I can begin right away. When I hang up, I am full of joy because I. HAVE. A. JOB! I have helped Mami clean houses and sell Avon, but this is my first official job in the US, and with it I can help my parents pay for tuition. I hold my head up high with pride.

It's 2002, and I'm a few months away from graduating from high school and starting my first semester of college. When we do the math, however, we realize that even with Mami, Papi, and me working, we don't have enough time to save up $3,400 for my first semester. But Papi is hopeful that tuition costs will change. He tells me he watched CUNY immigrant students speaking up against the policy change on Univision's evening news, which he is hooked to every night. "These students are like you. They are filing a lawsuit to change the policy, and they may win," Papi says. I'm skeptical. I'm curious about who these students are and how I can connect with them. In *El Diario*, New York's largest and oldest Spanish-language daily newspaper, Papi and I see a picture of CUNY students, professors, and representatives from community organizations and labor unions protesting. The article says three hundred students joined a rally at Hunter College, and they plan to hold a three-day hunger strike to push for the policy to change. Students accuse CUNY's administration of caving to racist and anti-immigrant politicians. We follow the development of this story on the news every day.

Republican state senator Frank Padavan argues that the new policy is about national security: "The CUNY Board of Trustees can't even really say how many undocumented aliens are enrolled at CUNY. Considering recent events, that's not only absurd, it's a matter of national security."[32] In the name of fighting this urgent threat, Padavan introduces legislation to ban undocumented students from attending public colleges and universities in the state. He argues that undocumented students should do it the "legal way": "When my grandparents arrived here at the turn of the century, they followed the law. They came through Ellis Island and were processed like hundreds of thousands of others. Why should there be two standards?" Conveniently, Padavan doesn't acknowledge that current immigration law is very different from when his grandparents came.

Countering Republican efforts, Democratic state senator Pedro Espada (Bronx) and Democratic assemblyman Adriano Espaillat (Manhattan/Bronx) introduce legislation in the senate and assembly to allow certain undocumented immigrant students to pay in-state tuition. Mirroring the in-state tuition policies from Texas and California, the legislation proposes that tuition rates be based on where students attend high school. Labor unions, students, CUNY faculty, and advocacy organizations pressure state policymakers and Republican governor George Pataki to pass the legislation. Pataki is running for reelection and knows he must back the policy to allow undocumented students to access higher education to get the support of Latine leaders and voters in New York City, which he needs to win. In June 2002, nearly two months before my first semester at Queens College, Governor Pataki proudly signs the tuition equity bill that allows undocumented students to pay in-state tuition into law, at the Great Hall at City College. At home, we are all in disbelief while watching the news on Univision. With tears coming down her cheeks, Mami thanks God for answering her prayers. "Ya vez, hay que tener fe!" she tells me.

Papi and I look at each other. "I told you the students were going to win," he says to me.

I'm in shock. I cry while my eyes are fixed on the TV screen. I slowly grasp that students like me, along with their allies, forced powerful politicians to change the law. Somehow these students found the courage to speak up in the face of injustice. If they can do it, perhaps I can find the courage within me to do the same. But I have no idea how to go about becoming as courageous as they are. I aspire to meet them and learn from them.

With the three of us working, we can see a more possible path to saving up $1,600 for my first semester. But then I get a tuition bill in the mail for the fall semester, and despite the new law, it still reflects charges for an international student—$3,400. I can't find any information online about what to do. There is no one I can ask for help. I could ask Ms. B, but it is summer and she is not teaching. Mami suggests I go to Queens College in person to find out how to apply the new law to my tuition bill. Years of neglect by public and private institutions in Ecuador have taught Mami that institutions can't ignore you if you are physically present. I'm afraid. People on the other side of the counter hold the power to open or close the door for people like me. Every question, every document, every interaction can lead to humiliation, a rejection, deportation, and family separation. The simple act of going to a public college to get information has high stakes.

But our family's dream of me going to college is stronger than the fear. I get on a bus to head to Queens College. It's a humid New York City summer day, and I'm sweating as I try to find my way through campus to the bursar's office. In my head, I anxiously play out the scenarios of my interaction with the person on the other side of the counter. How do I ask for help without sharing I'm undocumented?

The campus looks almost empty. Classes haven't started yet, and there are only a few people walking around. The trees all around, the colorful flowers in full bloom, and the birds singing have a calming effect on me. As I walk, I begin to imagine my life as a student here, heading to class, hanging out on the quad, and studying in the Rosenthal Library. I snap back to reality, realizing I'm lost. I return to the entrance gate, where there is a large sign with a map of the campus and its buildings. I finally find my way to Jefferson Hall, where the bursar's office is located. The building looks like a large old-world colonial house with a dark-brown wooden door and red-clay roof tiles. Inside, the first floor has shiny wooden floors and antique carved furniture that reminds me of Abuelita Esther's house.

I see the sign for the bursar's office. I begin to feel my heart beating faster and my hands getting sweaty. I open the door, and a white woman with glasses asks, "How can I help you?" Like my college advisor, this woman behind the counter has so much power. I'm paralyzed by her simple question. My mind is racing. I fear she may shame me for thinking that someone like me, an undocumented immigrant, could even dare to dream of a college education. I fear she will tell me, "Go back to where you came from." I fear she will call me "illegal." I fear she may report me to ICE. I find myself voiceless. I can't tell her I'm undocumented. Instead, with my voice trembling, I tell her Queens College "misclassified" me as an international student.

"Misclassified?" she asks.

I stay quiet, wishing this whole exchange could stop. But before her next question, a young Puerto Rican woman joins her behind the counter. She looks straight out of a Jennifer Lopez music video, with beautiful black hair that almost touches her waist, long red acrylic nails, and twisted gold hoops. "If you are not an international student, I know the forms you have to fill out," she says with a warm smile. Hearing Mami's voice in my head, I wonder if she has been sent by God. "I can help her," she says to the white woman. I don't know for sure if she is godsent, but I for sure thank God for her and all Puerto Ricans in New York City who come to our rescue. Our family encounters Puerto Ricans on the other side of the counter at hospitals, schools, subway stations, and the IRS offices in Queens. Throughout the city, they hold jobs where they can open or close the doors to newly arrived immigrants. They speak both English and Spanish, and they helped us apply for a tax ID number in the IRS office and helped Mami fill out the paperwork to get my vaccination card for high school registration. They also help us find our way when we get lost in the subway. Gracias por los Puertorriqueños, Diosito!

She asks me for my full name and date of birth and enters the information in her computer. Looking at her screen, she tells me they have my high school transcript in their system and the only thing I need to submit is the CUNY residency form, which includes an affidavit. The form must be notarized, she explains, as she hands it to me. To qualify for in-state tuition, students must show that they attended a New York high school for at least two years, graduated (or have a New York GED), and applied for CUNY or SUNY within five years of graduation. Students must also show proof of residency in New York and in the affidavit declare that the student will file for legal immigration status as soon as they become eligible. I don't read the form and quickly shove it in my bookbag. I don't know if I will ever see this woman again, so I take advantage of the few minutes I have with her and ask her if I can pay tuition in installments. She tells me about CUNY's tuition-payment plan and that I can sign up for the program regardless of immigration status. I freeze. It dawns on me that she has known all along that I'm undocumented. Neither one of us admits it. I feel ashamed. I want to find a place to hide. "Tragame, tierra," I pray silently. I can't look her in the eye. Instead, I look down at the tuition payment plan information sheet she hands me and say thank you, then rush out of the office.

As I read the CUNY residency form at home, my anxiety swells. My back tenses up and my chest tightens. Part A of the form asks my name, address, Social Security number; if I'm a US citizen, permanent resident, or international student; the information about the high school I attended; and my high school graduation date. Part B, the affidavit, entitled "Affidavit of Intent to Legalize Immigration Status," reads, "(Student's Name), being duly sworn, deposes and says that he/she does not currently have lawful immigration status but has filed an application to legalize his/her immigration status or will file such an application as soon as he/she is eligible to do so." This form forces me to come out as undocumented. Is this a trap? The semester starts in a few weeks, and I don't have much time to figure out what to do or find help.

I begin to feel suffocated. Suffocated by all the barriers and risks I face. Suffocated by the constant oppression at every single turn of my journey. I'm also angry. I'm angry that no matter how hard I work or how "good" of an immigrant I am, I'm not worthy of this country. I'm not worthy of an education. I'm not worthy of healthcare. I'm not worthy of opportunity. I'm not worthy of existing.

In the years to come, as a community organizer, I will learn that the requirements to qualify for in-state tuition and the questions on the CUNY residency form were the result of negotiations between Democrats, who controlled the assembly, and Republicans, who controlled the senate. Republicans, mostly anti-immigrant, wanted to make it harder for undocumented students to access higher education. I will also learn that my experience is not isolated. Poor and working-class people of color, regardless of immigration status, interact with people in institutions who have more power than we do. Whether we are applying for a job or trying to access healthcare, education, retirement, or other social benefits, the person on the other side of the counter has the power to make or break our future.

I sit down and take deep breaths. My righteous anger and strong commitment to honor my parents' sacrifices fuel my courage to fill out the form despite the risks. But the fear about how my information will be used stays. It will be with me for a long time. Perhaps it will be with me forever. The uncertainty about whether we can keep up with tuition payments is also in the back of my mind. This is the biggest bill our family has ever had. It's much more money than our combined rent and utilities. But I'm fiercely resolved to do all I can to go to college. With determination, I head to the pharmacy on the corner of our building with my passport to get the form notarized.

The man who is on the other side of the counter at the pharmacy is our family's friend. He works at the register, manages inventory, and notarizes documents. In his fifties, from the Dominican Republic, he is soft-spoken and kind. Over the years, he translates and notarizes all kinds of documents for our family—birth certificates, passports, baptism certificates, school and medical records. I know he knows we are undocumented, but he never says anything; and we don't say anything either. He never makes us feel less than, shamed, or judged. We just know that our secret is safe with him. He welcomes me with his usual warmth and asks how I'm doing. I tell him I've been stressed out about the college application process and ask him to notarize the form. He reads it and with a big smile says, "Of course. Congratulations! Your parents must be so proud you are going to college."

"They are," I say.

He doesn't even flinch at the contents of the form and stamps it with his signature. Our interaction is comforting. I feel supported and more at peace. I drop off the form at the bursar's office with the hope that this is the last obstacle I must overcome to go to college. Within a few weeks, I get a letter in the mail confirming my eligibility for in-state tuition and an updated tuition bill for $1,600 for the fall semester. I jump up and down, bursting with joy and excitement. I'm going to college!

6

WAKE UP

(Left to right) Selene, Cristina, Diana, and Jonathan proudly repping the Queens College Political Science Club, 2004 (courtesy of the author)

> *We have to confront our own internalized oppression in order to fully liberate ourselves.*
>
> —Cherríe Moraga

After all the hurdles, I'm finally all set to start my first semester in college. I'm excited about my political science classes and the opportunity to meet the undocumented students I have seen in the news. I'm nervous because I don't know anyone. My first class is Political Science 101 with Professor Bowman. I get to class a few minutes early, and being the nerd that I am, I sit in the front row, right across from the professor's desk. Professor Bowman is a tall white man in his fifties. He makes me think of Big Bird from Sesame Street because of his long, long, long legs. He greets me with a warm smile, but I'm so self-conscious of my accent that I don't say much more than hi. As students trickle in, I look around the classroom and notice a stark contrast with my high school classrooms. I'm one of only a handful of students of color in the class. Most of the students are white. Some of the girls are wearing fashionable clothes and Prada loafers. My college classmates have much more than me and my high school classmates. We are also mixed in age. Some students are older than me. They chat about driving to campus from Long Island and Westchester, complaining about traffic and parking. It dawns on me that my classmates here can afford expensive shoes, living in the suburbs, and driving to commute to school. I haven't felt like a minority in a school setting up until that day.

Class begins and Professor Bowman reviews the syllabus. He expects students to read the *New York Times* and assigned chapters of *American Democracy in Peril: Eight Challenges to America's Future*. He engages students in conversation. I try to focus, but I feel intimidated by my classmates. They speak very fast and use words that I don't know. I feel like I'm drowning in a sea of unfamiliar SAT words. I'm overwhelmed with shame. I become smaller and smaller by the minute. I pray for Professor Bowman not to call on me. I remain silent through the entire class, my sweaty hands clasped on top of my desk, feeling I am not ready for college after all and I don't deserve to be here.

The only way I can handle my feelings of shame, inferiority, and inadequacy is by working harder. I go to Rosenthal Library every day in between classes to work on my assignments until it closes at 10 p.m. The library becomes my refuge. I make a list of all the words I don't understand, and one by one I look them up in a dictionary. In an era without smartphones and audiobooks, I carry a heavy bookbag with multiple political science books, a notebook with notes and hundreds of vocabulary words, and two dictionaries: one for English definitions and the other for English-to-Spanish translation. I barely sleep six hours a night.

Years later, when I have access to therapy, I will understand that this was the way I coped with anxiety and depression. Experiencing poverty and migration, feeling ashamed of my skin color and how I look, and navigating a new country where we are exploited, racially profiled, and threatened with deportation have taken a toll on my mental health. These experiences of stress and trauma are widely shared by US-born and immigrant youth of color. For the Latine community in the United States, the legacy of colonialism, racism, sexism, economic inequality, poverty, migration, and fear of deportation and family separation have created a youth mental health crisis. Latine youth are more likely than their peers to experience anxiety, PTSD, and trauma. Studies from the Robert Wood Johnson Foundation find that 22 percent of Latine youth have depressive symptoms, more than one in four Latine female high schoolers think about committing suicide, 32.6 percent of Latine students report feeling hopeless and sad for more than two weeks (the highest rate among youth in the US), and 17.2 percent of Latine students report race-related bullying in school, with Latine parents naming bullying as their number-one health concern.[33]

In May 2023, ten-year-old Lukas Illescas from Westchester, New York, son of Ecuadorian immigrant parents, took his own life for fear of facing another day of bullying at school.[34] Systemic racism and oppression are literally killing us. Despite this crisis, Latine youth don't receive adequate mental health services. About 20 percent of the Latine community don't have health insurance, and many have health insurance that doesn't cover mental health services. Mental health is also a taboo subject in our community. Shame keeps families with mental health needs in silence and isolation. As I struggle with the highs and lows of anxiety and depression in college, I don't have anyone to talk to about it. There aren't mental health resources that I know of or that I can access at school. I think there must be something wrong with me and that I just need to push myself more and continue working hard, while numbing myself. No feelings, just keep working. *What else is there to do but to keep going?* I think.

"It's all in your head. Keep focusing," Mami says.

"Therapy is for locos," Papi says.

My parents don't know better. They also struggle with PTSD, depression, and anxiety. I can see it now.

Over the years, my work helps me understand how poverty, colonialism, systemic racial capitalism, sexism, and forced migration have created generational trauma, anxiety, and PTSD in my family and community. As an adult with immigration papers and a job that provides me with health insurance, I will finally be able to see a therapist. I will learn that working hard and overperforming are partly driven by my anxiety to distract myself from feeling pain and grief. I will also find therapists for Mami and my brother, Jonathan, who provide support on a sliding scale for families and communities with limited resources. Papi will continue to believe he doesn't need therapy, because he is not loco. Every week I show up to therapy to work on my healing, and Mami, Jonathan, and I get to have conversations about what we are learning about ourselves and our unprocessed traumas. But individual healing is not enough. As a society, we need to end systems of inequality, oppression, and injustice for our individual and collective healing and well-being.

In Professor Bowman's class, I'm shocked to read about how in the US, there is a long history of denying Black people, Indigenous people, and people of color equal participation in our democratic process; corporations have the power to influence the outcome of elections by donating to political campaigns; judges and Supreme Court justices make decisions aligned with political parties, instead of siding with justice; and the popular vote does not elect the country's president. I feel scammed. Our family thought we were fleeing poverty and a corrupt government in Ecuador to find stability, safety, and a better life in the "greatest democracy in the world," but I realize that this country's democratic system is far from providing equal participation for all people. I wonder how this country can be considered a global leader in spreading democracy while failing to uphold and practice democratic values at home. How hypocritical, I think.

I use the library's computer lab, which provides fast internet, to write my papers and do online research about resources for undocumented students. I also search for ways to connect with other undocumented students at CUNY. While searching, I come across two of the organizations that were part of the advocacy efforts for in-state tuition: the New York Immigration Coalition and the Latin American Integration Center, which later merges with another organization, Make the Road by Walking, and together become Make the Road New York. I leave a message at both offices, hoping to talk to someone who can connect me with the students. I learn that these organizations are advocating for the Development, Relief, and Education for Alien Minors Act, also known as the DREAM Act, a bipartisan federal bill introduced in 2001 by Senators Dick Durbin (D-IL) and Orrin Hatch (R-UT) to provide access to higher education and a pathway to citizenship to some undocumented students. I don't know much about how policy proposals become law, but finding out about this bill gives me hope. Naively, I think that a proposal that would allow young people to go to college and protect them from deportation would swiftly become a law. I will learn that in Congress, white supremacy, racism, xenophobia, and greed are far more powerful than good policy solutions that benefit not only immigrants but all of us.

In my Race, Class, Gender, and Law class with Professor Rollins, I learn about the Constitution and social movements that have pushed this country to live up to its democratic ideals. I learn about change makers from Black, Indigenous, LGBTQ, and Latine communities, and women who force the US to fulfill the promise of equality, justice, and freedom. A white man with shoulder-length gray hair that has a perfect shine, Professor Rollins has a sarcastic sense of humor, making his class my favorite. He is the first openly gay educator I meet. Raised by an Ecuadorian Catholic family and schooled by Catholic nuns, I was taught that being gay is a sin. This belief was reinforced when I joined an evangelical Christian church that one of my older cousins introduced me to after the passing of my sister. Attending Sunday services and joining praying circles helped me cope with the pain of losing her. The pastor and deacons of the church instilled in us the belief that gay people are possessed by demons that must be cast out. Prayer has the power to get rid of the demons, they told me. I imagined getting the demons out looked like a scary scene from *The Exorcist*.

Now as a college student, I watch Professor Rollins lecturing about how the values and protections named in the Constitution were only meant for white men with property. I refuse to believe that he is possessed by demons. How can someone who is teaching students about equality be possessed by demons? Weren't the teachings of Jesus all about justice and equality? Aren't we all, without exception, created in the image of God? Professor Rollins's class plants the first seeds of doubt in the religious beliefs that had been instilled in my childhood. I question the teachings from Catholic priests, evangelical Christian pastors, and nuns. My beliefs and understanding of the world begin to crack open and transform.

As I confront the truth of the origins and history of this

country, I feel betrayed and disappointed. But I'm also inspired by the leaders of social justice movements who have made this country better. They were ordinary people, committed to equality and justice, who didn't give up on the promise of this country and worked to create change. They have made possible the world that I live in now and the rights I have. As a Latina undocumented immigrant, I have access to K–12 public education and higher education only due to the work of people before me who courageously chose to speak up and unite with others to fight for change. People like Sylvia Mendez, a Mexican American girl in Orange County, California. In 1945, she wasn't allowed to enroll in her district's school because of her Mexican background.[35] Her father challenged the school's decision in court, and in 1947, *Mendez v. Westminster* became the first case in US history to force school integration. The court's decision held that separate but equal schools were inadequate but wrongfully held that Mexican Americans were part of the white race. The fight to end school segregation continued, and in 1950, Reverend Oliver Leon Brown tried to enroll his seven-year-old daughter, Linda Brown, in the local elementary school in Topeka, Kansas, but Linda wasn't allowed because she was Black. Instead, she was forced to ride a bus to a segregated school.[36] Reverend Brown became part of a group of thirteen Black parents who worked with the National Association for the Advancement of Colored People (NAACP) to challenge racial segregation in schools by filing a class-action lawsuit. In 1954, the Supreme Court ruled on the landmark case of *Brown v. Board of Education of Topeka* that school segregation and discrimination based on race were unconstitutional.

In 1975, the Texas legislature passed a law requiring the state to withhold funds to school districts that enrolled undocumented immigrant students. Some districts banned undocumented students entirely, while others charged $1,000 for annual tuition per student, making it impossible for undocumented parents to afford K–12 public education. The Tyler Independent School District began expelling students who did not have proof of US citizenship. The policy targeted the undocumented children of Mexican immigrant farmworkers. Alfredo Lopez was ten when he and his siblings were kicked out of school because they did not have US birth certificates.[37] Risking deportation, the Lopez family and three other undocumented families joined forces to work with the Mexican American Legal Defense and Educational Fund (MALDEF), a Latine legal civil rights organization, to legally challenge the Tyler Independent School District on the unequal treatment of immigrant students. After a long legal battle, in 1982, the Supreme Court ruled in *Plyler v. Doe* that denying access to students based on their immigration status was unconstitutional and in violation of the Fourteenth Amendment and the equal protection clause. Justice Brennan on behalf of the court said, "By denying these children a basic education we deny them the ability to live within the structure of our civic institutions and foreclose any realistic possibility that they will contribute in even the smallest way to the progress of our Nation."[38]

The Supreme Court's decision in *Plyler v. Doe* has ensured that undocumented students have had access to K–12 public education for over forty years. But a growing white nationalist movement, responding to a demographic shift that will result in nonwhite people becoming the majority in the country by 2044, has led to states and localities adopting policies to deny undocumented students access to public education. In 2011, Alabama enacted a law requiring school administrators to verify and report the immigration status of their students as well as their parents. Although civil rights and immigrant justice advocates filed a legal challenge that resulted in the courts blocking implementation, the damage in immigrant and Latine communities had already been done. The policy intensified fear and confusion among undocumented immigrants and their families. More than 13 percent of Latine students in the state, immigrants and US citizens, withdrew from public schools between September 2011 and February 2012.[39]

The legal fights courageously led by people like Sylvia Mendez's father and Reverend Oliver Leon Brown give me hope that the conditions faced by undocumented immigrants can change. My belief that I don't have the right to demand better because I'm undocumented is challenged. If everyday people find the agency to change this country, so can I. I aspire to understand more about how people create and join social justice movements and win. But I don't ask questions in class, because I'm still self-conscious of my English and accent. Instead, I write down questions in my notebook and stay after class to talk to Professor Rollins. He tells me that I ask smart questions and I should bring them into class discussion. The thing is, our class is intimate, with fewer than fifteen students, making discussions quite intimidating for me. I sit in the front row, but I am quiet and shy. One of my classmates, Azmina Jasani, speaks in class often and engages in back-and-forth conversations with Professor Rollins and other classmates. I observe her with curiosity and admiration. I see in her everything I am not. She is bold and confident, speaking her mind with the certainty I only dream of having one day. She is the first young immigrant woman of color I meet who actively participates in class and persuasively engages in debates with other classmates. She is not afraid of publicly disagreeing with other students and standing by her perspective. I want to be like her. I know there is a valuable voice inside of me too. I don't know what my voice sounds like yet, but I know she is there and wants to come out.

One day, Azmina smiles at me during class. Her warm smile

gives me the courage I need to approach her. I share with her that I'm struggling to write our upcoming assignment. She offers to help me by sharing her last paper as reference. She asks me what year I'm in, and we get to know each other. Azmina is an immigrant from India who came with her family as a young person seeking a better life. She is a junior, and like me, she grew up in Queens and wants to go to law school. We both love dancing. She tells me she is a dance minor and is rehearsing for an upcoming show. Before parting ways to head to our next class, she invites me to the dance performance and a Political Science Club meeting. I don't have that many friends at the time. Meeting her makes me feel less alone and hopeful that I can build a community of friends like I did in high school. I show up to the Political Science Club meeting, where I find out that she is the vice president of the club and a student senator. Afterward, we hang out for the rest of the afternoon in the student life building. We talk about our political science classes, her dance rehearsals, law schools, preparing for the LSAT, and our eyebrows. We both enjoy skin care, makeup, and fashion. We share makeup tips and the lipstick colors we get from MAC. Azmina and I become friends. My life in college will never be the same after meeting her.

We see each other almost every day, chat after Professor Rollins's class, and attend student meetings and events together. She takes me to her favorite eyebrow-threading spot in Jackson Heights, where I get my eyebrows threaded for the first time, and I'm hooked. I will never wax my eyebrows again. Inspired by her dance performance, I sign up for dance classes to complete my liberal arts credits and talk to an academic advisor about a dance minor. I crave a space, even if only an hour-long class, where I can be creative, find joy, and feel free. Luckily, once I start taking dance classes, from ballet to modern dance, I need to find time to practice the routines I'm learning. My grade is determined not only by written assignments and class participation but also by our final performance. I arrive on campus early every morning with a small group of other classmates to practice. My days start and close with dance.

Azmina introduces me to her friends in the Political Science Club, student government, and the New York Public Interest Research Group (NYPIRG). Many of them are also immigrants or children of immigrants of color. I meet students from Pakistan, India, the Philippines, Nigeria, Israel, and Mexico. They remind me of my high school Key Club crew. They all speak other languages, have all kinds of accents, and find joy in planning and hosting events to engage students in efforts to improve conditions on campus and celebrate our different cultures. At these events, I try halal and kosher foods for the first time. I love how tasty halal food is and end up becoming a regular at the Shah's Halal Cart on Kissena Boulevard outside campus.

The students I get to know through Azmina have meetings to talk about how to fight tuition hikes, increase funds for student support services, and improve food on campus, as well as the need for more space for student activities and events. I'm surprised to learn that students can make demands. They are outspoken, fighting for what they believe they deserve. I still struggle with the feeling that I don't have the right to demand anything. I am barely allowed into college. Why would I create trouble asking for more? But reminding myself of the social justice movements I learn about in my political science classes and spending time with these students crack the door open for me to shed the idea that I don't have the right to speak up and fight for a better life. They share stories of struggle—not having enough to pay for tuition, books, and transportation; raising families and going to school; and hustling in between jobs. I'm not used to sharing about my life, but I relate to their stories. I increasingly open up to them about my struggles as a student, too. I don't disclose that I'm undocumented, but I share how my family works multiple jobs to pay for my tuition. The more that I speak, the more I hear my voice, and the more I believe that I, too, deserve the changes students are demanding.

I have found my community. And it is in this community that I grow passionate about improving the lives of students on campus and ensuring that college is more affordable for me and thousands of other students at CUNY and those coming after me. Immigration status is only one of many barriers facing poor and working-class students in higher education. I join the Political Science Club and student government and start volunteering for planning events and participating in student meetings and my classes. I begin to let go of the shame about my English and accent bit by bit. When Azmina's term as vice president of the Political Science Club comes to an end, she encourages me to run. "I'm not sure," I say. The truth that I never tell her is that I don't believe I'm worthy.

"Come on, Cristina!" Azmina says. "You will be an excellent vice president. You're smart and capable."

It's hard to believe her words, but for the first time in college, I feel that someone who I look up to believes in me and sees something in me that I can't see. Maybe she is right. Maybe I'm smart enough to do this. Maybe this is my chance to make a difference in the lives of students and learn to have the confidence that Azmina has. I decide to take this leap and run for vice president. I ask her to mentor me on how to be the best club officer possible. "Of course," Azmina says with a big smile. I'm elected as the new vice president of the Political Science Club, beginning my journey as a student leader.

One of the first events I co-plan with other officers of the Political Science Club is a student debate about the war in Iraq.

Congress and President Bush accuse the Iraqi government of supporting Al-Qaeda, linked to the terrorist attacks of 9/11, and of having weapons of mass destruction that pose a threat to the United States. In 2002, Congress passes a joint resolution granting President Bush the power to use military force against Iraq, and in 2003, the US bombs and invades Iraq, overthrowing the government. Across the country and on campus, the debate about the war is heated. Some students support and others oppose the war, and some even call into question whether the war is legal. The Political Science Club is a nonpartisan student organization. This means our programming must engage all perspectives. I'm an undocumented college student that has been personally impacted and politicized by the country's response to 9/11, which turned immigrants into suspects of terrorism, dehumanized us, and made us targets of the war on terror. The same Republicans that use the attacks of 9/11 to justify the war in Iraq use 9/11 to target immigrants. I not only don't trust the Bush administration, but I'm against the war. In 2004, after a fifteen-month investigation, it is revealed that Iraq had no weapons of mass destruction.[40]

I struggle with the planning of this event. Not because of my views about the war, but because I'm afraid of Republicans. I am not friends with any Republican students on campus, and I don't know of many, but what I do know about Republicans is that they think I'm a criminal, a suspect of terrorism, and they want immigrants of color like me out of the country. In one of our club meetings, I meet Jonathan, a freshman studying political science, who is interested in joining the debate. I know he is Jewish because he wears a black yarmulke. He tells me he is a conservative Republican and eager to share his arguments for why the war is legal. He is the first openly conservative Republican I meet. I'm beyond freaking out inside. On the outside, I keep it cool, but on the inside, my heart is beating faster, and I feel a flare of cold sweat. Nobody on campus knows I'm undocumented, but I wonder if Jonathan, like other Republicans, is against my existence.

We don't have a lot of time left to plan the debate, and I, along with the other officers, decide to confirm Jonathan as a panelist. I try to keep him at arm's length, only engaging in conversations about the event, but he comes to the Political Science Club office every day. We can always count on him bringing food along. He often shows up with boxes of leftover kosher pizza that he gets from other student club events. It's his first year in college, and like me when I was a freshman, he is looking to find community. He is friendly and funny. He breaks into guffaws at his own stories. The jokester in me lets my guard down, cracking up at his jokes. I tease him about talking too fast. "English, please," I yell.

For many of us who live in small, crowded apartments with our entire families, the office is our second home. My family's studio apartment in Jackson Heights is six hundred square feet. The four of us share a tiny bathroom and kitchen and turn half of the studio into our sleeping space, leaving the other half for a living and dining area. My brother and I sleep in bunk beds to save room. It's hard to read and write my papers at home while Papi is watching the news, Mami is cooking, and my brother is playing video games. I stay on campus all day between my political science classes at Powdermaker Hall, the dance studio at Rathaus Hall, the library, and the student life building, where the Political Science Club has an office in the basement.

The club office smells like pizza and old books. It can't fit more than twelve people comfortably, but about twenty of us come in throughout the day to hang out between classes. We have a brown couch, donated by one of the former club officers, where we take naps, a small black fridge, and two cabinets where we keep books, gym clothes, banners, and snacks. Jonathan and

I will end up having some of the most intimate conversations in that room. We happen to be in the office alone a lot, and instead of catching up on schoolwork, we catch up on our lives. We talk about our classes, families, and how we'd rather be at school all day instead of at home. Jonathan comes out to me as gay, and I come out to him as undocumented. He shares with me that he also comes from an immigrant family. His maternal grandmother came to the US fleeing the Nazis and made Brooklyn her home. His dad came to the US with the help of a Jewish nonprofit organization supporting Jews fleeing persecution and poverty. We hold each other with humanity and love and become each other's safe space. We leave our closets behind and begin a journey of self-discovery, self-determination, and self-love together.

Jonathan joins the Gay, Lesbian, and Straight Alliance (GLASA). I join too and go with him to GLASA meetings and events. The GLASA office becomes our second hangout spot. We collaborate on events to raise awareness about homophobia and to celebrate queerness. Following in Azmina's footsteps, I also join the student government, and as a student senator, I become chair of the Student Government Minority Affairs Committee. I join senators from other CUNY campuses to advocate against tuition hikes and convene students to have conversations about equal access to higher education. I host my first event to talk about undocumented students in higher education and the need for policies like the federal DREAM Act. Jonathan and I are both trying to find ourselves and our voice. I meet other political science students, whom I recruit into our club: Selene, a Mexican immigrant who I later learn is also undocumented, and Diana and Andreana, both born in the US to immigrant parents. We are all Latinas with big dreams. They are passionate about college affordability, women's and immigrants' rights, and student activism.

We get to know each other while sharing our struggles juggling family, work, and school, and our aspirations to make our parents proud as the first people in our family getting a college education. We laugh and cry about our dating life, and from time to time, we turn the club office into a dance party, blasting soca, reggaeton, merengue, salsa, and bachata. We often join forces with the Black Student Union and the Caribbean Student Association, who have offices near us, to turn the hallway into our dance floor. The Caribbean Student Association has the best dancing playlists, but when they are not around, I designate myself as the DJ. I may be a nerd, but you can always count on me to be on top of the latest hits and throw a fun party. I play top songs from Ivy Queen, Daddy Yankee, Tego Calderón, and Aventura. Jonathan is my dancing partner. Even though he is still learning to keep rhythm, he is not shy about practicing shaking his hips to salsa and bachata.

In my junior year, when Jonathan and I are elected vice president and president, respectively, of the club, Diana, Andreana, and Selene take on other officer roles, and with that, the crew is complete.

We roll deep together through the rest of our time at Queens College. We cofound a new student political party on campus and the Model United Nations chapter, where we lead the first Queens College delegation to the Model United Nations conference. Our delegation is assigned to represent Sudan. It's a tough year to represent Sudan. The country is undergoing a civil war and genocide. All night long before the event, we prepare to represent Sudan in front of the Security Council. Here we are, a mixed group of Latines, Pakistanis, and a Jewish gay guy, some of us with accents, ready to defend Sudanese war criminals! Jonathan leads our delegation. He knocks it out of the park. We don't win an award that year, but we mentor the next delegation, and the Queens College Model UN will go on to become an award-winning delegation.

We celebrate each other's birthdays, support each other in our class assignments and projects, and help each other through difficult times. We become chosen family, loving on each other despite our differences, holding grace and compassion for our growing edges and mistakes, giving each other a real talk when needed (like when we tell each other to let go of a guy who is not worth dating), and supporting each other's dreams. We are friends to this day.

Jonathan and I plan meetings and events, coordinating with other clubs for club-orientation day and preparing for the club's main event of the year, War on Hate. War on Hate, a sarcastic twist on the Bush administration's "war on terror," is a weeklong series of events exploring issues surrounding inequality, racism, xenophobia, homophobia, and the negative impact of globalization, war, and genocide. We run around campus submitting paperwork for the college administration to approve event space, food, and honoraria for speakers. We are good at political analysis, but we both suck at budgeting. Developing budgets for events takes us days, and we often end up working through the night to meet deadlines. We get kicked out of the student life building at 10 p.m. and move to finishing the budget in the back seat of Jonathan's car. By the end, we are both tired and laughing deliriously. He often drives me back home before heading to Westchester, where he lives with his parents in a beautiful house with many rooms and a spacious yard.

We don't talk much about our class differences, but we both know his family has more than mine. I'm hustling in between selling Avon products and working as a receptionist at a chiropractor's office to help my parents pay for tuition, food, books, and transportation. Jonathan has his parents' support to pay for tuition and his expenses. Sometimes I don't eat because I don't have enough money. I don't know if he notices, but often he pays for my dinner when we go to our favorite Middle Eastern kosher spot, Grill Point, on Main Street. Our friendship bond is strong and deep. I go from fearing him to loving him. College, our lived experiences, and our friendship help us see each other's humanity, shape how we understand ourselves and our identity, and help us find our voice. He moves from identifying himself as a conservative Republican to becoming a progressive and one of my most vocal friends fighting alongside me for the rights of undocumented immigrants.

While I'm liberating myself from fear and gaining confidence in my student leadership and my voice, the Bush administration's war on immigrants continues to intensify. The administration increases detentions and deportations of immigrants, and in the news, it is reported that Congress is talking about an anti-immigrant bill that would make it a crime to hire and help undocumented immigrants. I'm overwhelmed by the news. But at the same time, Jonathan and I are eager to speak up in support of immigrants' dignity and rights. Jonathan suggests that the Political Science Club take a public stand on campus by holding a march around the quad. I agree with him, but I don't feel comfortable bringing too much attention to myself or sharing more publicly that I'm undocumented. Jonathan has my back. He leads all the public speaking and the small march holding an American flag and chanting, "What do we want? The DREAM Act! When do we want it? Now!" As we get closer to the end of the 2006 spring semester, Jonathan comes up with the idea of asking faculty and students to wear a white ribbon in support of the DREAM Act on commencement day. The administration doesn't want us to distribute ribbons during commencement, but Jonathan never takes no for an answer. There is always a way to get things done, he tells me. "Loopholes" is his favorite word. Spending time with him, I get to closely witness the privilege of being a white man in this world. Most of the time Jonathan does, in fact, find a way. He moves the college administration to allow us to distribute white ribbons. He even gets the president of Queens College to commit to wearing one. Watching him in action helps me build the muscle and the confidence to not take no for an answer and to speak up even when I'm afraid.

I'm growing in my understanding of my own political identity and voice, but this process has not yet pushed me to confront my internalized colonialism, racism, sexism, and self-hate. I find my path loving who I am and where I come from thanks to Mr. Hayes, a Black man in his fifties. He is the director of student development and supports me in my role as chair of the Student Government Minority Affairs Committee. He sees me, a young, short immigrant woman who is always running around between working, classes, student-event planning, and meetings with the administration advocating for student services. He sees something in me I don't see in myself yet: the need to connect with who I am and where I come from, and the potential for greater leadership. He calls me by my last name. "Jiménez, I'm recommending you for a leadership-development program," he tells me.

"What's the program about?" I ask.

He introduces me to the Model New York State Senate Session Project. A program run by the Puerto Rican/Hispanic Task Force of the New York State legislature and the State University of New York, it trains students in the legislative process and culminates with students debating bills on the floor of the senate chamber in Albany. I'm interested, but I tell him I can't do it. What I don't tell him is that I'm afraid of being rejected because of my undocumented status. I want to protect myself from the disappointment and shame that come whenever I must disclose that I'm undocumented. Letting go of some opportunities becomes my coping mechanism. Mr. Hayes is confused. Any other student would have jumped at the opportunity to get a free trip to Albany and get to meet members of the New York State legislature face-to-face. He insists on asking me to go into his office and even calls me at home. I avoid him, pretending to be too busy with schoolwork. I run into him in the student life building, and there is no more hiding.

He confronts me: "Jiménez, why don't you want to join? What are you concerned about?"

I feel cornered. In a rush of emotions, feeling exhausted about having to conceal my status and frustrated about dreams and opportunities that I've been denied, I decide to tell him the truth: "I'm undocumented."

"So? Who says you can't join this program?" he asks in a no-big-deal kind of way. I'm surprised at his reaction and feel silly for not having shared with him from the get-go. He tells me, "I don't think there is an issue with that, but let me call them and I will call you back. And pick up my phone call, Jiménez," he says. He calls me a few days later confirming I can join.

I go to his office to fill out the program's paperwork, and Mr. Hayes starts asking me about ways we can fix my status. "There is nothing I can apply to," I explain. He is frustrated to learn that our immigration system does not provide a way for people like me to adjust to lawful immigration status. Before I leave, he gives me the advice that sets me on the journey to understand who I am, where I come from, and to be proud of what all that means.

"Have you taken a class with Professor Flores from the English Department?" he asks.

"No," I say.

"You must register for one of her classes," he tells me. I don't question his recommendation. Mr. Hayes is an educator that not only believes in me but also chooses to use his knowledge and institutional power to help students spread their wings. I trust him, so I sign up for one of Professor Flores's classes for the next semester.

The first day of Professor Flores's women's literature class, she is playing hip-hop to welcome us. *This is different*, I think. She is half-Panamanian and half-white, proud of her roots and of living in the South Bronx. She greets us in English and Spanish. "Bienvenidos, estudiantes," she says. No other college professor has ever talked to me in Spanish before this class. I feel seen. I don't know her yet, but I immediately feel drawn to her. Her syllabus lists eighteen books as required reading. She admits that her class is a lot of work, but she is not sorry about it. "If you can't handle it, feel free to drop the class," she says. I feel overwhelmed by her syllabus, but dropping the class doesn't even cross my mind. She is the only Latina professor I have, and though I don't know until I take her class, I realize I'm craving a professor who looks more like me and my community, gets my culture and my language, and can speak to my reality and experience. We read books by Black, Latine, and Chicana writers: Toni Morrison, Angela Davis, Gloria Anzaldúa, Cherríe Moraga, Ruth Behar, Sandra Cisneros, Michelle Cliff, Elena Poniatowska, and Julia Alvarez. My mind and heart are being stretched and challenged in new ways. These writers give me a framework and language to understand and explore my identity as an Ecuadorian, a Latina, an undocumented immigrant, and a working-class heterosexual woman in a US context. They help me process the contradictions of not belonging, of feeling ni de aquí y ni de allá, of feeling not enough, of feeling ashamed of my accent and how I look, of feeling fearful and yet wanting to speak up, and of feeling homeless, uprooted from the country where I was born and rejected by the place I consider home. Slowly, I'm breaking free from the fears, shame, and lies that I've been carrying for a long time.

My papers for class explore the literature through a feminist lens, questioning gender roles and norms and the part religion and church play in defining what freedoms and rights women have. My inner voice that questions the religious beliefs instilled in me by the Catholic Church after taking Professor Rollins's class is now clearer and more confident about challenging the role of the church in society and its position on LGBTQ and women's rights. It is in Professor Flores's class that the veil finally comes off. I feel like I'm having my own *Matrix* moment. I see through the tradition and culture I was raised in and begin to realize why women in my neighborhood in Ecuador are told by priests and evangelical pastors to stay with their husbands and honor their marriages even though their husbands cheat on them and hit them when they come home drunk; why my tía Blanquita is shamed by society for choosing to stay single and not have children; and why Mami was told women don't go to school. I come to understand how religion, institutions, laws, and cultural norms keep women down, take away our freedom and agency, and concentrate the power over systems and institutions on men. I reject the idea that God created women to be submissive beings, controlled by the church and men, and only valued to please and serve men—an idea that is still alive in Latine tradition and culture.

Seeing the world with these new eyes feels overwhelming, but also empowering. I find hope that a different world is possible in the stories by the women writers of color I read in class. Their characters and narratives inspire me to imagine my own freedom and a society where women are safe and free. I fall in love with Toni Morrison's Sula, who takes pride in not conforming to gender roles and expectations of what a Black woman should be like. I'm inspired by the writers' courage in defining themselves, challenging the status quo and the patriarchy, and charting a path of their own. My first email signature will include this line under my name: "I am Toni Morrison's Sula."

After taking Professor Flores's women's literature class, I'm hooked and try to take as many classes with her as I can. In her twentieth-century global literature class, we analyze the impact of colonialism on both the colonized and the colonizer and explore mestizaje, the process of interracial and or intercultural mixing, counterhegemonic aesthetics, and new archetypes of the Americas. We read *The Invention of the White Race* by Theodore W. Allen, and works by Eduardo Galeano, Edward Said, Malcolm X, and the Combahee River Collective, a Black feminist lesbian organization active between 1974 and 1980 that pushed the feminist and civil rights movements to reflect the vision and needs of Black women and lesbians. One day as we explore mestizaje, Professor Flores engages the class in a discussion about internalized colonialism and how white supremacy has historically shaped how we think about beauty. This conversation really hits home for me. I think of the times growing up watching TV and not seeing people who looked like me, feeling I wasn't beautiful, my brown skin and black hair being a source of shame. I remember when as a child I heard family and friends talk about the need to better our race and the aspiration to look whiter—look more like the colonizer.

At the end of class, I tell Professor Flores I want to explore this more. She suggests readings from *Women Writing Resistance* and tells me I have a beautiful Indigenous face. Her words feel like a slap in the face. I'm offended and embarrassed. Nobody has ever looked me in the eye and said that to me. I don't respond, but her comment forces me to confront my own internalized racism, anti-indigeneity, and colonialism. There is nothing wrong with a beautiful Indigenous face. Why do I feel offended and embarrassed instead of proud? The women writers of color I learn from in her class help me make meaning of this moment. I feel uncomfortable and stretched because that's what colonialism does to you. It makes you believe the lie that you are less than the colonizer and that your Indigenous roots are something to be ashamed of. I break free from this lie and choose to learn more about the history and present of the Americas and my Indigenous ancestors. I choose to be on a lifelong journey to love myself, where I come from, and how I look. Over the years on this journey of learning and healing, I become proud of who I am and the process that it has taken to wholeheartedly believe I am enough, beautiful just the way I am, and worthy of love, freedom, and a life with dignity.

7

NOT ALONE

Cristina at her first rally in New York City to stop the deportations of Marie Gonzalez (from Missouri) and Kamal Essaheb (from New York), with Kamal, holding the microphone, sharing his story, 2005 (courtesy of Walter Barrientos)

> *Your silence will not protect you.*
>
> —Audre Lorde

I don't hear back from the groups I contacted that are advocating for the DREAM Act and other immigration reforms, but every time I go to Rosenthal Library's computer lab, I search for updates about the bill. I read in the news that there's a renewed effort to push Congress to pass it, and I really start nerding out, following every step of the legislative process, reading news updates, and even watching committee debates on C-SPAN online. I learn that the bill doesn't benefit every undocumented young person, but I want to see if my brother and I would qualify. There are strict criteria, including the following: (1) you must have entered the US before your sixteenth birthday; (2) you must have been living in the US for the last five years; (3) you must be a person of good moral character, which means young people convicted of a crime can't qualify (but what and who define what's considered a crime?); (4) you must have been admitted to an institution of higher education and have earned a GED or high school diploma; and (5) you must be under the age of thirty on the date the law gets passed. As the bill is written, I would qualify, which is a relief, but I think about the young people that don't meet these requirements. I wonder who came up with the criteria; they seem so arbitrary.

From reading the news, I learn that people who support immigrants see the DREAM Act as the most viable immigration policy proposal under a Republican-controlled Congress in an increasingly anti-immigrant political and cultural environment. Those against the DREAM Act argue that undocumented immigrant parents and children are criminals, should be punished, and would take "American" jobs and college spots—the same old stuff that anti-immigrant politicians have said generation after generation. Supporters make the case that the bill will enable immigrant youth to get a college education, get better jobs, and contribute to the economy by empowering them to work, increase their spending, and pay more in taxes. They point to the country losing the investment already made in undocumented youths' K–12 public education. They also argue that young people came to this country through "no fault of their own." Senator Durbin, Democrat from Illinois, who is a sponsor of the bill and its leading champion, makes the case that the government shouldn't punish young people for the decisions of their parents. I pause when I read this. This logic shames immigrant parents for migrating with their children and accuses them of being irresponsible or doing something wrong. Yet, when I remember what we were fleeing, I know my parents are heroes for leaving everything behind to seek a better life here. I don't have the language yet to fully explain how conflicted I feel about knowing my parents did what was best for their children yet feeling ashamed about being undocumented and living in fear of deportation.

A few years later, as a trained community organizer with a better understanding about power and this country's history, I will learn that the politics of "personal responsibility" are used to make us believe that any marginalized group is at fault for their own difficult situation, erasing and denying the systemic harm that they've endured. That somehow, it is our fault to have to flee our homes and therefore we must be punished. I will learn that "personal responsibility" is a tool used to keep us from challenging people in government and corporate power who create the systems and conditions that force us to flee our homes in the first place. I will also realize that the claims that immigrants are bad for the economy are not backed by research and evidence at all. Blaming immigrants takes the attention away from people in government and corporations responsible for defunding education and moving jobs overseas or hiring undocumented workers in the US to exploit workers for greater profits. I remember reading some of those anti-immigrant "research" reports blaming immigrants for everything from the housing crisis to traffic congestion.

The sad fact is that different waves of immigrants over time, particularly those considered "less white," have consistently been blamed for the ills of the country over and over again. In the 1920s, during the Prohibition era, German, Italian, and Irish immigrants were shamed as "not American," "immoral," and "drunks" and blamed for creating chaos and threatening public welfare. Nativists and those who favored Prohibition worked together to push for the Johnson-Reed Act of 1924, the first immigration reform. Every immigration reform since then has further criminalized immigrants for seeking a better life in the US, increased government resources to detain and deport them, and stripped them of their human, civil, and legal rights. Many of those immigrants have become "white" in the American story, and some of their descendants are now saying the same things about people like me and calling for the mass deportation of immigrants.

I get more and more involved in the Political Science Club, student government, and other student organizations. I'm feeling more comfortable in my own skin, and I'm slowly finding my voice. In meetings with college administrators, I talk about the need for student services on campus and more funding for student organizations, and I argue against tuition hikes. But the more I learn about the truth of the immigration system, the more empowered I become in every part of my life, except my immigration status. I'm still in hiding about being undocumented. I don't talk to anyone about it, and I don't know of anyone on campus who is undocumented. I had hoped the organizations I found online could help me connect with other undocumented college students, but I've still heard nothing, and I think that maybe I won't hear back from them at all.

When I've almost given up, I'm relieved to get an email from the New York Immigration Coalition (NYIC). Minerva Moya, an organizer and advocate with the NYIC, invites me to join an upcoming DREAM Act campaign meeting where other CUNY students will be present. I'm elated. I'm eager to learn more about the status of the bill and how we can help to make it become a law. The passage of this bill would transform my life. I also can't wait to meet other undocumented students. They may know about jobs, scholarships, and other ways I can fix my immigration status and pay for tuition, not to mention it would be nice to just have friends with whom I could share my whole self. As I read the email, my heart and body are overtaken by hope. I want to scream with excitement, but I can't, because it's mandatory to maintain silence in the computer lab. But inside, I'm doing a happy dance for sure.

The NYIC's office is in Midtown Manhattan. I don't travel there often, so I triple-check my foldable NYC subway map and leave Queens College two hours before the meeting to avoid being late. People who aren't from New York City may not know this, but the city is absolutely massive, and Manhattan might as well be a different world from Queens. Main Street in Queens is bustling, with people from a hundred different cultures coming and going to and from supermarkets, shops, and the subway station. I move quickly through the crowd to get to the train. I'm slowed down by a group of Korean friends who are unbothered by the pace around them, chatting, laughing, and drinking bubble tea. I pass them and run quickly to the subway station stairs where I, along with Latine immigrant construction workers holding coffee and Colombian empanadas, rush down to catch the Manhattan-bound train.

On my way, I think of all the questions I want to ask other undocumented students. *How can the DREAM Act become a law? Are undocumented students destined to graduate without being able to put their degree to work?* And I think of the personal questions I'd ask if we become friends. *Do you tell anyone else that you are undocumented? Have you ever been caught?*

I transfer from the 7 to the F train on the Roosevelt Avenue stop and get off at Twenty-Third Street. I don't exactly know my way through the streets of Manhattan and realize I'm walking in the wrong direction when I see the sign for Twenty-Second Street, so I begin walking back the other way. I make it to the right street, but now I don't know which way—right or left—is Seventh Avenue. I look more lost than a tourist. By the time I arrive, I am beginning to think that this whole thing is a big mistake. But in spite of my fears, I head into what looks like a typical austere office building and up the elevator. When the doors open, I'm welcomed by a warm smile. Minerva, the staff member from the NYIC, is a petite young Puerto Rican woman with glasses. She makes me feel comfortable from the get-go, offering me water and asking me about my trip in. She ushers me into a conference room filled with people. I start wondering if they know I'm undocumented. In spite of Minerva's warm welcome, fear closes in around me and all I feel is shame. I keep my gaze on the gray carpet and sit down in the first empty chair. I resolve to not say anything.

But again, the warmth of the folks in the room pushes some of the shame and fear to the back of my awareness just enough for me to say hi. All around the long conference table, people greet me and introduce themselves. They are from different organizations providing services to immigrant communities and advocating for immigrant rights representing Chinese, Korean, Latine, and African immigrant communities. I'm surprised to learn that New York is home to thousands of undocumented students from Asian and African countries. Up until that point, I have only seen Latine students on the news. A few of the people at the meeting are from labor unions representing CUNY faculty and the city's janitors, doormen, and school and food service workers. I'm so intimidated in the moment that I can't even remember their names except one: Walter Barrientos. Walter is a tall Latino student at CUNY's Baruch College and the first undocumented college student I have ever met.

Throughout the meeting, I am struck by how open and unashamed Walter is about his undocumented status. He references some of the times that he and other undocumented students met with members of Congress to share their stories. I sit there in disbelief. I get chills listening to him laying out plans to meet with more Congress members from New York, including Senators Chuck Schumer and Hillary Clinton. I'm in awe of his fearlessness and wonder how he found the courage to be public about his status despite the risk of deportation. I'm too afraid to share that I am also undocumented.

I'm both ashamed of my immigration status and ashamed of my shame and fear! I introduce myself as a Queens College student who is part of its student government and "interested" in joining the advocacy efforts for the DREAM Act. I don't speak much during the meeting, except to ask a few questions about the legislative process and to volunteer to help engage Queens College students in the upcoming congressional visits. The group talks about the current state of politics and the strategy to push the bill in Congress. I listen carefully. Nerd mode engaged, I am furiously taking notes; I feel like a student in one of my political science classes. They talk about the need to push New York senators Schumer and Clinton to become champions of the bill. Senator Clinton has publicly announced her opposition to undocumented immigrants' rights to drive and have driver's licenses. Advocates fear that in this new post-9/11 environment, Clinton's support for the DREAM Act will dissipate. Within the Democratic Party, Senator Durbin from Illinois is the leading champion of the bill. He is also working in partnership with Senator Ted Kennedy, Democrat from Massachusetts, on a bill to provide a pathway to citizenship for undocumented farmworkers. But in an environment where other politicians are pushing the lie that Muslims and immigrants of color are national security threats and in a Congress controlled by Republicans, both bills face an uphill battle.

The strategy is to get as many Democrats as possible to sign on to the bill, while also encouraging more members of Congress to champion it, actively organizing their colleagues to support the bill and speaking in favor of it publicly. Although it is harder to get Republicans to support the bill, the strategy includes working with Senator Hatch, Republican from Utah and cosponsor of the bill, to appeal to more members of his party. It's news to me that some Democrats need to be pushed to do the right thing.

Without Republican support, the bill cannot be passed in Congress and get to the president's desk. I feel overwhelmed by all the political information shared in the meeting, and the political obstacles seem daunting, but at the same time, my political science curiosity from class gets activated. I start to see the strategy and picture the task as a giant multidimensional puzzle to be figured out. I look around the room and I feel hopeful. All these leaders, immigrants and nonimmigrants alike, don't even know me, but they are fighting for my family. I wonder if these are the kinds of meetings that people like Reverend Martin Luther King Jr. and Larry Kramer, a legendary LGBTQ organizer during the AIDS crisis, were part of. I've since been in many of these strategy meetings—which aren't covered by the media or publicized—but it's the place where people impacted by injustice and representing different communities decide how they will combine their power and demand change.

Before the meeting ends, they also talk about the problems the DREAM Act is having in the Senate. Senator Jeff Sessions, Republican from Alabama, proposed over twenty amendments with the intention to kill the bill in committee. Still, the DREAM Act eventually made it out of committee with strong support from Republican and Democrat committee members. But white nationalist opposition to the DREAM Act is heating up, and organizational leaders agree to mobilize voters to call Congress in support of the bill to outweigh the opposition. They also agree to do an advocacy day in Washington DC, where undocumented students will share their stories with members of Congress. The goal is to show the human side of the DREAM Act. I sign up to join the advocacy day as a helper—not as one of the undocumented students who will tell their story.

Walter rushes out of the conference room to not miss the next train home to Long Island, where he lives. I run out and catch up to him in the elevator to talk to him one-on-one. The conversation continues as we walk together to Penn Station. It's the evening rush hour, and the city is bustling with people racing to the subway, yellow cabs honking, and cars stuck in heavy traffic, but it really feels like we're the only two people around. I learn that he's a business and organizational psychology major, and he is also a student senator. His family fled poverty in Guatemala and arrived in the US in 1996. He grew up undocumented on Long Island in Suffolk County, one of the most anti-immigrant counties in New York. I struggle whether to tell him that I am undocumented too. I feel conflicted.

Finally, with my voice almost cracking, I find the courage to tell him. "So, um, I'm undocumented too." I feel like a heavy weight has been lifted off my chest, but I'm simultaneously afraid of his reaction. Will he judge me or think less of me for not sharing my status during the meeting? But while this is quite literally one of the most important conversations in my life, Walter is just like, "Whatever." He keeps walking and rushes up to look at the screens with the train schedule. He acts as if what I shared is totally normal and not a big deal. I feel as if the unveiling of my biggest secret just fell flat. Maybe I've watched too many overly dramatic Mexican telenovelas and thought that all of New York City would stop to gasp at my secret, but what I get from Walter in that moment is serenity. The normalcy with which he receives the information starts having a calming effect on me. That ability to be unshaken by the storm is a quality of his that will comfort me over the years and bring us closer together. I'm relieved he now knows my truth, and he doesn't make me feel ashamed. He briefly looks back at me and says, "Look, I know it's hard, but it's okay. Let's stay in touch and keep talking." We exchange numbers before he jumps onto his train and zips away.

The next time I see Walter is on the advocacy day in Washington DC. He's still the only one who knows I'm undocumented, but I'm excited about meeting other undocumented students and going to the nation's capital for the first time. I have no idea what to wear, but knowing that I'll be on a bus for nearly five hours there and back, I choose to be comfortable: jeans, gray sneakers, and a black tank top. We meet early in the morning in Manhattan at the corner near the NYIC office to board a bus. I see a group of students in suits congregated down the block. I'm not dressed for the occasion, but by this time, I'm a little more confident and decide to not care about what the others may think. On the bus, there are Korean, Chinese, and Latine undocumented students. Most are from CUNY, representing their respective CUNY colleges. I'm there representing Queens College. On the way, Walter and other students lead a mini training, breaking down how the day will flow, our agenda and talking points for the meetings with members of Congress. They also review who is on what team and the US Capitol map so we don't get lost. I seize the opportunity to get to know as many of the other students as possible, and suddenly, instead of feeling shame, I become shameless in asking them deeply personal information. I'm sure they were like, "Who is this girl?" I ask when they came to the US, why they migrated, where they live, and how they found the courage to speak up and get involved in this work. I learn that, like me, they had to flee their homes when their families ran out of options and that they, too, hold on to the promise that this country will see us and change the laws.

Washington DC is sunny and humid. I'm sweating even though we're on the bus with air-conditioning. Through the window, I can see the government buildings and green lawns all around. We get dropped off by the Capitol. I'm amazed at the architecture and beauty of the buildings. They remind me of Columbia University's library with its tall round pillars. I'm part of the group that Walter is leading. We head to the Rayburn House Office Building. I think Walter senses that I'm becoming scared out of my mind because he turns to tell me there is nothing to be afraid of. Just follow the group, he says. I take a deep breath, and we're on the move.

The building is stunning—four stories with a white marble facade. Just about everything I've been learning in my political science classes has happened right in there. I'm intimidated and nervous. I'm an undocumented immigrant who, just a few years ago, was living in Ecuador. *Am I even supposed to be here?* I wonder. The rest of my group has been here before. They are more at ease. I closely follow their lead. Looking around, I'm in awe, staring at the marble walls and floors, the bronze railings, and the beautiful ceiling high above. I'm comforted that Walter keeps an eye on me. We get in a line of people in suits waiting to go through the metal detectors and get our bags inspected. Everyone seems like Walter, cool and calm, like this is the most normal thing in the world, but I'm freaking out inside, wondering when one of the Capitol security officers will stop me and question me about my immigration status. The security officers don't ask any of us anything and we make it through security.

We meet with members of Congress from the New York delegation. To my surprise, some of the congressional staff welcome us warmly. I certainly wasn't expecting this treatment. I thought we were going to be treated as if we don't belong in these buildings. The offices all have a TV at the entrance streaming C-SPAN live and very elegant cherrywood furniture. Charming in an old-fashioned way, they are very spacious, much bigger than our studio apartment in Jackson Heights. One of the members of Congress we meet with is Representative Joe Crowley, a Democrat who represents Jackson Heights, where I live. We know he supports the DREAM Act, but there is a big difference between saying you support the bill and fighting like hell to get it passed. Our goal is to get him to be a champion. I'm his constituent, but I have never met with him or gone to his office in the neighborhood. When we get to his office, his staff is friendly. They offer us water and candy and usher us into a room where we take a seat and wait for the congressman to arrive. While we wait for him to come into the meeting, Walter reviews the agenda with the group. I listen while following along on the agenda document in my folder. All around Congressman Crowley's office are framed pictures of him, his family, and other members of Congress, and there is a bookcase full of books. When he arrives, he shakes hands with every single one of us, while his staff pull up chairs to sit next to him and take notes.

Walter leads the meeting, introducing himself and explaining that our delegation represents CUNY students. Walter and one more student share their stories. Representative Crowley shares a bit of his story too. He comes from an Irish family that migrated like our families did, seeking a better life in the US. He was born in Woodside, Queens, and he tells us he is a Queens College graduate, like me. I perk up when I hear that he went to my college. We all look at each other and smile with pride. His story makes us feel affirmed and relatable. I'm encouraged to know that an actual member of Congress also comes from an immigrant family and went to a public university like CUNY. I listen carefully and observe the exchange between Walter and Congressmen Crowley. Before we leave, the congressman thanks us for meeting with him and conveys his support for the bill. He encourages us to keep up our efforts and presses us to focus on getting more Republican support. Walter had told me Crowley's office was friendly, but it still feels surreal that he was this welcoming.

Other offices aren't so friendly—they barely acknowledge us, and some don't even have a staff person meet with us and instead send an intern. All in all, observing the other students and advocates in action serves as my training ground for future congressional visits and public events where I will share my story in the months to come. I see how sharing our stories isn't only a part of the strategy to advance immigration reform—it's also an act of liberation. In telling our stories, we are reclaiming our right to exist. We are also pushing back against language that criminalizes us. In the media and the public debate about immigration, we are called "illegals." Some immigrant youth leaders who are also bloggers begin using the word "Dreamer" to identify themselves. Many of us follow suit, using the word "Dreamer" to reclaim our humanity and push back on reporters that insists on calling us "illegal" students.

At the time we naively believe that by sharing our stories, we will help members of Congress see that we are worthy of staying in this country. We innocently give them the benefit of the doubt and believe that if they get to know us and our dreams we will appeal to their values and morals and inspire them to support and vote in favor of the DREAM Act. Over time, as I become a more experienced organizer and strategist, I will realize that though our stories may morally influence some members of Congress, humanize the public discourse about immigrants, and expose the injustices of this country's laws, they are not enough to force people in government to act and change laws. Telling our stories isn't enough to dismantle the nativism and racism that drive a lot of politics. I will learn from painful experience that our stories and dreams can be co-opted by media and politicians from both political parties to advance their interests. I will see that words like "Dreamer" and our stories can be manipulated and used to actually perpetuate narratives to hurt the majority of immigrants. I will come to understand that stories and logic alone aren't enough to win a political fight. What you also need is organized power.

Walter adds me to an email list where updates about the DREAM Act campaign and dates for upcoming meetings are shared. I attend a few meetings, still feeling like an outsider and hesitant to get too involved. In an environment of heightened fear of detention and deportation, I increasingly fear that our family could be targeted. I feel safer being known as a student leader on campus engaging with college administrators than speaking up about my undocumented status and engaging with powerful people in government. Like many undocumented immigrants, I find myself hiding in plain sight.

It's 2004, and my apprehension about getting more involved and openly talking about my status begins to crack when I learn about a young undocumented student like me and her family facing deportation. Walter and Minerva convene a time-sensitive call about the deportation of a young woman named Marie Gonzalez who lives in Missouri. They share updates on her case and the need for people across the country to hold protests to demand that she and her family not be deported. I don't know Marie in person, and I don't even know where Missouri is on the map, but Walter knows her, and I hear all about it. He tells me that in the spring of 2004 they met in Washington DC on a day of action, at a mock graduation ceremony that had been organized by Josh Bernstein—an advocate and immigration policy expert with the National Immigration Law Center (NILC)—and advocates and organizers from a group called Community Change, formerly known as Center for Community Change, an organization dedicated to improving the lives of poor and working-class communities. Josh wrote the original version of the DREAM Act, inspired by his community of friends including his ex, an undocumented Mexican woman he loved dearly. Love for people and community moves advocates and leaders to act courageously and fuels this movement for justice.

Walter and Marie were a part of the mock graduation ceremony in front of the media with about fifty immigrant youths wearing caps and gowns. The idea was to show the students' potential and to point out just how ridiculous it would be to deport them. Marie was one of the speakers as the class "valedictorian" and shared her story publicly, calling on members of Congress to stop her family's deportation and pass the DREAM Act. They brought together advocates from civil rights organizations, educators, and undocumented students from across the country. At the event, Marie and Walter met undocumented students from Texas, Illinois, and California. Most of them were still very afraid of sharing their stories. Many of them were using an alias. Walter shared his story as "Carlos." The mock graduation got a lot of positive media coverage. In a country where the stories of undocumented students and their families are supposed to be invisible, here they were, telling their stories for everyone to hear.

I learn that Marie and her family came to the US from Costa Rica in 1991 seeking a better life. Her parents, Marina and Marvin, had owned a seafood restaurant that had to shut down due to a cholera epidemic crashing the local tourism industry. Marie was five years old when they arrived. They came in with tourist visas, which they overstayed, becoming undocumented. Her parents moved from Southern California to Missouri seeking job opportunities and settled in Jefferson City, Missouri. Marvin, Marie's dad, landed a job as a government mail clerk and actually found himself sorting packages for Missouri's governor. At the time, there was a series of biological attacks after 9/11 in which letters containing anthrax spores were sent to government officials and media outlets, killing five people. Marie's dad came across a package addressed to the governor with an unmarked envelope and a book about Osama bin Laden.[41] Terrified about the possibility of the package posing a threat, he reported the incident, and a formal investigation led by local authorities and the FBI began. The investigation determined the package did not contain anything hazardous, but the FBI continued to watch Jefferson City closely. Months later, Marvin opened a letter addressed to the governor that contained a white powder. Thankfully, the white powder wasn't dangerous, but the incident brought media attention and visibility to Marvin and his family. Shortly after, the governor's office received an anonymous call reporting Marvin's undocumented status. Marie's family didn't know if the anonymous call was intended to be a political attack on the governor or an attack on her family, but it led to the newly created Department of Homeland Security sending immigration agents to their home.

In December of 2003, the family got an order to appear in front of an immigration judge in Kansas City, the closest immigration court, two and a half hours away. The judge decided they had no claim to stay in the US and issued a deportation order for all of them, only allowing Marie to finish the school year before deportation. The family's lawyer worked with them to appeal and, in his research, found Josh Bernstein from NILC, who encouraged Marie's lawyer to have her travel to Washington DC to share her story with members of Congress and ask them to intervene in her case and advocate for the DREAM Act. Although it seemed that publicity was what led Marie's family into harm, leaning into publicity might be her only way out. Marie was afraid, but she courageously agreed to share her story with the media and members of Congress with the hope that it would stop her family's deportation.

Advocates hoped that by lifting up stories like Marie's and holding events like the mock graduation they would build up some good momentum for the DREAM Act to move in Congress, but unfortunately the 2004 congressional session ended without the passage of the DREAM Act and a resolution for Marie's family deportation case. Marie and her parents were given a deportation order set for July 5, 2005. Without the DREAM Act, Marie and advocacy organizations doubled down on efforts to get members of Congress to intervene in her family's case and launched the We Are Marie campaign, calling on immigrant justice organizers to lead rallies across the country. I don't know this at the time, but apparently the president and his top officials can stop people from being deported.

Walter explains all of this, and it's the reason why he, Minerva, and the others are planning a rally in support of Marie outside of the immigration offices in New York's Federal Plaza. I am afraid to join the rally, though. What if going to this rally leads to pictures and media attention, which lead to my family's deportation, just like what happened to Marie? But I know that if my family is ever targeted for deportation, I'd want others to fight for us, and I begin to realize that safety is not in hiding but in being public and in solidarity with a broader community. The truth is that most undocumented people just want to go about their lives, raise their kids, and work. But the broken laws put us in a catch-22: be public and risk exposure; be private and risk having no one to help you.

Deep down, I feel a growing anger and hunger for justice. I'm energized by the advocates around me, and I ask Walter about the risks of being part of the rally. As usual, Walter calms my fears. He patiently tells me that nobody needs to know I'm undocumented if I don't feel comfortable sharing and that, besides, ICE hasn't targeted him and other students so far for publicly sharing their stories at rallies. Of course, I tell my parents none of this. If I'm going to go, I don't want to make them worry. Ultimately, I decide to go for it.

It's June 2005, and I'm heading to my first-ever rally. When I get there, I see about a hundred people, and the energy is on fire. We are at Federal Plaza in downtown Manhattan, outside of a massive forty-one-story federal office building that houses ICE, immigration court, and application services. Walter gives me a black T-shirt with yellow words that say WE ARE MARIE. I put it on. I look around and see organizers and supporters holding signs with Marie's picture. One of the organizers greets me and holds a sign out to me. I timidly say hi and grab it. I'm surrounded by a hundred others wearing the same shirt, holding signs, and chanting, "We are Marie!" and "Education, not deportation!" Walter is standing by the sound system holding a microphone, leading the chants, and he is loud! I'm in awe. Most people at the rally don't even know Marie and her family. We're a thousand miles from Missouri, but we are here, working to fight for their right to remain in their home. I'm amazed that complete strangers are there on Marie's behalf and then notice that I'm one of them.

As I move around the crowd, I'm cautiously watching my

back, paranoid that police or immigration agents are going to show up. But as the crowd grows and the chants get louder, I feel safer and braver. I, too, join the chanting. "Education, not deportation!" I can't believe I am chanting. But I am. I hear my voice, and I get goose bumps. I chant, "We are Marie!" and as the words come out of my mouth, I realize that I actually *am* Marie, and I chant for her, I chant for me, I chant for Walter, I chant for my parents and my brother, Jonathan. We all are Marie, and as I chant, I get louder, and suddenly the girl and young woman who learned to not make waves, to live cloaked by shame, is literally screaming into the air. The fear of deportation remains inside of me, but it doesn't hold me back from tapping into my own power. I have a voice, and I feel proud to be using it to stand up for Marie and her parents—to stand up for justice.

The crowd then changes up the chant, and I hear "We are Kamal! We are Kamal!" I'm like, *Wait—what? There's someone else?* "Who is Kamal?" I ask Walter.

"Oh, he is our local Marie," he says. I see a young guy with a nervous smile and thick black hair get up to the microphone, and I hear Kamal Essaheb share his story. Here I am, nervous to chant in a crowd, and there he is at the mic, telling his truth. A young brown man, Kamal is shy and soft-spoken. I'm both shocked and in awe as I hear him share his story. His courage inspires me. I stand there holding a sign with tears in my eyes, wishing I could be as brave as he is.

Kamal shares that he came with his family to the US from Morocco and grew up undocumented in Queens. He graduated from Queens College in 2002 and was accepted into Fordham University's law school, but a government agent decided to put Kamal in deportation proceedings. He had followed the law, which, after 9/11, required men from Muslim-majority countries to register with the government. He registered without knowing that it was a trap. By 2003, an estimated eighty-three thousand men and boys registered with the government under this law, but government officials never disclosed any relationship between the registry and terrorist-related offenses. Nearly thirteen thousand Muslim men were placed into deportation proceedings, and Kamal was one of them. In April 2003, the government suspended some aspects of this law, but it did not cancel Kamal's deportation proceedings, which is why we are rallying.

The rally is a big success. We get national media outlets like the *New York Times*, the *Washington Post*, the *Wall Street Journal*, and National Public Radio, as well as hundreds of local press outlets, to cover Marie's and Kamal's stories, reaching millions of people across the country. We also recruit churches, schools, and other ally organizations to send letters to members of Congress, asking them to intervene with ICE. I send messages to CUNY students via various email lists, hoping to inspire more people to send letters to their representatives. Our goal is to increase the pressure on the ICE agents managing Marie's and Kamal's cases, because they have the power to decide if Marie and her family and Kamal get to stay or are deported. In a world prior to social media platforms, we also work on developing a website that is used to invite others facing deportation to share their stories under a section named "Meet Other Maries." Marie uses the website as a public diary, keeping people updated on her case.

I also join what seem like giant conference calls with lawyers, advocates, and undocumented youth from other states to coordinate efforts to stop their deportations. I am amazed. There are people from across the country on these calls, all organizing and fighting to save these two young people. On those calls, I meet undocumented youth leaders from Illinois, California, Florida, Massachusetts, Indiana, Oregon, Idaho, Kansas, Tennessee, New York, and Texas. I realize that there are thousands of young people like me, some of them facing even harsher realities in anti-immigrant states and dealing with the impact and trauma of having lost loved ones to deportation.

I begin to build friendships with Julieta Garibay, from the University Leadership Initiative (ULI) in Austin, Texas; Natalia Aristizabal, from Make the Road New York; Gaby Pacheco, Isabel Sousa-Rodriguez, Felipe Sousa-Lazaballet, and José Luis Marantes, from Students Working for Equal Rights (SWER) in Florida; and Carlos Saavedra, from the Student Immigrant Movement (SIM) in Massachusetts. They are friendly, outgoing, and funny as hell. Even though we just know each other through voice over the phone, I'm in awe of their courage and fierceness. They seem to have energy that just doesn't stop, and with each conversation, they make me feel less alone and more powerful. If we can organize ourselves to make calls, send letters, and host rallies for Kamal's and Marie's families, I imagine how many more people we can bring together to fight for all families facing deportation. I feel clearer that this work is not just about Kamal and Marie; it isn't even about my own family and me. The hunger for change grows beyond my self-interest to that of the freedom of Julieta, Walter, and all immigrants.

The nonstop pressuring and campaigning for Kamal to stay works. We get news that Kamal's deportation has been "administratively closed." This means ICE will keep his file but not prioritize him for deportation. While Kamal won't be deported, he will continue to live in limbo because he remains undocumented.

In the case of Marie, our work sharing stories publicly, leading protests and rallies, and pressuring members of Congress and DHS moves the ICE agent handling Marie's case to give Marie permission to stay for one year, but Marie's parents still face deportation. Marie gets a call from the family's lawyer on July 4, a day before the set deportation order, to share the bittersweet news. This is a heartbreaking moment for all of us. Her parents have a matter of hours with Marie before their deportation. And because of the 1996 immigration reforms, Marina and Marvin face a ten-year ban on reentering the US because they have overstayed their tourist visas and lived in the country without lawful immigration status. Before Marie's parents are deported, the family is featured in Jefferson City's Independence Day parade on the lead float. Ironically, the theme of the parade is "proud to be an American." People wave and cheer at them. But breaking a family apart is nothing to be proud of, I think.

The ICE agents on both cases have the power to make or break families and lives. Marie and Kamal are left to live in limbo. Even though Marie gets to stay in the US temporarily, there is no certainty that she will get to adjust her immigration status and be able to travel to Costa Rica to see her parents. Marie's family does not know when they will be reunited again. The senselessness of the ICE agents' decisions is enraging. This moment teaches me that no matter how "good" we are, the immigration system is designed to criminalize and deport us.

Living in limbo, not knowing if this will be your last day here in your home, is torture. I don't know how Marie has the strength to keep fighting, but she does, inspiring us all. She and Kamal will continue fighting to stay home and advocating for the DREAM Act and broader immigration policy reforms that would provide a pathway to citizenship for the undocumented. Marie's deportation will continue to get delayed and she will go to college and find her soulmate, eventually becoming eligible for a family petition. Kamal will graduate from law school and get protection from deportation when the immigrant youth movement wins the Deferred Action for Childhood Arrivals (DACA) program in 2012, and eventually gain lawful permanent immigration status through a family petition. He will go on to serve as a counselor to the secretary of the Department of Homeland Security under President Joe Biden's administration.

For the first time, I taste what it's like to have the power to shape or influence a decision made by government officials that impacts human lives. Up until this point, I have felt powerless and alone. Volunteering in these campaigns redefines what I consider possible. I wonder about the change that we can create by engaging more and more people. I begin to believe in the possibility of passing bills, and changing unjust laws to protect millions from deportation. I don't know it yet, but these campaigns will be my training to help stop thousands of deportations in the years to come, change immigration laws, and be part of building a powerful youth-led movement for immigrant justice.

One of the advocates from the NYIC asks if I would be willing to share my story at an event hosted by the New York City Bar Association and Mayor Mike Bloomberg's office. In addition to increasing support for the DREAM Act among members of Congress, the strategy is also to get more state and local officials to publicly support the bill and advocate for Congress to pass it. The event is open to the press. I worry I could be recognized by fellow students and professors and fear their reaction. Even though I've seen or heard Walter, Kamal, Marie, Julieta, and so many more share their stories, I still feel that if I share mine, I will have to explain to people that neither my parents nor I are "criminals." I've internalized the idea that immigrants are "bad" for coming here seeking a better life.

But then I think about Marie, Kamal, and their families. I think about their courage. I think about the tough reality that I could be the next Marie. ICE agents are increasingly coming after all of us. I may not be in this country tomorrow. I feel I have more to lose by not sharing my story. Alone, I'm in danger.

In community, I have a shot at staying here—to remain together with my family. I get in touch with Jennifer Kim, a lawyer from the New York City Bar Association, who is one of the organizers of the event. She is the child of Korean immigrants and a leader with the MinKwon Center for Community Action, an organization serving and defending the rights of Korean immigrants in Queens. I talk with her about the possibility of using an alias. That's what Walter usually does when he shares his story publicly. I tell Jennifer I'm willing to share my story if it can be as "Sandra." Jennifer is supportive and makes sure all press and public announcements reflect our agreement.

Now I need to figure out how to tell my parents. They know that I'm volunteering with community organizations advocating for the rights of immigrants and meeting other undocumented young people. They are supportive of me doing volunteer work. They've always believed in looking out not only for oneself but for our family and the community. They also like that I'm making friends who share my experience. But they don't know the details of our work stopping deportations. They don't know young people are sharing their stories and publicly defying ICE agents that want to deport them. They don't know that I'm about to also publicly share my own story. But I've been hiding for so many years that I don't also want to hide from my parents. Before the event, I tell them that I want to share my story publicly to pressure Congress to pass the DREAM Act. I explain that I've done my homework to figure out all the ways to protect our family, including not using my real name and not sharing the identities or stories of my parents. I also tell them that Marie and Kamal have found protection in being public and having a community fighting for them to stay. If I were to be the target of deportation, I'd have a community ready to fight for me and to protect us. Mami thinks it's too risky. She asks the same question multiple times: "Are you sure?" Papi is curious and excited. In Ecuador, Papi joined his coworkers at a car manufacturing plant to organize a union. He knows what it is like to pressure and confront those in power. He asks me who and how many people will be there. Papi reminisces about his years as a student activist fighting for funding for public education and the right of every child to have a school to go to. "Hay que luchar," Papi says. Although Mami still fears that this may increase the risk of deportation for our family, she agrees that it's safer to have a community around us ready to act if anything were ever to happen to us. They both support me. Mami helps me iron the blue blouse and black blazer I plan to wear.

The day of the event, I obsessively rehearse in front of the mirror at home and with Walter when I meet him before attendees begin to arrive. "Don't forget your name," he teases me. The event takes place at the New York City Bar Association building in Midtown Manhattan. When you enter the building, with its towering columns, elegant golden handrails, and walls made of white marble, you feel like you've been transported back to the Gilded Age. The room where we are gathering feels like a courtroom, with fancy paintings of judges on the walls. I am the only undocumented person on the panel, which also includes Josh from NILC and other advocates and legal immigration experts. My college friends, Jonathan and Diana, both children of immigrants, are here to support me. Over one hundred people are in the room, including New York City government officials and their staff, advocates, immigration lawyers, and reporters holding cameras, notepads, and voice recorders.

As I take a seat at the panelist table, I feel like my heart is going to jump out of my chest and break through my blue shirt. Trying to calm myself, I take out my notes and write *You can do this. You'll be okay. You can do this. You'll be okay. You can do this. You'll be okay.*

The other panelists arrive. We greet each other, and the event starts. I brace myself. When it is my turn, I can barely speak, but I get closer to the microphone and begin: "Good afternoon. My name is Sandra and I'm undocumented . . ." I'm fearful, but as I tell my story, I feel less afraid. I check out the crowd, and I see reporters taking pictures of me and writing on their notepads. Maybe it's the adrenaline of the moment, but I look straight at them, unashamed. I also see Jonathan, Diana, and Walter. They are beaming with pride. Before I finish my remarks, I tell the audience that I'm only one of thousands of undocumented young people in New York and across the country living in fear, urging them to press both state and national politicians to support and pass the DREAM Act. I close, feeling both relieved and empowered.

At the end of the event, Jonathan and Diana embrace me with admiration. Jennifer is almost in tears, and with a big smile, she hugs me while whispering in my ear, "You did it, Cristina! You are so courageous." I pause to take in the moment. I have just revealed my biggest secret. Everyone in the room now knows that I am undocumented. I feel lighter. The weight of hiding and keeping this secret is off my chest. I feel liberated. Even though I use a fake name, sharing my story publicly is an act of self-determination. It is an act of reclaiming my humanity, my dignity, and my place in this country. No matter what politicians and people think about undocumented immigrants—that we're "illegals," "criminals," "abusers of the system," "job takers," "free riders"—my family and I are here. We are human, and this country is our home too.

I don't see myself as a leader, activist, or community organizer. I don't quite know yet what those terms really mean. I simply see myself as a young undocumented student fighting for my family and immigrants like us to live in this country without fear.

This shifts when a couple of months later, I'm invited to join a training hosted by Community Change and immigrant rights organizations in the northeastern states. I have never been with so many undocumented young people in my life, and the feeling in the room is electric. Through icebreakers and story circles, I get to meet two hundred other working-class undocumented youths from different Latin American, African, and Asian countries. They live in New York, New Jersey, Virginia, Pennsylvania, and Maryland. We learn about our immigration journeys and our families. We talk about our dreams of a college education and our righteous anger over how the immigration system has shattered those dreams. Some young people are struggling to pay tuition, while most can't even afford it at all. I'm outraged to learn New Jersey, Virginia, Pennsylvania, and Maryland state colleges charge the undocumented more for tuition than other students. I learn that many of the young people at the training have lost loved ones to detention and deportation. I break down in tears as I hear their stories. I grieve with them.

But amid the sadness of our realities, we also inspire each other and share the amazing fact that the oppression we experience has not killed our spirts or our hope. We are young immigrants from different parts of the world, and despite our cultural differences, our stories make us feel connected and safe. We self-organize a space for joy and celebration. We begin with poetry and spoken word to express our emotions and dreams. I'm excited to realize that there are many artists, poets, and rappers among us. Natalia Aristizabal, an organizer who grew up undocumented and was able to get lawful immigration status through a family petition, and is also a poet, shares one of her poems in Spanish. She speaks about the longing for home, a home here in the US and in Colombia, where she is from and where her grandmother lives. Natalia's poem captures how many of us feel. She will become one of the best artists and popular education youth organizers I would come to know. Then, the dancing begins! Young people from the Student Immigrant Movement (SIM) based in Boston start a dance-off. They are Brazilian and start with samba, their feet and hips vigorously bouncing from side to side to the music. Most of us can't keep up with their moves, but we laugh at each other's efforts. I pair up with Walter and find out he is a great dancer. His body moves effortlessly to the sound of salsa, cumbia, bachata, and merengue. We also play some rock-en-español. Carlos, a musician and rock lover, leads us in singing "Oye Mi Amor" by Maná. We sing and dance the night away. We don't know this yet, but we are building a community of joy and solidarity. We are building lifelong relationships, bonding over our hunger for justice and our dreams of a world where all people, regardless of immigration status, can live with freedom and dignity.

We also learn about US immigration history, the immigrant justice movement, and community organizing. I learn that community organizing brings together people impacted by injustice to build power in solidarity and collectively take action to effect change. In one session, we walk around the room where handouts with historical facts about immigration laws are pasted to the wall in chronological order. I learn that the US has a long history of colonialism, systemic racism, and anti-immigrant policies, from European colonizers killing Native Americans, the enslavement of Black people, and the Chinese Exclusion Act of 1882 to Jim Crow and anti-immigrant policies like Proposition 187 in California, which was aimed at barring immigrants from accessing public education and health services. But I also learn about the social justice movements that pushed back against these unjust laws and won. This activity fills me with righteous anger. I feel a part of something bigger than myself and of a legacy of people who came together before me to fight for justice and freedom. These elders and organizers didn't know me, but they dreamed of me and our community being free.

Before we close the first day of training, Jaribu Hill, executive director of the Mississippi Workers' Center for Human Rights, joins us as a guest speaker. A Black woman in her fifties with a deep and powerful voice, she is a longtime community organizer and civil and labor rights lawyer. She speaks passionately about the role of young people in the civil rights movement. Listening to her, I learn about Ella Baker, a Black community organizer and leader with the NAACP and the Southern Christian Leadership Conference, and her work training and supporting the leadership of young people in creating the Student Nonviolent Coordinating Committee (SNCC) in the 1960s. SNCC leaders courageously led acts of civil disobedience, like sit-ins at restaurants and other businesses across the South, to push for the end of segregation. They were violently attacked by white people and law enforcement. They risked their lives to fight for the dignity and freedom of Black people. *This can be us*, I think. Mrs. Hill reminds us that we are part of a lineage of young people who have taken great risks for freedom and justice. She asks, "Are you ready to fight for freedom?"

"Yes!" we shout in response.

She starts singing "Ella's Song":

We who believe in freedom cannot rest
We who believe in freedom cannot rest until it comes

I feel as if I'm back in my evangelical church. Mrs. Hill's powerful voice touches my soul. When I hear the chorus, I get chills. I slowly sway from side to side, with my eyes closed and tears running down my cheeks, while I join her in singing. I am not at a church, but I know that I'm having a spiritual experience. I feel the arms of my blood and chosen ancestors—freedom fighters—around me. I commit to joining the long legacy of people fighting for the dignity and freedom of all those impacted by systemic racism and injustice.

8

PEOPLE POWER

New York State Youth Leadership Council youth leaders, with Cristina in the front row, holding large DREAM Act banner at the New York City May Day march, 2006 (credit: Kathy Willens, Associated Press)

> *Once social change begins, it cannot be reversed. You cannot uneducate the person who has learned to read. You cannot humiliate the person who feels pride. You cannot oppress the people who are not afraid anymore.*
>
> —César Chávez

Walter invites me to join him as a volunteer with the Latin American Integration Center (LAIC) in a campaign to get New Yorkers from working-class communities of color to vote. I'm managing too much with school and work, but I know I want to be part of this, and I'm excited to talk to voters in Queens. I get to meet the organization's executive director, Ana María Archila. She is an immigrant from Colombia following in the steps of her late aunt, who also migrated from Colombia and founded the organization. When she and I are introduced for the first time, she greets me as if she's known me all her life. She is in her twenties, and like me, she has an accent when she speaks English. I'm drawn to her with admiration and curiosity. I'm impressed that she leads an organization at such a young age.

Over the course of the next several weeks, Ana María and Walter teach me and the other volunteers how to use the voter database and have conversations with voters. We knock on the doors of voters and focus the conversations on the issues that are important to them. Before we leave, we give the voters a pamphlet with information on where they can vote. I'm good at knocking on doors and talking to people in my community. They are immigrants or children of immigrants, mostly from Asia and Latin America. I'm warm, outgoing, and people tell me I have a welcoming smile. Some voters talk to me for a long time. They even invite me in to have coffee with them. But I politely decline. I can't stay too long because I have a long list of voters to talk to. I realize people are eager to connect with others, find a community, and learn about organizations where they can access services. They are concerned about underfunded schools and the cost of rent being too high. Even though I'm undocumented and can't vote, it feels powerful to motivate voters to be part of the democratic process by electing their representatives.

The voter-engagement campaign is a success, increasing voter participation in Queens. When we are done with this campaign, Walter and Ana María invite me to join as an intern for the summer youth program. I'm excited about getting to work with other young people and learning about community organizing from Walter and Ana María. But I also feel intimidated because I haven't done this work before. I'm relieved to find out that the internship includes training and coaching with experienced community organizers.

Walter and I put our training into practice. We have individual meetings with the youth who join us for the summer program. They are all high school students who are immigrants or children of immigrants and come from working-class families. They are Black, Latine, Chinese, and South Asian. They are straight and queer. They come from families that have been separated by the immigration and criminal justice systems. They are vibrant, curious, resilient, funny, and shy at times. In our story circles, we learn about their migration stories; their experiences with bullying, police violence, and racial profiling; and their dreams of going to college. We talk about the emotional and mental impacts of being the target of criminalization by police and immigration agents. Muslim youth also share their experiences of increased bullying at school after 9/11. But they also make fun of the fact that they are considered terrorists in the country they call home. When we do a skit activity, a team of Southeast Asian and Muslim youth perform Yung Joc's "It's Goin' Down," which is one of the hit songs that summer. They change the lyrics of the chorus and insert their names: "Abdul is on the plane, it's goin' down; Iqbal is on the plane, it's goin' down." The room bursts into laughter. We remind ourselves that we are human beings worthy of joy, safety, and a life without fear.

In weekly political education workshops, Walter and I break down systemic racism and explore the root causes of gender, racial, and economic injustice. We also talk about social justice movements. We train the students in organizing, civic participation, and holding their elected officials accountable. We train them on how to volunteer to register voters and how to talk to people in the community about the issues most important to them. And after all the hard work of being out in the community in the heat and humidity of a New York City summer, we have fun. We have picnics at the park, where we listen to music, eat, and laugh together. The program ends with an art project in which an artist paints a mural and we throw a party at Terraza 7, a local café owned by a Colombian immigrant that's popular in the community, and dance the afternoon away. Many of the young people who joined us for that summer will go on to become community organizers.

While still going to school, I continue my involvement with LAIC as a volunteer, spending time with their staff and members. All of them are immigrants from Latin America. Most are women. They are warm and welcoming. The office, which is really more of a community center, smells like freshly brewed Bustelo coffee, making us all feel at home. There is salsa and cumbia playing in the background, though not when English or citizenship classes are in session. Yolanda, an immigrant from Colombia who is also a member of the organization and is in charge of keeping the space clean, often brings bread and empanadas to share with all of us. Every person that walks in is treated with warmth, and staff try to help every community member that has a need. They genuinely care for one another. *This is what community looks like*, I think. Ana María, whom I admire as a leader and community organizer, takes me under her wing and recommends me for an organizing fellowship.

The organizing fellowship, led by a training organization called Social Justice Leadership, hosts the trainings in their office in the Bronx. Rusia Mohiuddin, a Muslim immigrant living in the Bronx and a community organizer, is our trainer. She is known as a master organizer. On our first day, I'm intimidated by her deep voice and strong presence. She gives tough warrior vibes. But when we have our first one-on-one meeting, she breaks the ice by saying, "Yo, homie, how you doing? I'm so excited you are part of this fellowship." At this point, I've knocked on doors, organized community meetings, and planned rallies and press conferences, but I've only joined a day training on community organizing by the Midwest Academy. And I often feel insecure about whether I'm doing things right or wrong. But I'm hungry to learn more. I throw myself into learning the craft of community organizing. Rusia trains me for a year and becomes my mentor and close friend.

LAIC becomes my second home. Community leaders and I organize forums about the rights of immigrants, the elections coming up, and the ways people can join our fight. In our community meetings, we talk about the need for access to healthcare and driver's licenses for undocumented immigrants in the state. We recruit new members by visiting churches and talking to people at the 7 train stations along Jackson Heights and Woodside. Mami is concerned that I'm increasingly spending more time volunteering with LAIC. She now thinks that this is distracting from school. "You have to do well in school. You are also not getting paid for your time," Mami constantly tells me. I understand Mami's concern, but I feel frustrated and misunderstood. I don't let that discourage me, though. The members and organizers at LAIC are part of my chosen family now, and in them I find the courage, love, and support I need to keep going.

I invite my parents and brother, who is now twelve years old, to join me for a community meeting one weekend. I want them to see and feel what I do in the hopes that they will support and join me. That afternoon, they meet other immigrant workers, learn their stories, and by the end, we are all sharing food together, with cumbia blasting in the background. Mami is bonding with other immigrant moms who are domestic workers, sharing tips on cleaning products. Papi is cracking jokes, making everyone laugh. This is the first time we come together as a family to meet and develop relationships with other immigrants in our community. We feel very immigrant and proud. Papi begins joining me on weekends to walk the streets of Jackson Heights, giving out flyers and recruiting members. His charm and jokes make him one of the best recruiters. My brother joins the youth program. LAIC is the place where my whole family feels human and finds belonging, community, and joy. We have potlucks and dance away in a cramped multipurpose room in the organization's headquarters with hundreds of the members during holiday parties.

While I'm getting trained as an organizer at LAIC, Walter and I continue to build a network of undocumented CUNY students. The staff from the New York Immigration Coalition (NYIC) are very supportive of our work. They provide us with advocacy and communication trainings and an office space where we can hold our meetings. But we have a vision of building a group led by undocumented youth, where we can be autonomous about our campaigns and strategies. The NYIC staff encourage us to create something bigger and agree that starting a youth-led organization will build more power for the immigrant justice movement. They support us in creating our own undocumented youth–led organization: the New York State Youth Leadership Council (NYSYLC). Walter and I, along with other undocumented CUNY students, cofound the NYSYLC, the first undocumented youth–led organization in the state, to empower New York immigrant youth to organize and create change in their communities.

As immigrant youth build power, organize more people, and create new organizations like the NYSYLC, white nationalist members of Congress coordinate their efforts as well. They use 9/11 to pass one of the most draconian federal immigration bills ever in the House of Representatives in 2005. Called the "Sensenbrenner Bill" after its lead sponsor, Republican representative Jim Sensenbrenner of Wisconsin, the bill passes by a vote of 239 to 182 (not entirely along partisan lines), and it moves forward to the Senate. The bill is downright cruel and it would result in mass deportations and the arrest of US citizens across the country. It would label all undocumented immigrants as felons and make it against the law for anyone to provide undocumented immigrants with assistance. This includes churches providing food and shelter, medical facilities, community service organizations, even friends giving each other rides in their cars.

The passage of the bill has a galvanizing effect on immigrant communities across the country. Leaders from various faiths and charity organizations immediately condemn the bill, holding vigils and press conferences from coast to coast. Public polling shows that most Americans do not support the bill, and the fear and outrage generated by its passage fuel a national backlash. Immigrant families and workers across the country lead demonstrations denouncing the bill, and a wave of marches begins to take shape, and they are massive. The Illinois Coalition for Immigrant and Refugee Rights (ICIRR) is the first to organize a mass march, and over one hundred thousand people turn out, which inspires even more action. Churches, labor unions, community organizations, and students, along with Latine radio DJs, call immigrants and allies to megamarches across the country with the messages "We are America" and "Today we march, tomorrow we vote." On March 25, Los Angeles leads the largest protest—"La Gran Marcha"—with over half a million people taking to the streets.

The momentum spreads like wildfire. Anchored by the Fair Immigration Reform Movement (FIRM), a coalition of immigrant-rights, state-based organizations, there are rallies being planned in over one hundred cities from New York to Boise, Idaho, to Anchorage, Alaska, on April 10, 2006. In my immigrant community in Queens, you can feel the energy in the air. I work with other immigrant youth leaders and immigrant justice organizations in New York to promote the march at New York City colleges and universities. For the first time, I am responsible for recruiting enough people to fill an entire bus for a demonstration. I, along with friends from the Political Science Club and the student government, plaster the entire campus with flyers about the march and wake up early to chalk on classrooms' boards. The day of the march, I am nervous about whether enough students will show up. But within a few minutes, we have close to sixty people and fill the bus. When we arrive in Manhattan, there are thousands of people from all backgrounds marching. I can't see where the march begins or ends. I get goose bumps just looking at the crowd. As a new organizer, I know a bit more about what it takes to pull off a march, so I am in awe at the number of people who have turned out and at the amount of skillful strategy and organizing it must have taken to get them there.

We get off the bus, holding our NO HUMAN BEING IS ILLEGAL signs, and join the march. The energy in the air is brave, vibrant, and hopeful. As we march, we chant alongside faith leaders, teachers, business owners, students, and labor leaders. A stage and a large screen have been assembled at city hall for speakers, community leaders, elected officials, and faith leaders to address the crowd. No joke—it is like a rock concert. Standing blocks away, I get to see Walter speaking on the big screen. He courageously shares his story with the thousands of people who are standing with us. Being part of such a large crowd, the largest I have ever experienced, makes me feel not only powerful but as if change is inevitable.

The megamarches build national momentum and raise awareness about the extreme attacks on immigrants. People in immigrant communities experience a collective awakening—the same awakening I went through a few years before. They begin to face the contradiction that this country wants our labor but wants to deport us at the same time, and they realize that speaking up and acting collectively protects us and makes us powerful. The momentum keeps growing, and another large nationwide mobilization takes place on May 1, 2006—May Day, also known as International Workers' Day. Labor unions and community organizations call on all their members to join "A Day Without Immigrants," encouraging immigrants and allies to boycott work, school, shopping, and other economic activities. The goal is to disrupt business as usual.

On May Day, millions of undocumented and documented immigrant workers do not show up to work. Domestic workers; janitors; nannies; and construction, hotel, and restaurant workers join marches across the country. Students don't show up for class, or they walk out in the middle of the school day. The message is clear: you cannot function without us. Immigrants from all backgrounds march with their children and families in white T-shirts and with their heads held high. I feel powerful marching alongside a sea of thousands of immigrants and allies in the streets of Manhattan chanting, "Sí, se puede!"

Immigrant youth leaders in New York and across the country also use this as an opportunity to bring attention to the federal DREAM Act. Youth leaders from California, Florida, New York, Massachusetts, and Texas work for several days making huge banners for our respective marches. Our New York crew gets a roll of canvas fabric, blue and red paint, and brushes. Making the banner is an opportunity to bond, build relationships, and have fun. We compete with the other states on who can make the biggest banner—New York and Massachusetts take the prize! On the day of the march, the aerial shot of the protesters in New York City captures our giant DREAM Act banner held by twenty-five immigrant youths. We feel victorious.

The media and the country are shocked that millions of immigrant workers miss work and take to the streets in more than fifty cities. The country's biggest port in Long Beach, California, shuts down, and Tyson Foods, the world's largest meat producer, is forced to close about a dozen of its plants for the day. Behind the scenes, heads of corporations whose profits are impacted by workers not showing up call members of Congress to put an end to the bill.

That day, immigrants become visible. Our power becomes visible. The massive demonstrations unify businesses, faiths, and labor leaders in opposition of the bill. I feel positive change for immigrant communities is right around the corner. I'm not wrong. We—undocumented immigrants, youth, workers, and allies—successfully defeat the Sensenbrenner Bill as its supporters lose ground and fail to get it passed in the Senate.

The strategy works. Marie's and Kamal's stories inspire hundreds of young people like me to share our stories publicly, each story inspiring the next one, eventually moving hundreds of young immigrants to shed the fear and share their stories, in turn inspiring millions of undocumented immigrants to come out of the shadows and march across the country, demanding justice and dignity. Our power grows in numbers. We have moved the fight for immigrant justice from the private meetings in the halls of Congress into the public eye.

9

WALTER

Cristina and Walter celebrate their union at Walter's family home, Long Island, New York. 2009. (Courtesy of the author)

Love recognizes no barriers. It jumps hurdles, leaps fences, penetrates walls to arrive at its destination full of hope.

—Maya Angelou

The Bush administration's war on terror, which, for us, feels more like a "war on immigrants," keeps escalating. By December 2006, ICE triples the number of workplace raids compared to 2005. Under the ridiculous, Wild West–sounding name Operation Wagon Train, ICE raids six Swift & Company meat-packing plants in Colorado, Nebraska, Texas, Utah, Iowa, and Minnesota. Almost half of the workforce in the meat-packing industry is Latine, with immigrants representing over half of the workers in the front-line meat-packing occupations.[42] Homeland Security secretary Michael Chertoff says the raids are "a deterrent to illegal workers . . . We're going to try to make it inhospitable to break the law."[43] The mass raid arrests 1,300 undocumented immigrant workers, becoming the largest workplace raid in the country's history. Immigrant workers do not only lose their jobs. They lose everything. Their kids are left at home wondering what happened to their parents, who were locked away and deported. Entire families of low-wage workers are broken and traumatized for life, while the meat-packing company bosses—all of them white men—making millions of dollars in revenue every year face minimal fines.

At home, we are heartbroken and outraged as we watch the news footage of ICE agents handcuffing undocumented Latine workers outside the plants. The folks working in some of the most dangerous jobs were exploited for their labor, and now they are being exploited by politicians wanting to project a tough image. In fact, all of us are complicit, demanding cheap prices for pork chops and chicken breasts while never questioning the corporations and system that allow for the exploitation of immigrant labor. Now ICE agents in military combat gear violently arrest moms and dads, aunts and uncles, sons and daughters, detaining them in facilities without representation, guidance, or assistance and ultimately deporting them with nothing more than the clothes they were wearing that day. What will happen to their children? Could we be next? We are afraid and overwhelmed.

Every day that my parents go to work, they are choosing to risk deportation to sustain our family. By 2006 Papi no longer works in construction, and he and Mami work the night shift in the assembly line of a grocery facility. *When will la migra raid our workplace?* they wonder in anguish. During their thirty-minute breaks at work, they and their coworkers brainstorm different scenarios for running away from la migra. Far from their boss's ears, in whispered conversations, they map out all the exit doors in the back of the facility. When my parents come home from work, they can barely get undressed for bed because they are exhausted. The physical effort of their jobs and the tormenting fear of la migra weaken their bodies, minds, and souls.

In March 2007, another large-scale raid hits immigrant workers, this time at Michael Bianco, Inc., a garment factory in New Bedford, Massachusetts, that produces military backpacks under sweatshop conditions for soldiers serving in Iraq. Three hundred ICE agents are deployed to arrest 361 immigrant workers. A picture of two-year-old Tomasa Mendez crying out for her father who has been arrested by ICE becomes one of the faces of the inhumanity of our laws and the devastating impact of the US war on immigrants. But the campaigns to stop Marie's and Kamal's deportations and the megamarches have taught me that we can fight back.

Immigrant youth leaders from the Student Immigrant Movement (SIM) based in Massachusetts send an email alert for a rapid-response conference call to support the families impacted. The leaders from SIM recruit lawyers, community organizers, and other volunteers to travel to New Bedford to work with the families and children impacted by the raid. I can't travel to New Bedford, but I join the volunteers that are calling members of Congress to intervene for these families and contribute to the fundraising efforts for food and other financial help the families need. Every time we come together to act against injustice, I feel less alone and more powerful. I think that each of us feels this way. Day by day, we learn just how much more dangerous life actually is for us as undocumented people, and as our awareness of the dangers grows, so does our courage. As we advocate for the families in New Bedford—and some are reunited as a result of our efforts—I feel more hopeful that we can effect change. This is the transformational power of belonging to a community where you feel seen and cared for, and where the values of mutuality, justice, and freedom bring you and keep you together.

In this community, Walter is the person I feel the safest with. I don't have to hide my fears and my struggle with shame around him. I can be my full self. We find safety and joy in our friendship. His jokes and sarcastic humor, often making fun of our lives as undocumented people, make me laugh—the kind of laughter that brings tears to my eyes and leaves me feeling pleasantly tired. He is not the typical guy I'm used to. He is tender, kind, and respectful. He is not afraid of sharing his feelings and being vulnerable. Unlike my experience with most men, he doesn't objectify me. Walter is in touch with his fears and insecurities, and he shares those openly with me. He is afraid of deportation and fears graduating from college still undocumented with no hope that he can go to law school or be able to work. He is in search of real love, longing for the love of his life.

In our organizing work, he is collaborative, defers to women, and rejects gender power dynamics that center male leadership and visibility. He is intentional about not dominating the speaking time in meetings, and he never speaks over women. Walter is the ultimate community builder. He is constantly meeting one-on-one with immigrant students and families throughout the city, recruiting new CUNY students into the NYSYLC, and building relationships with ally organizations. Having grown up in the suburbs of Suffolk County, Long Island, he knows what it's like to feel alone and isolated, fearing anti-immigrant hate.

We work together almost every day. We text and chat and meet at his internship in Manhattan. We hear that some CUNY college staff are turning undocumented students away and not implementing the in-state tuition law that allows undocumented students to pay the same tuition as all other state residents. We decide to take action to hold CUNY officials accountable to implement the law and to improve how their colleges serve and support undocumented students. We collect testimonies and empower students to share their stories. Walter and I, along with leaders from the NYSYLC, meet with CUNY leadership and admissions and administrative staff to bring to light the lack of uniformity in the implementation of in-state tuition and to push CUNY to do better. CUNY commits to providing educational workshops for their staff and faculty on how to serve undocumented students and implement in-state tuition across colleges. Through this process, I learn that winning policy change—in this case, in-state tuition—is not enough. You also need to hold government and institutions accountable for implementing the change you've won, or they won't do it.

Walter and I love to empower immigrant communities with information about their rights and resources for young people to make it to college. We lead these workshops in New York City and travel to Long Island, Westchester, and Dutchess County, where immigrant communities don't have as much help because there are few or no immigrant-serving organizations. At every community event and workshop, we hear the stories of immigrant families facing so much adversity—deportation, family separation, racial profiling, exploitation, lack of access to healthcare—and yet we leave inspired by people's resilience, their dreams, and their hope to provide a better future for their children, a future with a college education. Afterward, we go for coffee or sometimes drinks. We talk for hours about the people we meet at the workshops and their stories. Sometimes we cry. We talk about our dreams of going to law school, becoming the first ones in our families with a college degree, going back to our countries of birth one day, and traveling the world. We dream of a country where immigrants and refugees can be fully free. We know things are hard, but we share a deep conviction that somehow, we can tap into people's humanity and create change—that we can make this country and the world a better place.

We share a love for food, music, and dancing. In the summer, we take advantage of free events throughout the city. We sing and dance to performances by John Legend, Seu Jorge, Puerto Rican Power, and Aterciopelados, one of our favorite rock-en-español bands. One time, we go to the Celebrate Brooklyn festival for a Manu Chao concert. It's a hot New York City summer day, and we are exhausted after running the youth organizing program. To top it all, we don't get a chance to eat before the concert, but the sacrifice is worth it. When we get there, there is a big crowd, and we bump into many college friends and social justice organizers we know. We all stick together, singing and dancing within the large crowd. Near the end of the concert, Walter and I venture closer to the stage and join a lively crowd of hardcore fans. Almost everyone around us is smoking pot. We look at each other and quickly snap out of singing and walk away. We know that being near people who are smoking pot could get us deported.

I take dance classes at school that require attending performances too. I get discounted student tickets for dance shows at New York City Center, and Walter and I both enjoy performances by the Alvin Ailey American Dance Theater, American Ballet Theatre, and more. We've never been inside this theater before. Most people don't really look like us. They are white, tall, and wear fancy clothes. At first, we feel like fish out of water, but after a few shows, we become more comfortable. We both get into modern dance and watch the performances with a critical eye. We follow the dancers' moves and coordination with the stage effects and the music so that I can write my assignments for class. We fall in love with Alvin Ailey's *Revelations*, which tells the story of enslaved Black people seeking freedom and finding liberating power in gospel music and the church. The music and the chorography touch our souls.

Our favorite Thai restaurant is near the financial district, but we can't afford to go there very often. We both work underground jobs and don't have much money to spare after covering tuition, books, and transportation costs. Eating out is a luxury, except for dollar-a-slice pizza. When we get to go to the Thai restaurant, we share fried rice, chicken pad Thai, shrimp and pork dumplings, and Thai iced tea. While eating, we get to know each other more deeply. We talk about the political science classes I'm taking on gender, race, and politics. Walter, who is taking mostly business classes, has not read books by Black and Latina feminist writers like Angela Davis or Cherríe Moraga. I tell him all about them, nerding out talking about decolonizing our minds and hearts, sexism, and reclaiming our senses of worth and humanity.

When we can, we also hit the dance floor. On Thursdays, we meet up with friends for drinks at Carlito's in East Harlem and pregame there while listening to poetry and the spoken word from local Latine artists, then we head to Camaradas El Barrio, a Nuyorican landmark pub, with live bomba y plena by Puerto Rican band Yerba Buena. We dance the night away. Every drumbeat, every drop of sweat, and every dance move bring temporary relief from the oppression our bodies and souls experience every day. We feel lighter, joyful, and free. We live in the present because we don't know if we will be targets of deportation tomorrow.

Walter also helps me overcome the fear of traveling. I'm a working-class undocumented immigrant New Yorker. My family hasn't left New York since we got here, except Papi, who commutes to New Jersey for work until he begins working full-time in New York City. Traveling puts us at a higher risk of deportation. I'm shocked when Walter tells me he is going to Florida with his friends for the summer. And it's not the first time! He and his family have traveled to Florida for vacation and to Chicago to visit family. I'm in disbelief. "Aren't you afraid? Did the authorities ask for your papers?" He tells me he has traveled with his Guatemalan passport, and though his fear has increased after 9/11, airport security has never asked him about his status. I'm embarrassed that my summer plans are not as exciting. I tell him I mostly plan to work to save up money to pay for the next semester and that I may try to make it to Rockaway Beach and our family barbecues at Flushing Meadows Corona Park.

Walter invites me to join him and his friends for their summer trip to Florida. I'm excited by the invitation, but I fear airport security will target me for deportation. He assures me that if I have a current Ecuadorian passport, I'll be fine. I feel conflicted. I can't wait to feel free to travel outside of New York, but what if this tiny taste of freedom leads to my deportation? I ask him to give me a couple of days to think about it. I tell my parents, and they, too, are afraid and not sure this is a good idea. But I've been in the country for eight years and never traveled outside of New York. I'm impatient to get to know other places. I also can't wait to visit Miami, the city I know only from movies like *2 Fast 2 Furious*. I want to see Miami Beach and Calle Ocho up close.

What if Walter is right? I decide to take the risk. If something happens to me, I know my community will come together to fight for me.

I ask Walter to talk to my parents over the phone to share with them his experience traveling. My parents don't know him in person but know he is a good friend and supportive of my undocumented struggles. Walter speaks to them in a polite and assertive way. They are impressed by his knowledge and candidness. We convince them! My parents and I chip in to buy my ticket. When it's finally time, my parents drive me to LaGuardia Airport and make sure to meet Walter in person. "Take care of our daughter," my parents tell him.

"No pressure," I tell Walter jokingly while staring at the floor, trying to make the moment less awkward. Mami me da su bendición and makes me swear to call her when I arrive and every day thereafter. I promise I will.

I have not been in an airport security line since 1998, when my family and I came to the US. I feel disoriented and clueless. Walter patiently explains step by step how the security-screening process works. He tells me that when the TSA officer calls on us, we will walk up to him together and hand the officer our identifications. If the officer asks where we are going, we will tell him we are going to Miami for vacation.

Finally, it's our turn, and my entire body is shaking. I try to keep calm while I give the officer my passport. A Black man in his thirties, the officer politely and slowly opens the passport and looks carefully at the first page, which has my information and headshot. He looks at the photo and then at my face twice. I'm afraid that he will ask me a question, because I don't have the strength to answer. He gives me back my passport and calls on the next person in line. I am so shocked that it takes me a minute to move. "Go ahead; thank you," the officer says. I look at Walter with relief and excitement. I'm discreet. I don't want to call attention to us, but once we make it through the TSA scanners, I jump for joy. I can't believe I'm on my way to Miami! As the plane takes off, I embrace the freedom to fly.

The first thing I want to do when we land is head to Miami Beach. Walter has been there a few times and seems to enjoy playing tour guide for me. Two years ago, in 2004, he lived in Miami for the summer as part of the New American Freedom Summer campaign. The campaign, hosted by labor unions and organizations working for racial and economic justice, brought together a group of volunteers including young people to engage voters in election. At the time, Senator John Kerry was the Democratic candidate running against President George W. Bush, who was seeking reelection. Immigrant communities urgently wanted to have their voices heard after experiencing the attacks led by the Bush administration after 9/11. Hundreds of young people knocked on doors in Miami-Dade and Broward Counties. They talked to people in these communities about their hopes and concerns. During his time in Miami, he checked out different beaches, restaurants, and bars and has a list of recommendations for places we should go to.

We go to Little Havana for Cuban food at Versailles, the self-proclaimed world's most famous Cuban restaurant, opened in 1971. The place is packed with tourists and locals. We order sandwiches, maduros, and classic mojitos, enjoying the amazing food while son cubano is playing in the background. Later, while walking on Calle Ocho, I finally get to see Celia Cruz's star of fame. Walter is a photography enthusiast, and we have fun taking photos of me in silly poses. When we get to Miami Beach, I look at the bright-blue sea and out to the horizon. With my feet grounded in the sand, I close my eyes and breathe in the sea breeze. I open my eyes and walk closer to the shore. People around us are in bathing suits, tanning and enjoying the waves. Walter and I are the only two weirdos without bathing suits. I'm wearing a short flowery dress, and Walter has shorts and a white shirt on. "Get in!" he shouts. "You've been wanting to be here; come on—just go in. Your dress will be dry in a heartbeat," he insists. I don't know how to swim, but I don't care. Encouraged by Walter, I run in until the water covers my knees. I laugh and cry at the same time. All that I've been through, living among the grime and sharp edges of New York City, the stress, and the anxiety, seem to both get lifted up to the surface and washed away at the same time. There are laughter and tears of joy. Walter smiles and takes photos of me in the water. We sit together on the warm sand, the sun hitting our brown skin, water dripping from my dress, talking about our dreams.

Sometimes you are the last to know what's happening in your own heart. Our non-undocumented friends notice the obvious—that Walter and I are spending quite a lot of time together. They think we're a good match. In separate conversations, they encourage us to date, but we both reject their suggestion. We are close friends and enjoy each other's company, but for Walter and me and our undocumented friends, there is an unspoken hesitation about dating other undocumented people. It comes from wanting to protect our hearts from unbearable suffering, and at the same time wanting to leave the door open for the possibility that falling in love may lead us to lawful immigration status. Falling in love with someone who is undocumented means choosing the insufferable uncertainty of you and your partner living in the shadows, fearing deportation, and being trapped within the legal constraints of being undocumented, without access to jobs, healthcare, credit, and in some states even education, housing, and driver's licenses. You may even lose the person you love to deportation. But falling in love with a US citizen or green card holder may potentially open a path to adjusting immigration status through marriage, depending on your immigration history. Walter and I don't have US citizen parents or siblings that can petition for us; we don't qualify for an employment petition; and in the absence of immigration reforms, one of the ways we may adjust immigration status could be through petitioning by a spouse with US citizenship or a green card. When you are undocumented, you are not free to date and fall in love without weighing the risks and immigration law implications. I try to avoid dating altogether. I am overwhelmed by the thought of having to deal with all these pressures when meeting guys. Instead, I immerse myself in building a movement that will allow us to have the freedom to love, and I try my best to ignore the feelings that are growing in my heart.

Back in New York, Walter, immigrant youth leaders from across the country, and I join conference calls hosted by Josh Bernstein and Raymond Rico from the National Immigration Law Center and Melissa Lazarin from the Children's Defense Fund in Washington DC to get updates on the process of negotiations on a new push for immigration reform. After the Sensenbrenner Bill is defeated by our movement, Senators Ted Kennedy (D-MA) and John McCain (R-AZ) work together on a bipartisan immigration-reform proposal. With renewed hope and urgency for Congress to act, we strategize on increasing the number of calls from voters to members of Congress to influence negotiations on the proposal and win reforms that provide a pathway to citizenship for the undocumented.

The policy proposal passes the Senate, but it gets stuck in the House of Representatives. The bill includes a pathway to citizenship for some undocumented people along with a pathway for future work permits, which sounds great, but we learn that it also includes more militarization at the border and, worse, more immigrant detentions and deportations. This combination of good things and bad things was a strategy decision by some members of Congress and some leading advocates at the time. The idea is that in order to get citizenship, you need to give in on deportations.

There are disagreements all around. People are against the deportations and border-militarization policies, some union leaders say that worker visas would hurt American workers unless there are labor protections, and most Republicans just want to beat up on immigrants. Some leading advocates and Democrats agree to "compromise" by accepting more detentions, deportations, and border militarization, and in exchange, they'd get a pathway to citizenship for some undocumented immigrants. But Republicans are playing a different game. They have no interest in ever agreeing to provide a pathway to citizenship for the undocumented. They are just playing the compromise game to lure Democrats and some leading advocates into accepting the idea of more and more deportations. The Republicans win as the compromise falls apart, but both parties agree that the country needs to increase immigration enforcement that detains, incarcerates, and deports more undocumented immigrants. The promise of citizenship is used to win real increases in deportations. I will come to learn that this game has been played over and over again for decades, and for almost thirty years, no wins for immigrants have come out of Congress, resulting in more pain and suffering in immigrant communities without any deportation relief.

By the summer of 2006, Walter graduates from college, a year before me. Walter's family throws a party for him in their backyard. His college friends, our friends from the NYSYLC, and I join to celebrate this huge achievement. He is the first one in his family to graduate from college. We eat, dance, and have a few shots of Colombian aguardiente. Walter's future is uncertain, but for that day, he chooses to celebrate. Even though he is a perfect candidate for a community organizer job, he can't apply for one. It feels shitty to not be able to get paid for work he loves and is already doing as a volunteer. But he must make money somehow to survive. He keeps his job at a tea shop, where he works under the table making teas and the most amazing strawberry-and-whipped-cream crepes, and he gets another job at a warehouse in Brooklyn. The afternoon and weekend work schedules allow him to still dedicate time to his purpose: empowering immigrant communities to fight for dignity and justice.

Meanwhile, in Washington DC, the massive "comprehensive immigration-reform bill" is dying again, and the DREAM Act seems to be the one immigration policy that continues to gain bipartisan support over the years. It would bring deportation relief to at least some people in our communities, while helping us build more power to get Congress to protect more people. To the immigrant youth on our conference calls, this seems to be a possible pathway to at least win something that would help immigrants without simultaneously hurting them.

We agree to meet in Chicago, where Kristin Kumpf, a community organizer with the Illinois Coalition for Immigrant and Refugee Rights, offers to host and support us with the gathering. Son Ah Yun—a sweet, funny, and savvy national organizer from Community Change in Georgia—and Walter take the lead on planning. Walter and I are supposed to represent New York, but something inside me just tells me not to go. With detentions and deportations around us intensifying, I am overtaken by fear once again, and I tell Walter I can't do it. He is disappointed but feels a great sense of responsibility as one of the main youth leaders planning the meeting.

He decides to take the train and heads to the Amtrak station in New York City on the evening of Thursday, October 19, 2006. While the train goes north along the Hudson River toward Upstate New York, he gets comfortable in his seat, sending a last round of reminder emails for the strategy meeting before falling asleep. I text him, asking him to keep me posted with updates about the trip. I have a bad feeling, un presentimiento, about this trip, but I think Walter would be weirded out if I mention it to him. To be honest, I am a little weirded out by my instincts sometimes too.

I temporarily forget about my worries and go out with my friends for salsa dancing to live music in the Bronx. Late in the evening, I notice my cell phone is dead. I get home exhausted and fall asleep before charging it. At three in the morning, I'm awakened by a nightmare. In my dream, Walter is being taken away by cops, and I can't do anything to stop it. I wake up in anguish and panicky. I struggle to go back to sleep.

At around six, just when I start dozing off, the landline phone rings at my house. It's one of our friends who tells me that Walter was arrested by ICE agents on the train and is being detained in a jail in Rochester, New York. Holy shit. The agents are starting the process of deporting Walter to Guatemala right now. I am paralyzed, and the world literally stops as I break into uncontrollable sobbing. I'm devasted at the possibility of losing Walter to deportation. I also feel guilty. Guilty for not sharing that I had a bad feeling about this trip. Guilty for not going with him as was originally planned. Guilty that I didn't charge my damned phone!

The Amtrak train to Chicago passes along New York's border with Canada. Border Patrol has the authority to stop and question anyone that they want about their immigration status within a hundred miles of the border. None of us connect the dots about the risk Walter is taking by traveling to Chicago by train. At two in the morning, while everyone on the train is sleeping and the lights are off, Walter is racially profiled by a Border Patrol agent while the train stops in Rochester. He is awakened by the Amtrak conductor, a Black woman, and the agent, a young white man in his twenties. They shake him, pointing their flashlights in his face. "Are you a US citizen? Are you a US citizen?" the agent shouts. Groggy with sleep, Walter says, "No." He is forced off the train and handcuffed. He is shaking uncontrollably; it's freezing and he's terrified. Four other immigrant men of color in the same Amtrak car are arrested with him. The agents put them in a white van and drive them to a nearby immigrant detention facility. Another van arrives with immigrants of color that were arrested at the airport. They are all Black and Latine immigrant men who were asked, for no reason, if they were citizens. Inside, they are divided into two small jail cells with a silver toilet in the corner. They are told they will be there for a long time, until everyone's case is entered into the system and processed. The agents search Walter's bookbag and luggage. They find a couple of books and make fun of him. "You know how to read books? You actually speak English?" they ask, laughing.

The agents ask Walter for his exact date of entry into the US. But he is too shocked to remember it. He also knows from the workshops that we do that despite what police and immigration agents say, he has the right to remain silent and contact a lawyer. Most immigrants do not know they have this legal right, and even if they do, most of them can't afford to hire a lawyer, and legal help is limited or nonexistent in the remote places where detention camps are located, making it hard for family members and detained immigrants to get help. Immigration agents also many times don't provide immigrants with interpretation services, even in the asylum cases where they are required to do so by law. Walter tells the agents he prefers not to answer any questions until he gets to talk to his lawyer. "Fine. The longer you take to provide us with the information, the longer you will be here; we could be here all morning," they tell him.

Walter has a few minutes to use his cell phone and make calls before they take away all his belongings. He calls me first, but my phone is dead. He calls his parents, Son Ah, and then Minerva, who secures an immigration lawyer for him. After four hours, Walter and the other detained immigrants are handcuffed and transferred to the federal detention facility in Batavia, New York. As soon as he arrives, he is told to take off his clothes in front of the agents and is given a blue uniform to wear. He is taken to another office for a medical exam, where an agent with gloves strip-searches him. His body and future are under the full control of immigration agents who just woke him up in the middle of the night, made fun of him, and stripped him of his clothes. He stands there naked, humiliated, and dehumanized. This is what the detention and incarceration process is all about—breaking us down.

After hearing about Walter's arrest, other undocumented youth leaders are afraid to travel, and the Chicago strategy meeting is canceled. We wonder if the government knows about our meeting and agents are targeting us to weaken our movement. We have valid and historical reasons to feel paranoid. In the late 1960s, the US government targeted Black civil rights leaders like Martin Luther King Jr., Elijah Muhammad, Malcolm X, and others with the intention to "expose, disrupt, discredit, or otherwise, neutralize" the movement fighting for the freedom and rights of Black people.[44] Yes, the country that claims to be the greatest democracy in the world has historically used these tactics to uphold white supremacy and weaken social movements. We aren't the first ones to be targeted.

That day, Kristin, Son Ah, and staff from the New York Immigration Coalition bring us together in a conference call to strategize on how to get Walter out of detention and stop his deportation. But before jumping into a strategy conversation, we talk about how we are feeling and how each of us is doing. We are committed to building a movement where our humanity comes first. We talk about how shaken and shocked we are. How we feel paralyzed by fear. We cry together. We remind ourselves that despite fear, we have come together to fight deportations before, and we have won. We can do it again.

Walter's lawyer walks us through the legal strategy: a petition to stop his deportation will be filed, citing the agency's own policy of prosecutorial discretion, which empowers ICE agents to decide if and how they will enforce immigration laws against an immigrant. The argument is for ICE to take into consideration that Walter came to this country as a child, has grown up here, and this is his home. His lawyer will also request a bond, allowing Walter to be released from detention and get a date to fight his deportation in court.

Most immigrants facing deportation don't have the money for bond, but even when they do, there is no guarantee that ICE will grant one. We must organize to force ICE to grant bond. We reach out to Walter's teachers and friends, immigrant rights and civil rights advocates from across the country, and faith leaders to call their members of Congress and ask them to intervene with ICE for Walter's release. We also ask them to send letters and place calls to the ICE regional and central offices. The NYIC reaches out to Senators Chuck Schumer and Hillary Clinton; Representative Steve Israel, who represents the district where Walter lives; and other members of New York's congressional delegation. Their offices agree to call ICE to intervene for Walter. Time is of the essence. The longer Walter is in detention, the lower his chances. ICE can deport him or transfer him to a different detention facility without informing his family or lawyer. If ICE denies him the bond request, we have a plan to escalate the pressure by protesting outside of ICE's administrative office at Federal Plaza and making the case public with the media, exposing the injustice and inhumanity of the Department of Homeland Security deportation force.

The hundreds of calls and the intervention from members of Congress work. After a massive sprint of activity, the ICE agents in charge give in and grant Walter release if he can pay a $10,000 bond to the government. Walter's family doesn't have the money, but they ask family and friends for support. Their family and network of friends come together to chip in and collect the money. A US citizen has to sign off on the bond, so Walter's aunt, the only US citizen in his immediate family, processes the payment for bond, and he is set to be released from detention. His parents can't go to meet him when he is released, because they are undocumented, too, and could be targeted for detention and deportation by ICE and Border Patrol agents. Deycy Avitia, a dear friend and also a staff member with the NYIC, is a US citizen and volunteers to pick Walter up. I anxiously wait for news of his release.

Early in the morning, after Walter has been in detention for four days, a prison guard announces via speaker the names of five immigrants to be released that day. Walter is included. He waits in the common use area to be called. As he waits to be called, a white female guard makes sure Walter knows ICE still has full power over his body and his future despite his impending release: "I don't know who you are, and I don't care who you are. I don't care if you are a big deal, and I don't care what's going on in your case outside. I want to remind you that I'm the boss here, and I decide if you are released or not. Go back to your bunk!" she tells him.

Throughout the morning, the four other immigrants are released one by one. The guard doesn't release Walter until lunchtime, just to be a jerk. When he comes out, he is ordered to get in a white van and is just dropped off at a Greyhound bus station near the detention facility, and Deycy finds him there, shaken but okay. I rejoice at the news from Deycy, and I'm in awe of our collective power. But I know the fight to keep him home is not over. The deportation case against Walter is not fully closed and could be activated at any moment.

I'm overwhelmed with emotions, knowing that we were so close to not seeing each other again. When I can finally see him, we hug and cry together, and we don't let go. We stay there embracing each other for a while. We don't say much, but our hearts and bodies know that the love we have for each other is beyond friendship. Facing the threat of deportation helps us clarify what we feel for each other. We are in love.

But right now, I want to know how he is feeling. He tells me he can't sleep. He is constantly awakened by nightmares of being in detention. He struggles with panic attacks and anxiety about whether he will be deported. He is also dealing with guilt—survivor's guilt. He can't stop thinking about all the immigrants he met in detention who didn't have legal support and a community fighting for their right to stay. He feels guilty that he made it out and they didn't. He feels guilty for not being able to do more.

He tells me more about his incarceration. This is how the post-9/11 immigration policies and emboldened deportation force work: After the medical exam, he is taken by an agent to a dorm building called Charlie 3. The guard tells him the jail holds people with federal charges, not only immigration violations. It is a long walk with multiple security doors, prison guards, and cameras. Walter is afraid of the people that will be on the other side of the door. He imagines he will be physically attacked by the other men held in the dorm, just like in the movies. Instead, he is given a warm welcome. As soon as the door opens, Walter sees a few heads popping up above the bunk beds, and the men in the dorm start clapping. They ask him where he is from. They shout, "Mexico? Guatemala? El Salvador?" He is assigned bunk 295, at the top right of the first set of bunk beds on the second floor. A Guatemalan immigrant in his forties approaches him. "Vos sos chapín, verdad?" he asks him. Walter nods, confirming he is Guatemalan. The man walks Walter to the second floor and helps him make his bed. Walter is physically and emotionally exhausted. He falls asleep as soon as his body touches the mattress.

Walter is awakened by the same Guatemalan man for lunch. He takes Walter to one of the tables where other Latine immigrants are eating. They are curious about how he got there. Looking around the room, Walter realizes half of the immigrants in detention are Latine, mainly from Mexico, and the other half are Muslims from different countries. This is not by accident. Most immigrants in detention barely speak English. Walter is the only one there who is fluent in English and Spanish. Whatever his fate will be, it is clear to him that he must help as many immigrants as possible to get out. He asks them about their stories and cases. They ask Walter for help talking to their deportation agents about questions they have regarding their cases that they have not been able to communicate for months because they don't speak English. None of the agents speak Spanish, and they don't provide interpretation services. Those with language barriers are destined to stay in detention without knowing the status of their cases or their fate. One of the men asks Walter to interpret for him when talking to his assigned officer. He desperately wants to know where his wife is. They were both detained about a month ago, and no one in the detention facility has provided information about where she is or about how he can request bond and a court date. Two other immigrants ask Walter to help them fill out a form that their immigration officer had given them. Walter is shocked to learn the form states the men are waiving their right to see a judge and are willing to pay for their own tickets back to Guatemala and Mexico, respectively. He asks them if they are sure about waiving their right to see a judge and agreeing to self-deport. The men say they can't take the mental and physical toll of being detained anymore. They have been there for several months and are desperate to leave, even if it means giving up the chance to fight their deportation orders. All of them have gone through a lot to reach the US. They have left behind their entire families and escaped death crossing the border, and some of them have been physically abused by Mexican and US authorities on the journey.

The laws and regulations around immigrant detention are very complicated and virtually impossible to navigate without legal help. Some immigrants can request bond hearings to secure release while their case is pending, whereas some immigrants are subject to what's called "mandatory detention" and can't be released while they fight their case. Immigrants in detention typically have three options: (1) some immigrants are subject to what's called "expedited removal," and aren't even given the opportunity to see an immigration judge for a hearing; (2) some immigrants are eligible for a hearing, but because of the backlog of cases in many immigration courts, it may take several months or even over a year for cases to be decided; or (3) some immigrants can waive their right to see a judge and sign for their "voluntary" deportation. Walter learns that most immigrants in detention trust America's justice system. They've heard America is the country of justice for all. They think judges will consider that they have been working, paying taxes, and supporting their children and families, some of whom are US citizens, when deciding on their cases. They think that because they are "good" immigrants, a judge will grant them the right to stay. The few immigrants who have already gone in front of a judge tell Walter the system is not just. Judges do not care about their children, family, and community roots here. They have been ordered to be deported and have been waiting three months to be sent to their respective countries of origin. Immigrants from Muslim countries who waived their rights and signed for "voluntary" deportation tell Walter they have been waiting to be deported for six months or more. The only European immigrant in the dorm tells Walter that Latine and Muslim immigrants are lucky to at least have a country to be deported to. He is from Kosovo, which, at the time, after the Kosovo war, is not a recognized country. Without a recognized country and a working government, this man is stuck in detention indefinitely.

The prison guards and ICE agents notice that Walter is helping other detained immigrants. They tell him he needs to stop and begin to monitor him closely and intimidate him. Walter doesn't stop, but in the interest of self-preservation, he is more discreet. Regardless, he is more limited with what he can do for his fellow detainees. He tells me, crying, that he feels guilty for not doing more. He had to protect himself because the agents could have deported him in retaliation. Walter can't forget the immigrants he meets in detention. He can't get their faces of defeat and their helplessness out of his heart and mind. He is fiercely committed to helping them get out of detention. Before he is released, he writes down their names, case numbers, and the contact information of their family. He works hard to get them out. He contacts lawyers who might be willing to take on their cases, talks to their families, and coordinates organizing and activist networks to take action to fight their deportations.

Walter also tells me why he couldn't make phone calls. One of the guards explained that to make a phone call, he must pay and "open" a phone account. A private company owns the phone lines and profits from people in prison. Opening a phone account means that the detention facility sets a unique identification number for you to use the phone. All calls are monitored and recorded. If you are lucky enough to have cash with you when you are arrested, you can tell the guards how much money you want to put in the account, but you can only call the people you put on your contact list when detained. If you want to call other people not on your list, you must wait a month to ask for other names to be approved. Immigrants that don't have cash when arrested can't open an account. Even when detained immigrants have cash, their application for a phone account is not guaranteed to be approved. Walter applies for an account but is never approved. He only gets to talk to his lawyer and his sister when they drive nearly seven hours to see him during visiting hours.

The more details I hear from Walter, the more outrage I feel, but also the more my commitment grows to fight for change and justice. I cry in rage and fear but also in gratitude that he is out. This is my first time hearing about the experience directly from someone who went through it and made it out. I hold his hand tightly to remind myself that it is not a dream. We talk for hours, processing his experience together. We talk about how Walter is probably one of the few immigrants who has the support of advocates, organizers, and a community to share his story and expose the inhumanity and injustice of the deportation force. He wants everyone to know the truth—that in the name of fighting terrorism, the president of the US and members of Congress design policies and use our tax dollars to fund a federal agency and a deportation force that indiscriminately target Muslims, immigrants, and people of color while benefiting corporations that own the detention facilities and profit from immigrant incarceration and advancing the vision of white supremacists and nationalists that dream of a white-only America. We talk about the pain we feel about some leaders and people in our own Latine community who claim detention and deportation don't affect us but are solely aimed at "Muslim terrorists" and "criminals." We feel the urgency for our Latine community to know that the detention system and deportation force are designed to go after all of us. We want them to know that one of the tools of white supremacy is using language and narratives to dehumanize a group of people, codify this dehumanization into law, and then use the law to justify government action against this group.

Walter's experience fuels our commitment to end this system. We know we can't do this one deportation case at a time. We begin dreaming about building a national movement, led by undocumented youth, for immigrant justice. In the months to come, Walter will convene a meeting in the basement of his home in Long Island to envision what a national network for and led by undocumented youth could look like. I can't be there, but Gaby, José Luis, Carlos, and Julieta are, and they develop a first draft of the vision for what can become an immigrant youth–led movement that would change politics, inspire the world, and improve the lives of millions.

When Walter and I see each other, we don't talk about our feelings, even though we know they are there. We focus on the organizing work. At night, we chat for hours online. Somehow it feels safer to talk about our feelings for each other on Google rather than in person. We acknowledge we like each other, but we both agree to resist dating. Walter's pending immigration case has turned the threat of deportation into a real possibility, and we don't want to put ourselves through that much pain. Ultimately, the ICE agent on Walter's case chooses to administratively close the case without a court date. This means that, like Kamal, Walter is stuck in a legal limbo without a pathway to gaining protection from deportation.

In the months to come we have a change of heart and decide

to give our love a chance. Our time together could be limited. Over chat, Walter tells me he doesn't want to be deported without having the experience of loving me and being loved by me. I feel the same. We are determined to not let this country's immigration system take away our freedom to love.

When we see each other in person after confessing our love for one another online, I wait for Walter to make the first move. I wait. And wait. And wait. We talk about work and meetings we have coming up, pretending the conversation over chat never happened. There is no kiss. No holding my hand. I'm confused. I know he is very respectful and wouldn't touch me without my consent, but I at least expect him to ask me.

Inside, I reason with myself. Even though guys I had dated in the past always made the first move, it doesn't always have to be that way. I feel confident in who I am and what I want, so as we walk to the subway to catch our separate trains, I reach for his hand. He welcomes it. I wrap my hand around his, tattooing the memory in my mind of how his hand feels on my skin. Still no kiss when we say goodbye.

The next time we meet is in Washington DC for an immigrant rights rally. We haven't told our friends and movement colleagues that we are dating. Our relationship is our cherished secret. On the bus ride back to New York, I ask him why he hasn't tried to kiss me. I'm starting to wonder if he is getting cold feet. My defense mechanism kicks in. I cut to the chase. "What's holding you back? Are you in or not?"

Walter is surprised by my question. "Of course I am," he responds. "I just wanted to take things at your pace and only do what feels comfortable for you." He admits this is the first time he has fallen in love with someone with strong feminist values, so he feels unsure about how to express his love without being imposing. So, I make the first move. Our first kiss.

We see each other every day, loving each other as if it is our last day together. Any day could be the last day I see him. We take trips together. For his birthday, we go to the east end of Long Island. It's my first time in Montauk. We take a long walk on the beach, enjoying the stillness and peace with the sound of the waves surrounding us. Although we have brief moments when we forget that he could be deported, I can see Walter struggling with the anxiety and uncertainty. He tries to not lose hope but sometimes falls into despair. The outcome of the 2006 midterm election gets our hopes up. Democrats win majorities in the Senate and House of Representatives, improving the chances for an immigration-reform deal in 2007. We intensify our organizing work. Secretly, our love becomes another reason to fight.

In May 2007, our friend Tam Tran, an undocumented graduate from the University of California, Los Angeles, travels to Washington DC to testify in front of the House Judiciary Committee's Subcommittee on Immigration, Citizenship, Refugees, Border Security, and International Law. Her parents are refugees from Vietnam, she was born in Germany, and the family seeks asylum in the US. Neither Germany nor the US will grant them asylum. Tam organizes students at UCLA for the DREAM Act and immigration reforms with the support of faculty and the UCLA Labor Center. Tam is an aspiring filmmaker, and after graduating, she can't pursue her dream of joining a PhD program, because as an undocumented student, she doesn't qualify for financial aid. Instead, she focuses her energy on organizing and filming undocumented students telling their stories while protecting their identities. She shows her film during the hearing. "I hope one day I can show this film without them hiding their identities," she tells members of Congress. I am in awe of Tam's courage. Even though I have gotten more used to sharing my story publicly, I can't even imagine sitting in front of members of Congress in an intimidating congressional room testifying. Tam is collected and poised. She tells her story with vulnerability and authenticity. Tam testifying in Congress makes our movement proud.

But Tam and Cinthya Felix, another undocumented leader from UCLA, will end up leaving us too soon. In 2010, they'll be killed in a car accident. I'm devastated that they make this transition without seeing policy changes in Congress. We feel the urgency to create change and to honor their legacy.

Despite the efforts of the immigrant rights movement to push Congress to pass immigration reforms, Democrats and Republicans can't find common ground, and negotiations fail to move forward again. We, immigrant youth leaders, convene to talk about our next steps. We believe the only strategic way forward is to push for the DREAM Act as a stand-alone bill. But the conventional wisdom among advocates is that the only approach forward is a comprehensive package of reforms. Some think we are too idealistic and even naive, but we don't get discouraged. We crave our own autonomous national space to strategize and train young people. We dream about creating our own immigrant youth–led national organization.

With no immigration legislative breakthrough in sight for the 2007 congressional session, Walter considers leaving the country. He tells me two of his college friends who are undocumented got student visas to go to Australia. They don't have family there, but at the time, they learn that the Australian immigration system provides work visas based on labor shortages. They have heard that students on visas with a degree in a labor area where the country needs more workers—like nurses and cooks—may apply to get a work permit and eventual legal residency in the country. Walter loves cooking and plans to apply to cooking school. He tells me he could keep fighting for immigrant justice from Australia and even start an international network of immigrant youth while there. I'm hesitant about the plan because if something goes wrong, he could end up without lawful immigration status in Australia too, and that would mean he could be trapped there or be sent back to Guatemala. He tries to convince me to go with him, but I can't leave my family behind. We agree that he will go. I don't have the heart to stop him. Staying in the US means living with the constant anxiety and uncertainty that he could be deported. One way for us to reunite after he gets lawful immigration status in Australia is marrying, so that he can eventually petition for me. We love each other and commit to staying together while considering marrying before he goes to Australia.

I begin to mentally and emotionally prepare for Walter to leave. There are moments when we are together and, out of nowhere, we look at each other and, without saying anything, start crying. We hold each other tightly. "Just imagine us together in Sydney or Melbourne," Walter tells me while he rubs my back. We spend as much time together as possible. Sometimes I join him and his parents for dinner in Long Island, and he drives me back home to Jackson Heights.

In the spring of 2009, one night after he drops me off, three men approach him, wanting to steal his phone while he is walking back to his car. They assault him, punching and kicking his head and back multiple times. They leave him unconscious on the side of the street. A taxi driver passing by stops and helps Walter get in his car. The taxi driver calls 911, and the cops and an ambulance show up. When Walter calls me, I first think he is joking, but when I realize he is not, Mami and I frantically run out of our apartment building to join him. The cops ask him to describe the incident while we are driven in an ambulance to the Elmhurst hospital's emergency room. Walter and I look anxiously at each other because the cops could ask about his immigration status, but they just ask him to sign a police report before leaving. We can breathe more easily when they are gone. I'm relieved to learn from the doctor that Walter is likely to feel better with painkillers, rest, and physical therapy. We find comfort knowing that it could have been worse.

A few months after the incident, Walter gets a letter from the court asking him to appear to testify about the assault. We fear that showing up in court or declining will activate his deportation case. Walter calls one of our friends who is an immigration lawyer and who collaborated on the legal strategy of his case to understand the implications. She asks Walter to send her the police report and calls within a few minutes of Walter emailing her the document. She explains to him that, given the specifics of the incident, Walter could be eligible for a U nonimmigrant status or U visa. A U visa is for victims of certain crimes who have suffered mental or physical abuse resulting from the crime. We are shocked at the silver lining to this violent and traumatic experience. A dear undocumented friend has called incidents like these "unlucky lucky breaks." We also have conflicted feelings because we know the criminal justice system is not just. We dream of a world where people who make mistakes are held accountable in a restorative way and not through torture, incarceration, punishment, and deportation.

Our lawyer friend is one of the few people who know we are a couple and Walter is considering going to Australia. She explains that if Walter is married at the time of his US visa application, his spouse could be included on the application. He and his spouse would get work permits while the application is pending review, and if approved, he and his spouse would be eligible to apply for permanent resident status after three years. Walter hangs up the phone, and we look at each other in disbelief. We don't need much discussion. We know this is our chance to stay home and be together. Our love will have the opportunity to exist, live, and grow.

We decide to get married within a week at city hall. It helps that neither one of us is attached to the idea of religious ceremonies and traditional weddings. Mami didn't raise me to wish for the day a guy gets on his knee with a diamond ring or getting married in a white dress. She raised me to dream of a college education and becoming a professional, self-sufficient, independent woman. In my women's studies college classes, with the values instilled by Mami as my foundation, I realize how the experiences of women in my neighborhood in Ecuador who survived verbal and physical violence from their own husbands are connected to the broader role that the legal institution of marriage has played throughout history in oppressing women. I know women who have been forced to marry because of a one-night stand, pregnancy, or to make their parents happy. Having a deeper awareness and understanding of why women's lives are not equally valued, I increasingly become skeptical about the institution of marriage. Yet I choose to marry Walter. I love him, and marrying means we have a chance at staying home together. It is a decision rooted in both love and survival. I want to be in equal partnership with him, and I'm committed to not recreating traditional gender roles in Latine culture with women destined to live under the shadow of their husbands. Walter and I talk about how I feel. He feels the same. We are determined to define our partnership on our own terms. My heart feels safe taking this step with him.

Walter and I have only a few days to get ready. We rush to get a marriage license and figure out what we will wear. We get our wedding bands at a jewelry flea market. Walter gets a blue suit from a local shop in Long Island, and I walk through the mall over the weekend to find a cute dress. I want a yellow dress, but Mami insists on white. I choose to not argue with her. I recognize this is all happening too fast, and she is still in shock about her oldest daughter getting married and leaving her side. I negotiate with her. I'll get a white cocktail dress, but I'll wear red pumps and a white feather headband. She doesn't love it, but in negotiations, you must give something up. Mami and Tía Rosita make the bouquet with pink lilies from the neighborhood flower shop.

We text our closest friends and invite them to join us. They are shocked. "Bitch, I thought you would never get married!" Rosa texts back with a crying-face emoji. We don't expect people to be able to drop their commitments and show up so last-minute. But they do. Ana María and Andrea, her partner at the time, are our madrinas. Nearly thirty of us, family and close friends, go to New York City Hall on a Monday morning for our elopement. We are the largest group there. They make us wait for the biggest room available for all of us to fit. Everyone is joyful. Some are even crying out of happiness. In front of our blood and chosen family, we say yes to each other, our love, and our commitment to building a powerful movement for immigrant justice together. Thirteen years later, Walter and I will welcome our first child, becoming the first in our household to be born in the US—although Santi, our fur baby, born in Vermont, may disagree.

10

LEARNING TO FLY

Cristina is interviewed by local news station NY1 during a press conference for the passage of the DREAM Act at the New York Immigration Coalition. 2007. (Courtesy of Walter Barrientos)

> *Every moment is an organizing opportunity, every person a potential activist, every minute a chance to change the world.*
>
> —Dolores Huerta

Back in May 2007, before getting married, it's graduation time. I had hoped that by the time I graduated, this country would have deemed me and my family worthy of immigration papers, but here we are, still undocumented. As an undergraduate, I am haunted by the thought of having a college degree without the ability to work and put my degree to use. I try not to think about it to avoid torturing myself, but as commencement gets closer, I am forced to face the hard reality: I'll be an undocumented college graduate with no future. The fact remains that my family and I could be deported any minute. It doesn't matter that I am a "good" immigrant graduating cum laude with awards for my student leadership and community engagement. I've heard similar things from lots of marginalized people (immigrants, people of color, and queer folk alike)—that somehow, we can "hard work" our way out of systems of oppression, but that just isn't the way things are.

My friends feel accomplished and are excited to join the real world, find a job, and move out to live on their own. Although some of them are going to law or graduate school, we talk about feeling relief that there are no more books to read and papers due. No more midterms and finals to keep us up late in the library. I'm bogged down with mixed feelings. I'm proud to be the first one in my family to graduate from college. But I'm heartbroken that I can't put my degree to use, and in the days leading up to graduation, I have a full-on panic attack. I'm lying down in my bed in the living room of our studio apartment. I think about my parents' sacrifices. I think about all those years working at the supermarket, selling Avon, and cleaning houses with Mami to help pay for tuition, books, and my MetroCard, and I ask myself, *For what? What was the point?* I cry uncontrollably. My heart is racing, and I have a hard time breathing.

Even though I've found a lot of new personal power through my organizing experiences, I've found a new community of immigrant youth, and I have a new chosen family with Walter and my friends, in this moment I feel completely alone. I think sometimes there is an expectation that empowerment is like a switch that gets flipped, like suddenly you aren't ashamed or alone and the story comes to a quick, happy ending. But my journey isn't like that.

Mami tries to calm me down. She brings me water and holds me in her arms until I can finally speak. "Por qué lloras, mijita?" she asks me. I want to keep this pain away from her. I don't want her to have one more thing to worry about. I know all the sacrifices she is making for me and our family. Mami is working three jobs: she cleans homes, sells Avon, and works at a nail salon five days a week for ten hours for sixty dollars a day. She is constantly mistreated by her bosses, who tell her to work more hours without pay, force her to work faster, and threaten to fire or expose her. And yet every morning she gets up to prepare our meals before she goes to work. And she comes home late at night exhausted, with her arms and hands in pain.

But I can no longer hold my despair alone, and I tell her how I'm feeling. Mami helps me lie down and asks me to take deep breaths. She tenderly rubs my legs and feet while telling me she is proud of me. She reminisces about being a young woman working while also trying to graduate from high school in Ecuador, dreaming of going to college and becoming a teacher but having to give up on this dream because she didn't have the means. Mami reminds me that graduating from college is a historic accomplishment in my family lineage, breaking a generational cycle of denied access to higher education. "Regardless of your immigration status, nobody can take your education away," she says. She insists that I must have faith; God will find a way for us to get immigration papers. "Ten fe, mija." I want to believe that she is right as I finally drift off to sleep.

A few days before commencement, I get a call from Judith Torrea, a reporter from *El Diario*, the largest Spanish-language newspaper in New York. She wants to interview undocumented students graduating from college. We meet for an interview at a café in Chelsea, and she asks if I would be comfortable being interviewed for a front-page article about me. Her question opens my eyes to see this moment in a new light. I've been so clouded with feelings of hopelessness about my future that I had not realized the opportunity I have to use my graduation story to inspire other immigrant youth—just like those young people who shared their stories years before inspired me. I feel I have nothing to lose. In community-organizing training, I learn that keeping a drumbeat about our stories in the media and exposing the injustice that undocumented students and families face help our movement empower undocumented communities and allies, reach more people, raise awareness, and spark a conversation about the contradictions between the values that the country professes and how it treats communities of color.

On commencement day, Judith and a photography and video crew from *El Diario* come to our family apartment early in the morning. They plan to follow me throughout the day to take pictures and interview my family, friends, and commencement speakers for the story. My parents don't want their pictures taken but agree to be interviewed. The hope that sharing their stories will add to the movement's efforts to change the laws gives them the courage to join me in speaking up and using this painful moment for our family to push for change. Judith and I agree that I will be the only person from my family being photographed to mitigate the risk of my parents and brother being targeted for deportation.

Mami welcomes Judith with a cafecito and invites her and her team to join us at the table for breakfast. Mami and Papi drink their coffee standing up because we can't all fit at our small table. Our dining area turns into an obstacle course crammed with humans and photography equipment. My parents are nervous, but Judith breaks the ice by sharing the story of her journey to the US from Spain. Soon, I realize we are running late. I hastily leave the dining table to begin packing my cap and gown. The photographer takes pictures of my every move. At first, I feel exposed and uncomfortable. I have become used to being interviewed and photographed by reporters at public events, press conferences, and protests, but this is the first time I'll be exposing my small apartment and my family to the media. As I pack and put my shoes on, I keep my head down, wanting to hide. But I find ease in hearing my parents and Judith share stories and laughter. I am reminded that in speaking up, I reclaim my humanity and, in the process, inspire others, including my own parents, to reclaim theirs. We are human. We have the right to feel feelings, to exist, and to live with dignity.

On campus, I'm welcomed by my friends Jonathan and Andreana, who are giving out white ribbons to all the graduates to raise awareness about the experience of undocumented students and show support for the DREAM Act. Jonathan and I did this last year too, but this time, we get our college president to acknowledge and celebrate undocumented students and their families in his speech. Our strategy here is not only to make immigrant students feel seen, but also to put pressure on the politicians in the audience to do more work for the DREAM Act. Weeks before commencement, Jonathan and I, along with our Political Science Club friends, had spent hours making ribbons for the close to four thousand students graduating. Jonathan pins a ribbon on the left side of my black gown while Judith interviews him. His family also came to this country seeking a better life. He tells the story of his grandmother, who fled the Holocaust in Poland. "It is truly sad and ridiculous that the US denies immigrants like Cristina and her family the opportunity to be fully part of our country," he tells Judith.

President James Muyskens gets his white ribbon and approaches my parents to congratulate them. My parents look up at him—he is almost twice as tall as they are—beaming with pride. There are nearly ten thousand people—students and their loved ones—gathered in the quad for the eighty-seventh Queens College graduation ceremony. The crowd is a microcosm of

Queens and the communities CUNY serves—people from all over the world, with different backgrounds and different languages and some wearing their traditional clothes, coming together to celebrate the graduates and the collective effort that it takes for working-class families to support their loved ones to go to college.

It's a hot day, topping ninety degrees, and I'm roasting under my black gown while waiting for my name to be called. Finally, it's my turn. I walk across the stage and hold my college diploma in my hands. My parents embrace me in tears when I return to my seat. "We did it. We did it," I tell them. Judith asks me how I feel. I'm proud. I'm proud of and grateful for what my family has sacrificed to get me to this stage. I don't know what my future holds after graduation; the only thing I know for sure is that I will keep fighting for the dignity of immigrant communities. "Solo queda seguir luchando," I say. I cannot imagine in that moment that seventeen years later, I will come full circle as a Distinguished Lecturer at CUNY's City College, teaching and empowering students from poor and working-class communities of color, many of whom are the first ones in their families to attend college.

On June 7, 2007, my story appears on the paper's front page. It includes information about a national week of action called "Don't Just DREAM, Act," which our network of immigrant youth leaders is planning in Washington DC to pressure members of Congress to support the DREAM Act. My hope is that some of the thousands of Spanish speakers who read *El Diario* will be inspired to join us, and I come to learn that other graduates in other cities have done similar articles to get their communities to rise up.

Immigrant youth leaders and organizers from across the country work around the clock to recruit undocumented immigrant youth to join our national week of action. We join multiple weekly calls to track recruitment from each state and identify the transportation and lodging needs for each state delegation. National partner organizations like Community Change and the National Immigration Law Center support us with part of the funding for transportation. But we're immigrants, so we know how to hustle, and we raise money by selling food and hosting car washes. We support youth leaders from farther states with flights and recruit allies in DC, mostly advocates and churches supportive of our movement, to open their homes to host immigrant youth for a night or two. If we end up not having enough allies to host leaders, the churches agree to let our leaders sleep on the floor. We plan on having sleeping bags and blankets.

Each state has a youth leader responsible for recruitment. Our New York crew fills up two buses of students and allies and takes off to DC. Together, we mobilize over four hundred immigrant youth and allies from as far away as Oregon and California to Kansas, Idaho, Tennessee, and Florida, to participate in congressional visits and a mock graduation and rally outside the Capitol. We wear caps and gowns, symbolizing the over sixty-five thousand undocumented students graduating from high school every year and the thousands starting to graduate from college, like me. I'm proud and inspired by the hundreds of young people that I meet in DC. The hopelessness I felt before my graduation is transformed by the courage of hundreds of undocumented youth speaking up and organizing to effect change.

It is inspiring for all of us—and just wild and epic, with people packed into churches and apartments, twenty people taking turns to shower in one bathroom, staying up all night talking, romances starting and ending, taking turns to sleep at a motel, surviving days on a couple of slices of pizza and the energy we give each other. Our strategy is to raise the heat and make progress.

Our efforts force members of Congress to debate the DREAM Act and other policy reforms, but ultimately, they once again decide to stall any immigration reform. Was this a failure? No. We were changing the culture among ourselves—from feeling hopeless to feeling like victory is inevitable. This is real political power to create change that is undeniable to anyone with eyes to see.

In the winter of 2007, the leaders from the established immigrant rights organizations in Washington DC and across the country, who are a mix of older immigrant and white professional advocates, organizers, and lawyers, convene a meeting to strategize about how to keep pushing immigration reforms forward. As part of the organizations in our respective states, many of the youth leaders from across the country get to go to the meeting, and we start getting concerned about what we are hearing. It seems like the consensus is focused on things that have been tried but have failed over and over again. The idea is that the only way to get citizenship is through "comprehensive immigration reform," which means that there would be one bill that includes good things (like citizenship) and bad things (like more money for deportations). This strategy has been tried year after year, but the only result has been more deportations. Anti-immigrant politicians would basically play us, and to us, this approach feels like we are being asked to go along with this same strategy once more.

Some of our core group of young leaders—folks like Julieta, José Luis, Gaby, Isabel, Carlos, Walter, and me—are growing frustrated because there seems to be an expectation that the youth should just sit and listen but not shape the strategy. The state and national groups provide us with training and volunteer opportunities. This helps us grow in our leadership and skills, but we want to do much more. We want a seat at the table where the strategies that will impact our lives are being decided on. We challenge the paternalistic expectation that young people must follow, without question, the strategy set by the older folks in leadership. But they feel uncomfortable sharing power. If immigrant youth leaders can't share a seat at the strategy table, then we will create our own. We are determined to have autonomy to develop our own strategies. We ask for a room where the youth can meet to discuss our strategy, but the organizers feel challenged by us wanting to meet without them. After a lot of scrambling, they end up letting us meet in the coatroom.

We feel the immigrant justice movement is stuck and that at least we, the youth leaders, have a new strategy that seems to be gaining momentum. Our thought is that a narrower approach—one focused on the youth—could win and change the momentum from decades of losing to a new momentum of winning. The DREAM Act would grant citizenship to some young people without any increase in deportations. It is an approach focused on helping people without hurting people. There is public support for it, and we have the energy to make it a reality. But all of us young leaders don't really have a say in the strategy. We are interns or staff at larger organizations and leaders of youth committees, and we're basically there to provide help but not to provide input on decisions. So, at our closet meeting, we talk about the need to declare our independence before the end of the gathering, and we appoint José Luis to deliver the message the next day in the closing session.

Born in Miami, Florida, to Cuban immigrants, José Luis is a US citizen and one of our fiercest allies. He is a youth organizer with the Florida Immigrant Coalition (FLIC), where he has gained the respect and admiration of immigrant youth leaders and advocates. Everyone likes José Luis. His Cuban charm, courage, and magnetic charisma are contagious. When he speaks, he channels the spirit of his Christian faith and the practice of call-and-response used in evangelical and Baptist churches. He dreams of becoming a pastor one day, but in the meantime, he is devoted to serving the immigrant youth movement.

José Luis is the last speaker at the closing session. "How many of you believe in the youth movement? Raise your hand if you do," he says from the podium. Most adults in the room raise their hand, looking at each other with a *What's going on?* look on their faces. "How many of you believe that this movement can't win without the power of the youth? How many of you are willing to give up your jobs to make way for youth to lead this movement forward?" The room is suddenly silent. There are a few folks in the audience smiling, including Josh Bernstein from NILC, who is looking at José Luis, beaming with pride. Julieta, Walter, and I are sitting way in the back of the room, trying to hold back our tears. It feels both sad and liberating to break away from the older leaders. It is also intimidating. But our trust in one another and our determination to win for our communities move us forward.

The tensions between immigrant youth and older folks leading some of the more established organizations are rooted in strategy and generational differences. Some of the leaders from the established organizations tell us and each other that we are naive and unsophisticated. A few years later, one of them, in a hostile way, will accuse me and other immigrant youth leaders of being selfish, caring only about ourselves and leaving other undocumented families behind, during a meeting in front of representatives from state-based organizations. Each of us—Julieta, Gaby, Carlos, Walter, and other youth organizers—have similar experiences. Those leaders think that the only way forward is to win citizenship for as many undocumented immigrants as possible through a big, comprehensive immigration-reform package. We think our movement doesn't have the power to win this yet, and we must start somewhere by advancing a pathway to citizenship for some. If we can at least get protection from deportation for some undocumented people, it would be better than nothing and would help us build more power to win protections for the whole community.

The reality is that our communities cannot take an "all or nothing" approach. Those of us who are undocumented feel the urgency to win protection from deportation because we feel the fear of deportation in our bones. We are here today, but we may be deported tomorrow. I feel frustrated and angry that many seem invested in putting out our fire instead of considering our fresh perspective on strategy, our unwillingness to take no for an answer, our hunger for finding breakthroughs, and our willingness to take risks as valuable contributions to strengthen the immigrant justice movement. This is why young people have been key in every social justice movement around the world throughout history! I'm disappointed that it is not only people in government who count us out, but also leaders within our own movement.

As we continue our conversations about how to build our own organization, we feel increasingly optimistic about the future and the upcoming elections, and even though we can't vote, all of us get busy mobilizing our communities to make their voices heard. Senator Barack Obama, the son of a Black man from Kenya and a white woman from Kansas—with a background in community organizing!—is running for president. Walter led a delegation of undocumented youth that met with Senator Obama before he announced his run for the White House. In the meeting, he committed to supporting the DREAM Act and to being a public champion. His presidential campaign message of "hope and change we can believe in" is contagious. It energizes and inspires youth in our movement and people from all backgrounds across the country. After graduating from Columbia University in 1983, Obama moved to Chicago to organize poor and working-class Black communities on the South Side of the city. Knowing that he intimately understands the work of bringing about change from the bottom up makes me feel hopeful and confident that he can make this country better for all people, including immigrants.

Obama designs a different kind of presidential campaign, integrating digital tools and community-organizing practices to empower and recruit campaign volunteers on a mass scale. His campaign partners with Harvard professor Marshall Ganz, a former organizer with the farmworker movement under the leadership of César Chávez, to train campaign volunteers and staff. Marshall, who also trains immigrant youth leaders, trains the Obama campaign in using the power of personal story and narrative to develop relationships and inspire people to join the campaign. Obama feels reachable, with only one degree of separation between him and our movement of immigrant youth.

In his campaign speeches, Obama calls on people to join him in working toward a vision of a country where all people, immigrant and native-born, can live with dignity and accomplish their dreams. I'm moved to tears when I watch him talk about how, together, we can achieve this vision, and he calls the audience to join him in chanting, "Yes, we can"—"Sí, se puede," a chant born out of the farmworker movement and coined by movement leader Dolores Huerta. I believe Obama when, on the campaign trail, he commits to supporting the DREAM Act and immigration reforms. And my optimism goes through the roof when, in an interview with Univision anchor Jorge Ramos, who is the most well-known and trusted anchor among Spanish-speaking Latines in the US, Obama commits to making the passage of a comprehensive package of immigration reforms a priority during his first year in office.

But it is not just Obama's promises on immigration that give me hope. Obama represents a historic opportunity for a country with a shameful legacy of slavery and systemic racism to elect its first Black president, and I can see a path toward relief under an Obama presidency for Muslim and immigrant communities of color that have been targeted as part of the war on terror. Even though I can't vote, I join thousands of everyday people in hoping he will become the next president of the United States.

Senator Hillary Clinton, who is also running for president, publicly makes the same commitment to immigration reform, but I feel doubtful that she would keep her promise. After 9/11, Senator Clinton opposed allowing undocumented immigrants to access driver's licenses and is reluctant to champion the DREAM Act and other immigration reforms, despite representing New York, one of the top five states with the largest undocumented population. I also don't forget that her husband, President Bill Clinton, signed the 1996 immigration law, the IIRIRA, which further criminalized immigrants, increased deportations, and took away immigrant rights to due process.

We, along with immigrant youth leaders and allies across the country, volunteer in nonpartisan efforts in New York, Virginia, Florida, Colorado, Arizona, and other key states to engage voters in the election. In June 2008, Obama becomes the Democratic Party's nominee. The alternative to Obama is Republican senator John McCain from Arizona, who supports the Bush administration's war on terror, and as a presidential candidate, he shifts to a more restrictive position on immigration, advocating for further militarization of the border first before any other policy reform is considered. The John McCain that partnered with Senator Ted

Kennedy to propose reforms that included a pathway to citizenship for the undocumented is long gone.

With only a few months left before the general election in November, we get to work. I organize with CUNY students and immigrant youth leaders of the New York State Youth Leadership Council. We host community and house meetings in Latine and immigrant neighborhoods to educate voters on the presidential candidates and their positions on immigration, healthcare, the economy, and the war. Young people volunteer to talk to voters about this historic election in states like Florida, Colorado, and Pennsylvania. On Election Day, NYSYLC leaders gather at the offices of the New York Immigration Coalition in Chelsea to call all our family, friends, and voters we had engaged with throughout the year to remind them to keep undocumented communities in their hearts and minds when they vote.

After hours of phone banking, we all head to a local bar to watch the coverage of the election. Seeing images of people gathering across the country in parks, churches, and community organizations to follow the results makes me feel we are part of a historic moment. I breathe hope and optimism for the future. When Obama is announced as the winner, the crowd in the bar breaks into cheers. Walter and I hug each other, ecstatic and in tears. We know that Obama's victory offers a chance to change the lives of millions of immigrants. Obama wins with the support of nearly 53 percent of the popular vote, with record-breaking voter participation. Sixty-five percent of Americans eligible to vote participate in the election, the highest percentage in fifty years. He also gets 66 percent of the youth and Latine vote. Crowds of people gather in the streets to celebrate. In New York City, people gather in Times Square, waving American flags and chanting, "Yes, we can." In his victory speech, Obama tells the story of a 106-year-old Black woman in Atlanta, whose parents had been enslaved and who was denied the right to vote because she was a woman and Black, voting for the first Black presidential candidate. I'm in awe at the historic meaning of this election for Black people in this country and for all of us. Obama's victory inspires an entire generation of young people to believe in our power to change the country. I believe this is our movement's chance.

After the election, we—immigrant youth leaders—come together for various meetings in New York and Washington DC. We are energized to be reunited in person. Everyone is feeling optimistic about the future and eager to get to work. In New York, the New York Immigration Coalition (NYIC) lends us their office space for our meetings, and their staff are supportive of us building a youth-led national organization. In one of the meetings we hold in Washington DC we talk about the exciting idea of starting our own organization but feel overwhelmed about what it would take. We will need to file paperwork with the government, create a structure, raise money, hire staff, and more. We aren't able to get paid for our work, so most of us will have to continue to juggle school and our underground jobs while building the organization. Some immigrant youth leaders feel hesitant.

Talking about all the challenges brings the energy of the room down. It is suddenly very quiet. I'm afraid of breaking the silence. My fear feels like walking against the winds of a fierce storm, but I push through and share what I think. I remind them of social justice movements we all have learned from in our trainings. I remind them that other young people have done this before. We are standing on the shoulders of courageous young people that have led social movements and created their own organizations like the Student Nonviolent Coordinating Committee (SNCC). We have the opportunity to build an organization that will develop thousands of immigrant youth leaders and effect change. Why would we walk away from that? Others like Julieta, Walter, and José Luis speak up, too, and people come around to the idea of developing a plan the next day. Having made the decision, we take a break to go out for dinner. I feel excited about our decision and proud that I spoke up to help the conversation move forward. As I'm packing my bag, a leader who is a US citizen ally from a Mexican background and is known for his big macho vibes, approaches me. With a smirk on his face, he tells me, "Eres una bocona" (You've got a big mouth). I'm outraged at his audacity. Before I respond I think of Julieta and what she would do in this moment. In the years of getting to know her I witness and admire her courage. Julieta is the woman in the room who would always name the thing that everyone is thinking about but is afraid of saying aloud. She speaks the truth even when afraid. Even when her voice trembles. Inspired by Julieta, I'm unshaken by his comment and determined to not let him intimidate me. Looking straight at his face, I tell him with a smile, "I know you are not saying that as a compliment, but I don't care what you think." I walk away and join the rest of the group for a fun night of food, margaritas, and salsa dancing. Walter and I dance the night away. This will not be the first or last time that men in our movement would try to bully me and other women to quiet us down and challenge our voice and leadership. But the sisterhood we build with Julieta and other women in the movement sustains me. Having each other's backs and being in solidarity with one another gives us the courage to overcome these moments and the determination to speak up and lead.

The next day, we dream of building a national network led by undocumented youth. We want to create a community of solidarity and empower young immigrants to fight for a country and a world where people of color, regardless of immigration status, can live with dignity and thrive. We intimately know the feelings of shame, loneliness, and hopelessness that undocumented youth experience, and we hope to empower them to shed the fear and find their voice and collective power. My wish is for everyone to go through the same transformation I did in our movement, shifting from a place of shame and fear to proud and feeling empowered. Over the years, we have learned that national campaigns for the DREAM Act inspire undocumented youth to participate in our work, but every time members of Congress failed to pass the legislation, young people would become disheartened and disengage. Sometimes we would never see them again. But we know we're in a long-term struggle, so we want to build an organization that would disrupt this cycle and train generations of leaders to build power and create change, regardless of what the politicians do.

In the weeks to come, we cofound the United We Dream network (UWD). This organization will go on to transform the immigrant rights movement and win. It will shift the visibility and leadership to people who are directly impacted by the immigration system, and we will be the protagonists in our own stories. Building on the legacy and teachings of the civil rights movement, we will go on to make history.

11

THE NEW MOVEMENT

United We Dream immigrant youth leaders lead a sit-in in the Hart Senate Office Building to push Congress to vote on the DREAM Act. 2010. (Courtesy of United We Dream)

Power concedes nothing without a demand. It never did and it never will.

—Frederick Douglass

It's 2009, and Walter and I are married and broke. We are undocumented college graduates with underground jobs, waiting for immigration to process our U visa applications. We can't afford a place of our own. But we don't fit in my family's six-hundred-square-foot studio in Jackson Heights, so we move in with his parents on Long Island and make their basement our new home.

CUNY professor Robert Smith, a sociologist who uses his academic work to advance community organizing in the Mexican immigrant community in New York City, encourages Walter and I to apply for the Master of Public Administration (MPA) program at CUNY's Baruch College, where he teaches. He tells us the program wants to support the development of leaders of color, advancing equity in immigrant and working-class communities. Walter and I decide to apply and get accepted! We are back to being full-time students, commuting forty miles each way on the Long Island Rail Road every day. We take most of the same classes together, saving us a lot of money in books. I'm good with words but suck at numbers and struggle with statistics and economics classes. Walter, on the other hand, is a genius with numbers and science. It just comes naturally to him. He has a lot of patience tutoring me with our statistics assignments, and I have a lot of patience proofreading his papers. This is when I learn that although Walter is a great public speaker, as a writer, he uses a lot of run-on sentences! Get to the point, Walter!

In the MPA program, I gain more context for how to create strong nonprofit organizations, and I learn about the inner workings of government, budgeting, evaluation, management, and policy analysis. I use what I'm learning in school to inform how we build UWD. I decide to focus my master's thesis on how the civil rights and farmworker movements built organizations to create spaces where people impacted by injustice find belonging and community, realize their agency to create change, and strategize together to accomplish their vision. Organizations helped them sustain their movements for the long term. I envision UWD to be a key organization powering a vibrant movement for immigrant justice.

Over twenty immigrant youth leaders and allies come together around the vision of building a national network of immigrant youth. The group includes Julie Gonzalez from Colorado; Matias Ramos from California; Raymond Rico from Kansas; Gaby, Isabel, Felipe, and José Luis from Florida; Julieta Garibay and Rebecca Acuña from Texas; Tolu Olubunmi from Maryland;

Carlos from Massachusetts; Josh, who is now working at the Service Employees International Union (SEIU); Adey Fisseha from NILC; Bill Shiebler and Angela Peoples from the United States Student Association (USSA); Walter and me from New York; and other youth leaders from across the country. We create a national leadership committee made up of immigrant youth leaders representing each of their local or state organizations to ensure that the network's vision and strategy are led by immigrant youth. We also form committees tasked with developing proposals for the network's structure, campaigns, training and organizing, fundraising, and digital organizing. I want to support the work of all the committees, but I'm juggling too much. I'm hustling between graduate school and working different gigs to pay for tuition. I join the committees for fundraising, designing organizational structure, and leading campaigns.

A smaller group of us, including Walter and me, volunteer to take greater ownership and responsibility for building the organization, becoming the first group of board members. We elect Matias, a UCLA graduate and immigrant youth leader from IDEAS, as our first board chair. In this role, we lead the work of building the operations of the organization; managing our partnership with the National Immigration Law Center, which offers to be our fiscal sponsor; and fundraising to support our meetings, trainings, and hiring of staff. It's quite intimidating to ask philanthropic organizations to support our vision. I fearfully prepare for meetings and write proposals about our plans, wondering if they will reject us. But our first funding partner, Unbound Philanthropy, turns my uncertainty into hope. Taryn Higashi, Unbound's executive director, a longtime leader in philanthropy shaping strategies for immigrant and refugee rights, is kind and encouraging. She believes in the power of immigrants themselves leading the way and is inspired by UWD's work. Taryn holds our hand tightly and helps us navigate this new world of philanthropy.

I find that feeling intimidated by fundraising work doesn't go away easily. The first time I have a meeting at the Ford Foundation, I'm suddenly paralyzed when I arrive at their headquarters in Midtown Manhattan. The building is massive, taking over nearly half the block on Forty-Third Street between Second Avenue and the United Nations headquarters. I look up at the building with its imposing glass-and-granite facade, and I can't get myself to go inside. I'm at the entrance of one of the world's largest foundations supporting social justice work. Their support has catalyzed social change across the globe. As an undocumented young woman from Queens, I'm second-guessing myself. I feel small. What credibility do I have to come into this building representing our movement and vision? Will this foundation find our dreams worthy? Thankfully, I'm warmly ushered in by Mayra Peters-Quintero, the program officer I'm meeting with. She gives me a friendly welcome in Spanglish. I'm relieved. I feel more at ease meeting an inspiring Latina who works in philanthropy supporting justice for communities of color, including immigrants and refugees. Unbound and Ford go on to become close partners and supporters of the immigrant youth movement.

Now with resources from philanthropic organizations we can hire our first staff. Most of us are undocumented but luckily Carlos, from the Student Immigrant Movement, gets lawful immigration status through a family petition and applies for the position. He becomes UWD's first national coordinator. Carlos came to this country with his family from Peru, growing up undocumented in Boston. He has long hair, loves soccer and rock, especially the Beatles, and plays the guitar. Carlos is an outgoing and charismatic guy, obsessed with learning everything about organizing. He is trained by Marshall Ganz and faith leaders from the Industrial Areas Foundation, a national community-organizing network known for its intensive organizing training.

Even though we have some money, it is not enough to host the many in-person trainings and meetings we need, but as poor and working-class immigrant kids, we know how to get creative to make things work. Carlos moves to the Columbia Heights neighborhood of Washington DC, the heart of the immigrant community. His studio apartment turns into the main hub for hundreds of immigrant young people coming in and out of the city for trainings, protests, visits with members of Congress, and strategy meetings. Carlos befriends everyone. When the doorman in his building sees immigrant youth with bags and luggage, he knows they are going to Carlos's apartment and enthusiastically shows them the way. One time when Walter and I, along with other youth leaders, stay at Carlos's place, there are so many of us that some people sleep in the kitchen, and one person even snuggles up in the bathtub! In our pajamas, we dream about our movement growing in numbers and power, and we sing along as Carlos plays songs by Coldplay, the Beatles, and Enanitos Verdes on the guitar. Walter and I sleep on a navy blue sleeping bag in the living room alongside about ten other people, all of us sharing one bathroom. So many of us pass through Carlos's studio that there is a lost-and-found box by the entrance full of socks, scarfs, beanies, T-shirts, cell phone chargers, and toiletries.

Our whole operation is grassroots and scrappy. We can't afford an office space in DC, so we turn to our partners and allies for support. NILC, whose staff and executive director, Marielena Hincapié, are very supportive of our leadership and efforts to build a national organization, lets us use some office space. Over time we need a bigger space, and we connect with our friends at the United States Student Association (USSA), the largest college-student-led organization, where many immigrant youth leaders in our network have learned to organize and served as student leaders. Our friends Greg Cendana, president of USSA, and Lindsay McCluskey, vice president of USSA, let us sublet office space and give us access to a conference room for a minimal fee. For larger meetings and trainings, we use churches and office space that ally organizations, including labor unions representing janitors, maintenance staff, and teachers, share with us. Our movement is also supported by Latine and immigrant restaurant owners. They donate food and offer their spaces for gatherings and events. Haydee's, a Salvadoran restaurant in Columbia Heights, becomes our go-to spot for food, hanging out, and karaoke nights. UWD trainings, meetings, and rallies in DC are powered by bangin' Salvadoran pupusas, Mexican tacos, quesadillas, rice, beans, and aguas frescas.

We also reach out to staff from civil rights and immigrant rights advocacy organizations based in DC who, by now, have become close friends. They host immigrant youth leaders in their homes when we have meetings and donate food and winter clothes. Immigrant youth from southern states aren't prepared for DC winters. When undocumented youth from Florida and other southern states are in Washington DC for our meetings or to meet with members of Congress, all they have with them are light sweaters and sandals. The donated winter clothes help us keep them warm. One winter, Gaby heads over to the Capitol for meetings and walks through the snow-covered streets wearing sandals, the only dress shoes she has. By the time she gets to the Rayburn congressional office building, her toes are starting to turn blue. Telemundo reporter Lori Montenegro sees Gaby and quickly reaches out to Congresswoman Ileana Ros-Lehtinen (R-FL), who is Cuban American and a supporter of the DREAM Act. The congresswoman is shocked to see Gaby's toes. She immediately brings her into her office, offers her a cafecito, and urgently calls on her staff to help her constituent. They storm out of the office on a mission and return with a pair of Payless boots and a winter coat that belonged to the congresswoman's mother. Regardless of political party affiliation, our movement's leaders and some members of Congress and their staff can find common ground on our shared humanity.

Carlos is tireless and recruits groups of immigrant youth from fourteen states to join UWD. The next step is to empower them with organizing and leadership skills. UWD partners with Community Change and other immigrant rights organizations to lead trainings across the country. Carlos, Matias, and José Luis join the training team and hit the road to train hundreds of immigrant youth in organizing, storytelling, and campaigning for immigration reforms. Immigrant youth and adults get in a circle, share their stories, and build relationships. They learn how their stories can inspire people to join the movement for immigrant justice and how to organize to pressure members of Congress. Having fun is always part of the mix. Representatives from each state compete on the best chant, and each training closes with a party.

Meanwhile, it's the early days of the Obama administration, and the new president is assembling his team. He recruits some veteran immigrant rights advocates. We hope this means he is aiming to keep his promise on immigration. Cecilia Muñoz, an advocate for Latine and immigrant rights from UnidosUS (formerly the National Council of La Raza), the largest civil rights Latine organization in the US, joins the administration's senior staff as director of Intergovernmental Affairs. In her role she becomes the president's lead advisor on immigration. Cecilia is the child of Bolivian immigrant parents and one of the most well-known and respected Latine and immigrant rights advocates in the country. Esther Olavarria, an immigrant from Cuba with a long career as an immigrant rights advocate and lawyer and lead immigration staff for Senator Ted Kennedy (D-MA), joins the Department of Homeland Security to lead the review and drafting of immigration policy.

But the optimism we feel about the administration and the advocates that are now in the White House soon begins to dwindle. The economic crisis, known as the most severe economic crisis since the Great Depression, and the birth of the right-wing Tea Party movement become greater concerns for the administration. The Tea Party, rooted in white supremacist ideology, gains momentum as a clear backlash against Obama, the country's first Black president. Across the country, the housing market collapses, home prices drop dramatically, and working-class people, targeted by predatory lenders, start losing their homes. By the summer of 2009, the unemployment rate tops 9 percent (the US average is about 5 percent). The Tea Party opposes anything President Obama wants to do, from healthcare to immigration reform. Wearing colonial-era hats, Tea Party protesters wave US and Confederate flags and hold signs that say NO MORE ILLEGALS; ILLEGALS GO HOME; NO TO GOVT HEALTHCARE; and WE CAME UNARMED (THIS TIME). The "birther movement" emerges, promoting the lie that Barack Obama himself is an "illegal alien" and not born in the US.

The first year of the administration comes to an end without Obama delivering on his promise to prioritize immigration. We think that with Democrats holding majorities in both chambers of Congress, we will finally get to pass immigration reforms. Not so. Democrats avoid the issue altogether. White House chief of staff Rahm Emanuel, a key advisor to President Bill Clinton on the 1996 law that further criminalized immigrants, believes immigration is a "third rail" issue that could hurt Democrats in the upcoming elections and encourages Democrats to not move on immigration at all.[45]

Those of us who were inspired by Obama and volunteered to mobilize voters in the election are disappointed—we thought that if we poured our hearts into the election, he would deliver reform. But we quickly come to understand Frederick Douglass's quote: "Power concedes nothing without a demand. It never did and it never will. If there is no struggle, there is no progress."[46] So we gear up to take action and hold President Obama accountable to his promises. In early 2010, we convene a national strategy meeting to escalate the pressure on Obama to prioritize the DREAM Act and immigration reforms. Mariano, an undocumented volunteer youth leader with the Minnesota Immigrant Freedom Network, a new affiliate of UWD, offers to host the meeting in Minneapolis. The network is growing, bringing together forty-five immigrant youth leaders and allies representing fifteen states. I can't go, but Walter joins, representing the UWD board of directors and New York. The group reflects on the last ten years of movement work, which many of us have been involved with since we started college, and envisions the next ten. They strategize how to up the pressure on the administration and Congress.

In the meeting, undocumented leaders from Chicago with the Illinois Youth Justice League (IYJL) present their plan to hold a "coming out" action where undocumented youth would publicly share their stories. In 2007, IYJL had led a "coming out" rally on the anniversary of the mass mobilizations against the Sensenbrenner Bill and inspired other youth leaders to share their stories. IYJL undocumented queer leader Tania Unzueta speaks to how IYJL organizes youth with the idea of an "intersectional lens," centering on discrimination due to not only immigration status but also gender identity, race, ethnicity, and class. Her story reminds me of my conversation with my friend Jonathan, when he and I revealed our darkest secrets and discovered the power of coming out. Inspired by their work and the experience of leaders coming out as undocumented and queer, the group decides to lead a series of "Coming Out of the Shadows" rallies across the country. We want to shift attention from the professional advocates in Washington to the stories and voices of the undocumented. The "coming out" actions aim to challenge the country's dominant notion of who is worthy of being considered an "American." The idea is to use our stories to present the country and political leaders with the moral dilemma of what to do with us. *We are here. This is our home. Will you deport us all?* Walter and the others leave the meeting feeling energized and hopeful that the rallies will escalate the pressure on members of Congress and President Obama.

When Matias heads back to DC, a TSA agent at the Minneapolis airport does not accept his consular identification card and requests another kind of identification. He flew to Minneapolis with the same consular card without any issue. The agent, who has the power to determine Matias's future, calls a supervisor. They decide that Matias needs an extra review by ICE. He is detained and taken to an ICE cell inside the airport. They don't take his phone away, so as he is sitting alone in the cell, he starts texting our network, asking for help. He texts Adey Fisseha, an experienced advocate and immigration policy expert who works at NILC. A petite Black immigrant woman from Ethiopia, Adey is a sharp thinker—and one of our fiercest allies. Adey is also at the same airport heading home and is boarding her flight when she gets Matias's text. Matias is a self-described goof, so at first, Adey thinks he is joking. When she realizes it is not a joke, she tells the flight attendants that she needs to get off the plane immediately. Adey stays at the airport and begins to make phone calls to DHS headquarters in Washington DC and to members of Congress to intervene and get Matias before he is transferred to a detention facility, where it would be harder to advocate for his release. The federal government is shut down due to a snowstorm on the East Coast, and nobody picks up Adey's calls or responds to her emails. ICE agents take Matias away to a detention facility bordering Iowa and put him in deportation proceedings.

Adey keeps us updated, and Carlos is ready to coordinate efforts for a public campaign to stop Matias's deportation. Like we did with Walter and with so many others when one of us was taken by ICE or CBP agents, we circle up and take action. We become a giant pain in the ass to administration officials, and our calls and the pressure we put on members of Congress to act work: Matias is released. He gets a one-year reprieve from deportation and is ordered to check in periodically with ICE agents. A few weeks after Matias is released, we get the news that Mariano, who hosted the strategy meeting in Minnesota, is racially profiled and stopped by Minneapolis police when he is driving immigrant youth leaders home after a meeting. He is jailed and ICE begins the process to deport him. We come together to fight his deportation too and keep him home. Here we are, fighting for justice and trying to build an organization when at any moment, one of our leaders could be picked up and taken away for any reason.

After the one-year deportation reprieve, Matias has to do an ICE check-in where agents interrogate him about his work in the movement. He is told that he will be placed under ICE surveillance, and they put an ankle monitor on him to track his every move. Our network mobilizes community members, advocates, lawyers, members of Congress, and organizations across the country to publicly demand that the agency stop the surveillance and close his deportation case. Matias continues to play a leadership role as UWD board chair, but the uncertainty of what could happen to him takes a toll on his mental health. When he feels down, he is reinvigorated by speaking with other immigrant youth leaders fighting their deportations. Leaders like Rigo Padilla, an undocumented youth leader from Mexico and cofounder of Chicago's IYJL, who is also courageously fighting his deportation by organizing and sharing his story publicly. Matias has to focus on fighting his deportation. He transitions out of his chair role and remains on the board of directors.

Board members and UWD member leaders have a lot of work to do! We are leading trainings in four states and preparing for a national meeting in North Carolina with eighty leaders. My New York bluntness, get-shit-done spirit, and strategy chops get me elected as the new chair. I am the first woman to have this leadership role in the network. My job is to support Carlos as he organizes the leaders of the network, raise funds to sustain our work, and partner with José Luis to create our internal structure and operations. The nerd in me feels excited to have another opportunity to integrate what I'm learning in graduate school into how we are building UWD. I also feel a great sense of responsibility to my friends with whom I'm building this organization and to all immigrant youth and their families. I don't know what it means to be the chair of a board of directors. I don't know what I don't know. But I am eager to learn, ask for help, and do the best that I can. I reach out to organizing trainers and mentors. Folks like Rusia and Ana María, who have experience serving on boards and building organizations.

Meanwhile, it will take two years for Matias's deportation case to finally close and for him to get on a path to lawful immigration status through a family petition when Matias and Lindsay, who are in love, get married. Another story of undocumented love in times of mass deportation. We celebrate them at Haydee's, where immigrant youth from our movement share moments of freedom and joy, singing Selena's songs at the top of our lungs for karaoke nights, dancing to the contagious sounds of cumbia, salsa, merengue, and reggaeton, and sometimes finding love and romance on the dance floor. Lindsay and Matias move to Boston to start a new chapter together and continue their work in social movements. Matias will join SIM to support and mentor the next generation of immigrant youth leaders and carry on his work to advocate for equal access to higher education for undocumented youth. The immigrant justice movement in Chicago successfully stops Rigo's deportation, and he will go on to become a leading voice for immigrant justice in Chicago and nationally before leaving us too soon and passing away due to brain cancer in 2023. Rest in peace, Rigo. Inspired by your courage, we will continue to fight for justice.

The Obama administration that we thought would be our pathway to liberation is instead targeting more and more people for deportation. Matias, Mariano, and Rigo are among thousands of immigrants being detained and processed for deportation. I'm deeply disappointed in President Obama. Perhaps I'm naive, but I feel betrayed and heartbroken. The hurt and anger fuel my commitment to show him that he can't take the voters that supported him for granted. This moment teaches me that elections can help us build support for the change we seek, inspire people to join us in seeking that change, develop leaders along the way, and push candidates to commit to our demands. But this is only half of the work. The other half, and perhaps the most important part, is to hold our government and elected leaders accountable to their commitments and our country's aspirational values of freedom, justice, and equality for all. This is how democracy comes to life. Practicing democracy means all of us owning our role and power—the power to voice the change our communities need, and the power to elect our representatives and hold them accountable. We now need to do the work to hold Obama accountable to his promises.

While we push Congress and Obama to pass the DREAM Act, we also know that the administration, regardless of congressional action, can do more to stop out-of-control deportations. Presidents have the decision-making power to increase or end deportations. Our movement has been successful at stopping deportations through deferred action, a decision that ICE officials have the power to make to temporarily delay the deportation of immigrants not deemed high priority, so what if we push the administration to use deferred action more broadly? We begin exploring this question with movement organizers and lawyers we've worked with over the years. Subhash Kateel, who has led and organized with Families for Freedom in New York—an organization created to defend Black and brown immigrants wrongfully incarcerated and deported after 9/11 and is now working in Florida—shares with us that based on his experience, our movement can push Obama to take more proactive action. Subhash suggests that our movement could demand deferred action for anyone who is not deemed a priority for deportation, even if they are not currently under a deportation order, providing them with work permits and protection. I know Subhash from his work in New York, having partnered with him to train the members of Make the Road New York on how to fight deportations, detentions, and the collaboration of ICE and police in our communities. He is one of the country's leading strategists at the intersection of incarceration, immigrant detention, and criminal justice. His thinking resonates with me and other UWD leaders.

The threat of deportation facing Mariano, Matias, Rigo, and now Gaby's family inspires UWD immigrant youth leaders in

Florida to take more radical action. Gaby, who is from Ecuador, and Carlos Roa from Venezuela, Felipe Sousa-Lazaballet from Brazil, and Isabel Sousa-Rodriguez from Colombia announce they are walking fifteen hundred miles from Miami to Washington DC to urge Obama to stop deportations. Isabel and Felipe are both undocumented and queer. They plan to walk despite the risks of sharing their stories throughout some of the most right-wing Southern states, a region of the country that has long been one of the epicenters of racism, xenophobia, and anti-LGBTQ sentiment. Isabel has been undocumented for fourteen years, and right before the walk, she gets her green card through a family petition. Having protection from deportation doesn't change her mind about the walk. Most of Isabel's family members have been deported. She knows this fight is beyond her individual case, and she is fiercely committed to winning protection from deportation and freedom for all immigrants. For Carlos, the walk brings hope back into his life after the passing of his mother and his struggle to find a job and a place to live. Gaby's parents and sisters are facing deportation. She is the only person in her family with lawful immigration status. Gaby has a student visa, which she can keep renewing as long as she is going to school. But Gaby decides to drop out of Miami Dade College to walk, effectively giving up her student visa and becoming undocumented. For Gaby, this is a risk worth taking because the walk may help our movement win protection from deportation for all.

Immigrant rights advocates think the walkers are crazy. Many beg them not to do it for their own safety. Walking will put them at greater risk of deportation. But with the always-eager support of María Rodriguez, executive director of the Florida Immigrant Coalition, and various state legal and advocacy organizations, they launch the Trail of Dreams. The name of their walk is inspired by Martin Luther King Jr.'s "I Have a Dream" speech and the resilience of Indigenous communities that were forcibly displaced from their lands in the mid-1800s to Oklahoma by the US government on what is known as the Trail of Tears. They hope to bring to light the shared struggle faced by Black and brown people in the US for racial, gender, and economic justice. The walkers have some more unexpected allies too—Republican members of Congress from the Florida delegation: Ileana Ros-Lehtinen, Lincoln Diaz-Balart, and Marco Rubio, all from Cuban immigrant families.

This isn't just a lucky coincidence—it is part of the strategic brilliance of their plan. Growing support for our cause among Republicans is a key part of our strategy, and the walk creates the conditions for Florida Republicans to publicly support the need for action on immigration and the DREAM Act. It should be noted that Marco Rubio's support is short-lived, and once he is elected to the Senate, he will move to stab our community in the back. But in 2010, the strategy is to generate just enough Republican votes for the DREAM Act to pass. Gaby, who will go on to shape UWD's advocacy strategy, leads the bipartisan strategy as a master bridge builder.

Local and national reporters are captivated by Gaby, Felipe, Carlos, and Isabel. Their stories appear on national TV and in all major national publications. Papi and Mami are proud to see Gaby, a fellow Ecuadorian, on TV. At every stop along the way, the walkers meet with immigrant communities and allies, creating spaces for undocumented immigrants and families to share their stories. The walkers bring hope to immigrant communities in the Deep South living in fear of deportation. They want to make visible the connections between the struggles of Black and Indigenous people and immigrants who, along the arc of history, have fought against white supremacy, systemic racism, and colonialism.

Building on the momentum of the Trail of Dreams, other groups of immigrant youth launch marches and other actions. The National Korean American Service & Education Consortium (NAKASEC) leads an eighteen-mile walk in Los Angeles, and immigrant youth from Santa Ana, California, Milwaukee, and New York City follow suit. Some of these walks are coordinated within the network. Some are not. That's part of the beauty of movements. The trainings coordinated by UWD empower hundreds of young immigrants with the tools and skills to act and provide them with a sense of belonging to something larger than themselves and their local groups.

IYJL leads a "Coming Out of the Shadows" action in Chicago's Federal Plaza, and several other youth groups do the same. These actions in plazas, schools, city halls, and churches are recorded on video and posted on Facebook, Twitter, and YouTube. They are also promoted on our website and Tumblr, which was the closest thing at the time to Instagram. Through these digital platforms, we reach thousands beyond our network. The marches and coming-out actions have a ripple effect. Across the country, hundreds of undocumented young people in states where we have no presence yet start sharing their stories. They declare themselves undocumented and unafraid, claiming their voice, humanity, and place in this country. They post videos on digital platforms, where they spread like wildfire. This upsurge moment catches the media's attention. Our stories break into local and mainstream media. Our movement arrives.

In tears, in front of my computer, I watch video after video on YouTube of undocumented youth I don't even know sharing their stories publicly. I have been in their shoes, afraid and ashamed, living in hiding. Our collective work, grassroots and scrappy, has unleashed a movement of fierce young people with the ganas and courage to fight for our communities. We have successfully brought the voices of undocumented young people to the center of the movement.

But as our movement gains power and momentum, so does the anti-immigrant movement. The Tea Party grows and enlists candidates with extreme anti-immigrant stands to challenge Democrats and more moderate Republicans for the 2010 midterm elections that fall. In Arizona, Republican governor Jan Brewer signs into law SB 1070, the Support Our Law Enforcement and Safe Neighborhoods Act, which is the most anti-immigrant bill in the country. The legislation was introduced by Republican senator Russell Pearce, former chief deputy to Sheriff Joe Arpaio. This is a huge victory for anti-immigrants like Arpaio. Even before SB 1070, he was in the headlines for leading raids targeting Mexican neighborhoods and immigrant day laborers in Arizona. Arpaio, proud to be compared to the KKK, was elected sheriff of Maricopa County in 1993 and quickly gained local and national media attention for building a tent city outside of the local jail, where men were imprisoned in extremely high temperatures of over one hundred degrees and forced to wear striped jumpsuits and pink underwear.[47] Under his leadership, law enforcement deputies were deployed in immigrant neighborhoods to arrest people who "look undocumented." Deputies targeted immigrants and people of color for traffic stops, arresting Black and Latine drivers for having cracked windshields or broken taillights. People without immigration papers were turned over to ICE for detention and deportation. Lydia Guzman, an activist from Phoenix, Arizona, witnessed one of Arpaio's deputies pulling a Mexican immigrant over for a cracked windshield and arresting him in front of his thirteen-year-old son.[48]

The new Arizona law allows local police to stop and ask about a person's immigration status based on "reasonable suspicion." The "show me your papers" law also makes not carrying immigration papers a crime. The passage of SB 1070 sparks a domino effect. Behind the scenes, Kris Kobach, a key architect of these racist policies, coordinates with values-aligned Republicans in state legislatures across the country to enact similar polices in Alabama, Utah, Indiana, South Carolina, and Georgia. SB 1070 and copycat laws foment a climate of fear and uncertainty for undocumented immigrants. But these attacks ignite our movement and a hunger for change and justice. Immigrant youth, activists, and organizers from the broader movement travel to Arizona to support the organizing efforts against SB 1070.

The Florida walkers—Felipe, Gaby, Isabel, and Carlos—arrive in DC feeling victorious, despite their exhaustion and the blisters on their feet. They want to personally deliver the thirty thousand signatures they collected demanding Obama stop deportations. The White House declines, stating that the president cannot meet with undocumented people. This isn't just a public relations issue for the president—most of the walkers also don't pass the security protocols to enter the White House, which require state or federal identification and background checks. The four keep pushing. On May 1, in honor of International Workers' Day, the entire immigrant rights movement mobilizes for a march and rally outside of the White House. Over thirty immigrant rights advocates, members of the state-based organizations, and Representative Luis Gutiérrez (D-IL), the most prominent immigrant rights champion in the House of Representatives, are arrested while protesting the rise in deportations by the administration of Barack Obama, the man who we thought would save us.

When asked whether he would push for immigration reform, President Obama says that after Congress has passed healthcare reform, there may not be an "appetite to immediately dive into another controversial issue,"[49] and we know that is code for "no." In these political conditions, we know a comprehensive bill of immigration reforms would be nearly impossible to move forward. But the DREAM Act, the least-controversial immigration policy, could have a chance. Our movement decides to give all that we've got to push for a vote on the DREAM Act. Beyond pushing for this bill, we continue to build the case that Obama can use deferred action to stop deportations.

Within the network, we know that our efforts need to push the DREAM Act through the finish line, but there is internal disagreement within the broader movement on how to get there. Some youth groups are ready to take greater risks by having undocumented youth use civil-disobedience tactics like sit-ins. Others feel more hesitant. Sharing our stories publicly is one thing, but refusing to comply with the law by staging sit-ins in government buildings is another. What if we can't stop the deportations of those who take this risk? We also disagree on whether we should be investing energy and time in building a national organization.

While we navigate these disagreements, Carlos, Gaby, José Luis, and I meet with the leadership of immigrant rights advocacy organizations in DC and state-based organizations as well as with the Democratic leadership to persuade them to support a vote on the DREAM Act. We want to unite the entire immigrant justice movement behind this demand, but some veteran immigrant rights leaders and advocates insist that we must keep pushing for a comprehensive immigration-reform bill and try to delegitimize our movement by questioning our experience and sophistication. We are called "selfish" and "petulant" children, but we persist and demand that the DREAM Act be introduced and passed as a stand-alone bill without anything else attached to it. In our view, it is our only shot.

Sometimes I'm the youngest woman in the meetings with high-ranking leaders from the Democratic Party and immigrant rights groups. I feel intimidated. But I'm not alone. Either Adey, Carlos, or José Luis are usually with me. When I'm with Adey, I pay close attention to her. In her career as an advocate, she has years of experience leading these kinds of meetings. A role model for me, Adey is poised, speaking the truth with love. She has the ability to listen keenly, even to those who disagree with us, and yet seamlessly bring the conversation back to the question of strategy. One time, I join a meeting with the leadership of various labor unions via Skype. This is my first time meeting with them. The leaders are mostly white, with some Black and Latine leaders, who look like they are my parents' age. When I introduce myself, my voice cracks, but I keep speaking. I share my undocumented story, explain the strategy, and ask for their support. Sometimes, I have to just fake it until I feel more comfortable owning my voice and power. A few weeks later, the executive council of the AFL-CIO, the country's largest union, issues a resolution supporting the passage of the DREAM Act as a stand-alone bill.

The DREAM Act and any bill in the Senate needs a supermajority—sixty votes—to overcome the Senate filibuster. In 2010, there are forty-nine Republicans and forty-nine Democrats, with two independents that caucus with Democrats. This gives Democrats control of the Senate. But this congressional makeup and voting rule still mean we need to win over Republicans for the bill to pass. With Arizona becoming ground zero for the immigrant justice movement, we focus on Senator McCain.

He had supported the DREAM Act in the past, but he refuses to sponsor the bill. In an election year, he is facing an anti-immigrant primary challenger. Despite McCain's backtracking on immigration, we think he can be persuaded to vote in support of the DREAM Act.

I first met Senator McCain in person in 2006 when he stopped in New York to build support for a proposal of immigration reforms that he cosponsored with Senator Ted Kennedy. He came to talk to the leaders and members of the immigrant rights and labor movements at the headquarters of 32BJ Service Employees International Union (SEIU). Eight hundred workers gathered in the auditorium, holding blue signs that said WE ARE AMERICA. Before McCain spoke, I shared remarks as part of a lineup of immigrant leaders. I was the youth representative. Wearing my blue I LOVE IMMIGRANT NEW YORK T-shirt, I shared my story and rallied the crowd in support of reforms that would provide a pathway to citizenship, chanting, "Sí, se puede." I got a brief chance to talk to him about the DREAM Act, and he shook my hand, committing to continue working with Senator Kennedy to pass the DREAM Act and other reforms.

Even though immigrant youth leaders have not reached consensus on taking more risky actions, undocumented youth leaders from Illinois, Michigan, California, and Missouri spring into action in Arizona. In May, five courageous leaders—three of whom are undocumented—symbolically wearing graduation caps and gowns, stage a sit-in in McCain's Tucson office and refuse to leave until the senator commits to vote in favor of the DREAM Act. This is a turning point in the history of our movement. For the first time, undocumented youth lead an act of civil disobedience, risking arrest and deportation. The "Coming Out of the Shadows" actions, the Trail of Dreams, and the passing of Tam Tran and Cinthya Felix inspire immigrant youth to be bolder. Local police arrest the four that decide to remain seated in McCain's office. We anxiously wait for news after the arrest. The police do not transfer them to ICE for deportation. In a testament to the power that our movement is building, they are released. Our stories and courageous actions have built the moral pressure for local police and ICE to not target these leaders for deportation. McCain doesn't commit to voting for the DREAM Act, but the sit-in in his office generates wide media coverage and sends a message to other legislators: the next sit-in could be at their office. This raises the tension between our movement and members of Congress, especially as Democrats are bracing themselves for the midterm elections and fear losing to Tea Party–backed Republicans.

In June, President Obama meets with immigrant rights advocates from established national and state-based organizations. Isabel from the Trail of Dreams, who is the only walker with lawful immigration status, is also invited to join. She receives the call about the invitation the day before the meeting as the walkers are speaking about their journey at a social justice conference in Detroit. At first, Isabel wants to decline because she feels that Gaby, Carlos, and Felipe should also be there. But this is the first time an immigrant youth leader would meet with the president of the US, and they agree it is best for our movement to be represented and for Isabel to attend, bringing with her the demands of the immigrant youth movement. Isabel doesn't have money to get a flight from Detroit to Washington DC and anxiously calls Adey from NILC. Adey does what she does with so many of us—she listens to Isabel, helps her calm down, assures her that it is a good decision for Isabel to attend, and reaches out to allies to help with getting her a flight. Our movement shifts from the margins to meeting with the most powerful person in the country. We are both proud and inspired by the leadership of Isabel and the Trail of Dreams crew.

The goal is to use the meeting to keep pressuring the administration and Congress to pass the DREAM Act, while also asking the president to stop deportations through deferred action. We don't know if Isabel will be given the opportunity to speak, and the walkers fear that Isabel could be used as a political photo op, so Gaby suggests that Isabel refuse to shake the president's hand to convey our message. This will be a strategic move to bring attention to our demands. During the meeting, when Isabel looks at the president and doesn't shake his hand, she is reminded that Obama is responsible for all the deportations that we are experiencing in the community, and she tells him that. Everyone is shocked. The mood in the room becomes tense. The meeting moves from an anticipated friendly engagement between the White House and immigrant rights advocates to a conversation about deportations and our movement's demands. The majority of advocates view Isabel as disrespectful and attempt to shift the focus of the conversation to the need for passing immigration reforms in Congress. A few other advocates from established immigrant rights organizations support Isabel's message, echoing our demands and pressuring the president to explore the use of deferred action to protect as many people as possible from deportation. By the end of the meeting, the president does not commit, but he leaves the door open for more conversations about deferred action.

The pressure our movement puts on Obama to stop deportations is working. On June 30, 2010, at the request of the president, the assistant secretary of the DHS, John Morton, issues an internal memo providing guidance to ICE agents, making it clear that only immigrants who represent a threat to national security or have been charged with violent crimes are a priority for deportation. We know this guidance is not enough, because the criminal justice and immigration systems wrongfully criminalize and charge immigrants, but it is a step forward toward our demands and our fight to dismantle the deportation system. It is a testament to the power that our movement is building. The memo, however, also includes this clause: "Nothing in this memorandum should be construed to prohibit or discourage the apprehension, detention, or removal of other aliens unlawfully in the United States. ICE special agents, officers, and attorneys may pursue the removal of any alien unlawfully in the United States, although attention to these aliens should not displace or disrupt the resources needed to remove aliens who are a higher priority."[50] The guidance outlined by the memo is not followed by ICE and CBP agents, and across the country, immigrant youth leaders continue to get calls from people asking for help to organize campaigns to protect their loved ones from deportation.

ICE and CBP agents refusing to comply with the new guidance further exposes the deeply embedded racist and white supremacist culture of the agency. By the end of 2010, the Obama administration expects to deport four hundred thousand immigrants, close to 10 percent above levels during the Bush administration and 25 percent more than in 2007.[51] Obama is on his way to becoming the president with the highest number of deportations, and we give him a new name: the deporter in chief.

The clock is ticking. We have less than six months to get Congress to pass the DREAM Act and win permanent protection from deportation and a pathway to citizenship for thousands of youth. Before the end of the summer, the leaders from the established immigrant rights organizations agree to send a letter to congressional leadership, including Senator Harry Reid

(D-NV), who is the majority leader of the Senate and decides which bills will be scheduled for a vote, asking Congress to vote on the DREAM Act as soon as possible. We successfully coalesce around one demand: a vote on the DREAM Act. We launch coordinated protests across the country, demanding that Congress vote on the bill before the end of the year. From Texas to New York, immigrant youth lead hunger strikes, walks, marches, vigils, rallies, and study-ins, in which immigrant youth take their school books to study while sitting in the offices of members of Congress.

In New York, we stage daily vigils outside of Senator Chuck Schumer's main office in Midtown Manhattan. Senator Schumer supports the DREAM Act, but he's refused to champion the bill. He is a key senator to pressure because, as part of the leadership of the Democratic Party, he can influence Senator Reid. Walter and I, along with dozens of immigrant youth, wear graduation caps and gowns, holding candles and banners that say PASS THE DREAM ACT NOW. We chant. We sing. We share our stories every evening for a week until his staff tell us he is committed to making the DREAM Act a priority. But we are very familiar with lip service by now and we refuse to stop until Senator Schumer makes this commitment public. Senator Schumer's staff are increasingly annoyed by us. They stop being friendly and refuse to respond to our emails and calls. I will later learn that Senator Schumer called the more established immigrant rights advocates in New York, asking them to stop our vigils. "Get these kids off my sidewalk!" he said. What Senator Schumer didn't know is that we were not controlled by the older immigrant rights leaders. Nobody could tell us what to do.

In Washington DC, we mobilize close to two hundred immigrant youth for twenty days to hold public teach-ins on the steps of the US Capitol. Inspired by the civil rights movement's work to build desegregated schools and universities in the 1950s, we launch "Dream University," sending the message that if the government won't allow us to go to school, we will build our own. With limited resources for housing and food, we create a hub for supporters, educators, congressional allies, immigrant business owners, faith leaders, and others—allies and friends—to help our efforts, including free housing and food for immigrant youth. The young people sleep on the floors of local churches and on couches in the homes of friends and allies. Major national media outlets, including the *Washington Post* and CNN, cover our actions. With energy building outside the Capitol, momentum for a stand-alone DREAM Act vote gains traction. Still, Senator Reid does not move to schedule a vote on the bill.

The next wave of actions is focused on Senator Reid and the Senate. Neidi Dominguez, an undocumented youth leader from DREAM Team Los Angeles (DTLA) and one of the fiercest organizers in our movement, helps lead the actions along with dozens of undocumented youth from across the country. Twenty-one undocumented youth, including Isabel, dressed in caps and gowns stage a sit-in in the offices of Senators Reid and McCain as well as in the atrium of the Hart Senate Office Building in Washington DC. Dozens more show their support by rallying outside of the Senate building. Immigrant youth refuse to end the sit-in until the senators commit to scheduling a vote for the DREAM Act. Capitol police arrest them but do not refer them to ICE for deportation. They are released. We all can breathe more easily.

Senator Reid is facing a competitive general election campaign against a Republican challenger who is backed by the Tea Party. This is the toughest reelection campaign of his political career. The growing Latine electorate in Nevada makes it a critical bloc of voters for his reelection campaign. Immigration is a top concern for Latine voters who voted for Obama and are increasingly frustrated about deportations and Democrats' refusal to pass immigration reforms. Our public pressure on members of Congress had turned the DREAM Act into a litmus test for Latino voters on whether politicians were in support of or against the Latine community. Reid's campaign is struggling with creating enthusiasm among Latine voters. A Latino Decisions poll finds that only 41 percent of Latine voters are "very enthusiastic" about voting, and over 50 percent are less excited about the Democratic Party than they were when Obama was elected.[52] Senator Reid knows that a vote on the DREAM Act could energize and mobilize Latine voters to the polls. He publicly commits to including both the DREAM Act and a repeal of "Don't Ask, Don't Tell"—a policy that allows the discharge of members of the military if their sexual preference becomes public—as part of the package of policies in the National Defense Authorization Act, which is a "must pass" bill. The idea here is that Congress must pass the defense bill because it includes all of the money for the military. So, one tactic used by members of Congress is to load up "must pass" bills with things that might not pass on their own. With Senator Reid's commitment, our movement knows that the future of the DREAM Act depends on the outcome of his race. Immigrant youth leaders from Nevada and other parts of the country volunteer to mobilize voters for the election.

The LGBTQ movement is also mounting pressure on the administration and Congress to end the ban on same-sex marriage and repeal "Don't Ask, Don't Tell." Increasingly, as immigrant youth leaders come out as undocumented and queer, our movements come together to coordinate and support each other's demands. On September 21, 2010, the Senate votes on the DREAM Act, achieving a fifty-six-to-forty-three vote, winning a majority of votes but falling short of the sixty needed to break the filibuster. But this isn't the last chance for the Senate to vote on the bill; Congress is still in session for two more months.

UWD convenes our first national congress in Lexington, Kentucky, hosted by the new UWD affiliate, Kentucky Dream Coalition. UWD continues to grow, bringing together 120 leaders representing twenty states. We strategize on our plan for the last months of the congressional session.

This is our largest national meeting ever. I know some of the leaders in the room, but there are young people from Connecticut, North Carolina, Arizona, and Kentucky that I meet for the first time. Sitting among all these new faces, I'm in awe, witnessing our vision coming to life. The meeting starts with building community. Sitting in a circle, everyone shares their stories, starting with, "Hi, my name is . . . and I'm undocumented." We see each other in our stories. *You are me, and I am you.*

We develop a plan to sustain actions until we get a vote, even if it means having to mobilize through the holidays. New leaders from North Carolina, Kentucky, Arizona, and Connecticut commit to recruiting more people. I develop a close relationship with Lorella Praeli, an undocumented student leader from Peru who lost her right leg in a car accident when she was two years old and came with her family to the US seeking medical treatment. Lorella and I are both in school; she is an undergraduate student studying political science at Quinnipiac University. We get to know each other more while waiting for the bathroom and nerd out talking about our thesis projects on social movements. Lorella's cousin, Hafid, and Carolina and Camila Bortolleto, who are twins and are also in the line, are excited about building out an organization led by undocumented youth in Connecticut. They are a short drive away from New York, and I'm excited to support them in their work to build a youth-led organization. They will go on to found Connecticut Students for a Dream

(C4D), becoming one of the leading young-people-of-color organizations fighting for racial, gender, and economic justice in the state.

At the end of the three-day gathering, some of the UWD board members come together to reflect on the meeting and the moment. We had dreamed of rooms with hundreds of young undocumented people sharing stories, loving on each other, and finding their power in spite of fear. It is no longer a dream. It is a reality. We beam with joy. We are tired, but we feel accomplished. We look at each other in awe, relief, and wonder. We take a picture of the crew together—Julieta, Carlos, José Luis, Matias, Josh, Walter, and me—capturing years of friendship, comradery, struggle, highs and lows, joy, dreams, and miracles. A moment in movement history.

Meanwhile, Walter and I get an email from the Department of Homeland Security notifying us that our U visa case is moving forward. The agency has approved our work permits. We don't have permanent immigration status yet, but having temporary work permits and Social Security cards protects us more from deportation and allows us to work. It is not guaranteed that we won't be deported, but at least we have one more tool to fight back. Walter and I hug each other and sob. I feel a sense of relief but also survivor's guilt. I have protection now, but my parents, brother, and most of the immigrant youth leaders in United We Dream are still undocumented. When we get the work permits in the mail, it feels anticlimactic. I had imagined I would feel ecstatic and overjoyed. But holding the card in my hand, I can't help but think that the absence of this plastic card has trapped us in fear for so many years. This pocket-size card holds so much power. Walter, an eternal optimist, reminds me to also recognize the huge changes this card will bring to our lives. We can finally apply for organizing jobs, help our families, eventually petition for my parents, and move out of his parents' basement to a place of our own!

Three and a half years later, in February 2014, Walter and I will finally get our green cards via mail. We both get to go back home to Guatemala and Ecuador. Home is both there and here. Home is in the heart. When I go, I feel a connection to the land and the mountains of the Andes that I can't explain in words. It's the feeling of home. I'm joyful to see my cousins, tías, and tíos. All of us have changed physically, but our connection feels the same. I get to go visit my sister and abuelitas Julia and Esther at the cemetery. On behalf of my parents, I bring a heart broken by the pain that they can't come with me and by the grief that they didn't have the opportunity to say a last goodbye to their mothers before they passed. But I also bring with me colorful flowers, the joy of being able to reconnect with them in spirit, and the hope that one day my parents will get to come too.

On Election Day 2010, the Latine vote delivers the victory for Senator Reid. He wins with 50.3 percent of the vote. Sixty-eight percent of Latine voters cast their ballots for him, making their vote 5.7 percent of Reid's advantage in the race. Democrats retain a slim majority in the US Senate with fifty-one seats, while Republicans win six additional seats for a total of forty-seven. The Tea Party, with its small-government and anti-immigrant agenda, wins a total of forty-four congressional seats. The election results legitimize the Tea Party in mainstream American politics and lead to the Republican Party becoming more extreme in its anti-immigrant and xenophobic views. The new makeup of Congress means action on any immigration reform will be nearly impossible. Our last real chance is the lame-duck session of Congress, which consists of the weeks between the election and when the new Congress is sworn in early the following year. During the lame-duck session, members of Congress have less influence over their colleagues, while also having the freedom to make decisions without much fear of consequences. Our hope is that members of Congress will feel they can vote with their conscience.

The lame-duck campaign is on! We make a national call to the entire network and our allies to descend on Washington DC for sustained action. UWD affiliates and allies also recruit immigrant youth within their local schools and communities. Those of us who are in school are in the middle of final exams, but it is an all-hands-on-deck moment, so we leave our finals behind. Walter and I send emails to our professors. They understand. Immigrant youth are making history, they say, granting us extensions. We hop on buses down to Washington DC. In the meantime, Carlos, Julieta, and José Luis, along with other co-founders and immigrant youth leaders from across the country, turn the conference room lent to us by the National Immigration Forum, an advocacy organization in DC, into our lame-duck war room. They create different teams. There is butcher paper all around the walls with a calendar of the congressional session, each day showing the actions youth are leading and the lists of names with the different delegations of young people coming to DC with their arrival and departure dates. The digital team makes posts on Facebook and sends emails to our lists. Carlos and Julieta host national calls to recruit as many young people as possible, while others are making confirmation calls. The room feels and sounds like a calling center.

We plan to keep a sustained presence in the Capitol and the halls of Congress until they give us a vote on the DREAM Act. More than three hundred youth sign up for the lame-duck session. Young people come from as far away as Texas, Arizona, and Washington state. We raise enough money to cover travel and food. Not everyone can join us in DC, but the network supports groups to lead action in their home states too. In San Antonio,

Texas, immigrant youth hold a hunger strike for forty-three days to pressure Republican senator Kay Bailey Hutchison to vote in favor of the bill. Senator Hutchison offers a more conservative proposal that would give temporary protections to some youth. We don't support her proposal, but her openness to negotiations signals that perhaps if we pressure her, we can move her. It's a long shot, but we need every single vote we can get. Carlos Amador, an undocumented youth leader from Mexico who is with the UCLA Labor Center and completing his master's degree at UCLA, leads a group of undocumented youth in a fifteen-day hunger strike outside the office of Democratic senator Dianne Feinstein in Los Angeles. Carlos, who will become a UWD board member, is soft-spoken and a true organizer—always focused on empowering others, not interested in the spotlight.

Those of us in DC lead actions every week. Hundreds of immigrant youth wearing caps and gowns lead actions in the US Capitol. We hold vigils, rallies, study-ins in the cafeterias of the US Capitol, and marches with faith leaders. We also follow members of Congress through the halls of the Capitol, asking them to commit to vote for the DREAM Act and capturing their responses on video to then share online. We use online platforms to mobilize supporters to call and sign petitions asking their members of Congress to support the DREAM Act. Every day we send emails and social media posts urging people to generate as many calls as possible to members of Congress. Supporters share them online via Facebook and Twitter to reach more people. Mainstream media and Spanish TV networks cover our presence in Washington DC every week. Our movement is not only visible but the most vibrant youth movement at this time.

The pressure we exert on members of Congress leads the House of Representatives, under the leadership of Speaker Nancy Pelosi (D-CA), to vote on the bill first. We work with

Democratic leadership and members of Congress's staff to review the language and negotiate final details of the bill. Adey helps us advocate for broadening the bill so it can benefit as many youth as possible. We focus on getting rid of the age requirement. Every year that Congress decides to not vote on the DREAM Act since 2001 when it was first introduced, young immigrants have gotten older, and over time, many of them have turned thirty-five. Julieta is one of them. But Democrats refuse to get rid of this requirement. They argue that moderate Democrats who are more conservative on immigration won't vote in favor of the bill if the age-cap requirement is taken out. We have to decide whether to take the risk that we may or may not succeed in changing the requirements when the bill moves to the Senate. It's a difficult decision. Carlos hosts a call with UWD board members and leaders to make a collective decision. Julieta cannot contain her tears. The rest of us cry too. Julieta loves us, this movement of immigrant youth, so much that even in this moment, she inspires us to step into our courage. With her voice quavering, she shares with us how painful it is to know that she may not qualify, but she reminds us that this is not only about her but about thousands more and the broader movement of immigrant youth we are building. At this moment, I think about that older leader who said that immigrant youth were "selfish" and see Julieta step into the most courageous and humble act of leadership I've ever seen before or since. She reminds us that we have gotten this far. We can't and shouldn't turn around. Let's fight with all our might to pass this bill in the House and make it better in the Senate. Every single one of us on that call commits to keep fighting for Julieta and all immigrants regardless of the outcome.

Carlos, Adey, Walter, and I meet with Representative Gutiérrez before the House votes on the bill. He is mostly worried about the Senate and feels hopeful that the House will pass it. Speaker Pelosi will never bring a bill to the floor if she doesn't have the votes, he says. Sitting in his office, he tells us, "We got this, familia." Our movement is determined to keep pushing members of Congress until the last minute before the vote. We are fiercely hopeful. Advocates, on the other hand, feel uncertain that we can get the votes to win.

On December 8, we follow the votes closely from the House chamber's upper balcony, where guests are allowed. It's my first time there. The chamber is a large assembly room with armchairs in a semicircle facing a rostrum in the middle of the room with a US flag and black marble columns behind it. It feels surreal to be in the room where decisions about our lives are made. Representatives are walking in and out of the House chamber floor. We all hold hands. To the shock of some advocates, the DREAM Act passes in the House of Representatives with 216 votes (208 Democrats and 8 Republicans vote in favor). Most Republicans, now highly influenced by the Tea Party, vote against the bill with 160 votes. We embrace one another, shedding tears of joy. We feel proud, victorious, and unstoppable.

After the House vote, Senator Hutchison sends a letter to her party stating that she will not support the DREAM Act. Her letter is meant to send the clear message to her party colleagues and Democrats that they cannot count on her vote; she hopes it will also influence other Republicans and conservative Democrats to vote against it. Hutchison may be a no, but we keep pressuring Republicans, especially Senators McCain and Hatch, who had supported the DREAM Act before.

Senator Reid schedules the vote for December 18, right before the Christmas holidays. Our presence in DC is strong. Hundreds of immigrant youth wearing caps and gowns are rallying, marching, and leading sit-ins inside the Capitol building. The day of the vote, we organize a virtual meeting for hundreds of immigrant youth across the country to follow the vote together on C-SPAN, and those of us in DC gather in the Senate gallery to witness the ballots being cast in person. The Senate gallery is a semicircular room with fancy wooden desks facing a rostrum. Each senator is assigned a desk, but most of them are walking around the floor and coming in and out of the room with their staffers. The Senate parliamentarian sits by the rostrum reviewing the process of the votes and begins the roll-call vote. In a monotone, she calls each senator by their last name. In response, some senators give a thumbs-up or thumbs-down, and some call out "yea" or "nay." We stand up, holding each other's hands, virtually and in person, tracking the vote count on the screen by the rostrum, praying, with our hearts full of hope.

The bill fails to get the sixty votes needed to stop the filibuster, with fifty-five to forty-one votes. The filibuster is a rule in the Senate that allows senators to delay voting on a bill by keeping the debate going. The vote is mostly along party lines, but five Democrats vote against it: Kay Hagan of North Carolina, Mark Pryor of Arkansas, Ben Nelson of Nebraska, and both Montana Democrats, Jon Tester and Max Baucus. Joe Manchin of West Virginia, who publicly opposes the DREAM Act, misses the vote. Three Republicans vote in favor: Senator Richard Lugar from Indiana, Senator Lisa Murkowski from Alaska, and Senator Bob Bennett from Utah. Senator McCain does not show up for the vote. The repeal of "Don't Ask, Don't Tell" is up for a vote next, and the bill passes by a margin of seventy-seven to twenty-two, with one voter abstaining.

The votes on both bills move too fast for my mind and body to process. I'm holding Walter's hand, and I turn my head to Josh. "Is that it?" I ask him. "Was the decision over our lives made in what felt like less than five minutes? Can somebody pinch me?"

Josh looks at me with sorrow. He tries to hold back his tears. "I'm sorry, friend," he tells me.

I start to cry. I'm not the only one. Over one hundred of us are in the Senate gallery crying. Though we are glad for the passage of the repeal of "Don't Ask, Don't Tell," it is a devastating moment for our movement. We gather in the lobby of the Senate building and form a large circle, hugging each other. In the middle of that circle, in tears, I feel in my soul that this loss will not stop us. We head to the United Methodist Building, which has become our base for our days of action, and form a circle. We cry. We sing. We chant. Everyone who speaks is in pain about the loss but also deeply committed to our movement. This loss does not represent a defeat. I think of it as losing forward because our movement is stronger, with hundreds of leaders committed to keep fighting for justice. This is not the end. We will be back.

12

UNDOCUMENTED AND UNAFRAID

United We Dream leaders and staff (from left to right: Yadira Dúmet, UWD organizer; José Cáseres, leader with Dreamers of Virginia; Julieta Garibay, UWD cofounder; and Greisa Martinez Rosas, UWD executive director) block traffic outside the White House to demand President Obama stop deportations. 2014. (Courtesy of United We Dream)

We are freedom bound.

—June Jordan

We are committed to keeping up the fight for immigrant justice, but we also grieve the loss of the DREAM Act. To say that the preceding period was intense would be a complete understatement. We are physically and emotionally exhausted. Some of us fall into depression, but we hold on to hope and each other. We come together in conference calls and meetings to reflect on our work and discuss our strategy moving forward. We remind ourselves that our worth is not defined by a piece of legislation and that we are on a long journey toward freedom.

We talk about the lessons we've learned. One of them is that despite trying everything we could think of to build a network that is inclusive and democratic in making decisions, we made mistakes.

None of us have run or built national organizations before, much less tried to imagine what a democratic organization can even be. As survivors of laws and experiences that have silenced us and made us invisible, we go through growing pains in creating processes that listen to and value every idea and every voice. In 2010, things move too fast, and in the midst of it all, we don't pause to talk about our different perspectives on how to win change for our communities. As a result, some groups and leaders feel unheard, and distrust grows between some leaders, staff, and cofounders of UWD. Deep down, I wish we had the mental and emotional capacity to talk through our disagreements, acknowledge mistakes and harms done, hear each other's ideas, and maybe rebuild trust, but it is hard. The divisions grow, and we can't find a way to build a bridge, so we decide to go our separate ways. In January 2011, a few groups split from the network to build their own, while most groups within United We Dream stay together. We commit to growing the network and coordinating a national strategy incorporating the lessons we've learned.

Immediately after the split, we know that the most important thing is to provide young leaders with an opportunity to be in community with one another and to talk about the movement's strategy. In times of deep strategic questioning, the answer always lies with our people. So we decide to plan the largest national meeting our network has ever had. We—UWD staff, the leaders of UWD's National Coordinating Committee (NCC), and the board of directors—design a process to include all UWD leaders in developing the network's strategy.

The process starts with representatives from UWD affiliates meeting in Arizona. The group includes some of the most seasoned and talented leaders in UWD: Felipe Sousa-Lazaballet from Florida and Natalia Aristizabal from New York, as well as up-and-coming leaders from California, Missouri, Texas, Colorado, Massachusetts, Wisconsin, and Arizona. They are part of a new generation of leaders that have joined the movement in the wave of protests for the DREAM Act vote in 2010, bringing fresh leadership, boldness, and creativity. During this meeting and in conference calls with groups across the country, we talk about the fact that the new makeup of Congress, which now includes extreme anti-immigrant and xenophobic representatives, makes it unlikely for any immigration reform to be passed this year. But if Congress won't pass legislation that would protect us permanently from deportation and provide a pathway to citizenship, the president can, at the very least, stop deportations. We have been building the case for the administration to use deferred action to provide undocumented people with temporary protection from deportation and a work permit. This is how we have successfully stopped deportations one by one. Given the broad national bipartisan support that immigrant youth have earned through the fight for the DREAM Act, we could start with demanding deferred action for immigrant youth. If we can get the Obama administration to grant this, we can win deferred action for all.

We require all UWD affiliates to have strategy meetings with immigrant youth leaders in their states before they arrive at our March national strategy meeting in Memphis, Tennessee, hosted by affiliates Youth for Youth and the Tennessee Immigrant & Refugee Rights Coalition. While affiliate and NCC leaders work on the recruitment and agenda for the meeting, the members of the board of directors focus on logistics and fundraising. In my role as chair, I work on raising the funds to cover the costs of food, transportation, lodging, and our meeting space. I make phone calls and write letters and grant proposals, asking for financial support, reaching out to philanthropic organizations and more established progressive organizations and labor unions. The labor unions AFL-CIO and SEIU come through with financial support, helping build momentum for other organizations to help out. Many of the advocacy organizations that once disagreed with us and underestimated our leadership make donations too. The tides have turned, and we raise most of the funds to cover everyone's transportation, lodging, and food.

Two hundred and fifty immigrant youth from over thirty states register to join the national strategy meeting in Memphis. We chose Memphis strategically because we want to ground immigrant youth leaders in the vision, history, and courage of Black leaders in the civil rights movement. We plan for them to visit the National Civil Rights Museum and have the chance to speak with civil rights movement elder Hollis Watkins, an organizer and member of SNCC. We hope being in Memphis gives them an opportunity to learn more about the history of the city as the site of the sanitation workers' strike and the assassination of Martin Luther King Jr. In 1968, over one thousand Black sanitation workers went on strike demanding higher wages and better working conditions after two sanitation workers were crushed to death by a malfunctioning truck. The strike captured national attention and galvanized the civil rights movement and prominent leaders like Dr. King to expose the urgency for economic justice and the Poor People's Campaign.

Dr. King traveled to Memphis and addressed the workers and supporters in what would be his last speech, "I've Been to the Mountaintop." King told them, "I've looked over. And I've seen the Promised Land. I may not get there with you. But I want you to know tonight, that we, as a people, will get to the Promised Land."[53] The next day, April 4, 1968, Dr. King was fatally shot at the Lorraine Motel, where he was staying. In 1991, the motel became the National Civil Rights Museum. We hope our leaders will be inspired by the perseverance of civil rights movement leaders and keep fighting with an eye toward freedom.

On March 4, 2011, immigrant youth arrive in Memphis for our three-day strategy meeting. The meeting brings together seasoned leaders and young people new to the movement. Based on the input from the affiliates, we provide workshops and trainings on topics ranging from nonviolent direct action to organizing, communications, grassroots fundraising, accessing college, being an undocumented artist, and building your own business. Jesús Iñiguez and Julio Salgado, from the California-based undocumented artists collective Dreamers Adrift, create a space for other undocumented artists to get to know one another. Julio, an undocumented, queer Mexican artist and activist, draws portraits of leaders from across the country. People wait in a long line for Julio to draw them. The portraits, on white legal-size pieces of paper, feature each of our personalities and expressions. Julio creates an art installation of all the portraits along the hallway walls, which somehow helps all of us to see one another: We are no longer in hiding. We are undocumented and proud. Julio will go on to become a nationally recognized artist and an inspiration for immigrant and queer artists.

At the end of the first day, Hollis Watkins from SNCC joins us. He shares his experience as a young Black man growing up in Mississippi, joining SNCC, and leading the first lunch counter sit-in in the city of McComb. He acknowledges the pain of the DREAM Act loss but reminds us that our shared struggle is much more than a piece of legislation. It is about freedom. He tells us, "To get the job done, you must keep a certain kind of mindset.

Portraits of United We Dream (UWD) leaders, drawn by undocumented, queer artist Julio Salgado, attending the UWD National Congress in Memphis, Tennessee, 2011 (photographed by Stephen Pavey, courtesy of United We Dream)

How did you wake up this morning?" The room is confused and silent. He starts singing: "I woke up this morning with my mind stayed on freedom." He calls on us to join him. We all move to the front of the room and form a large circle, singing in unison. It is a spiritual experience. Some of us sing and cry at the same time. Through our tears, we let go of the painful DREAM Act loss, and our spirits are reinvigorated. We will continue learning from movement elders who value and believe in our leadership, building a close relationship with the SNCC Legacy Project and movement elders, including Bob Moses, Judy Richardson, and Courtland Cox. Sadly, Bob Moses passes away in 2021 and Hollis Watkins in 2023. But we gain movement ancestors that will continue fighting for freedom with us in spirit. Rest in power and in peace, Bob and Hollis.

This is a historic national meeting for UWD. Not only because it's the first gathering after the failure of the DREAM Act vote, but also because undocumented queer leaders hold a plenary session to center the role of "undocuqueer" leadership in the network, affirming UWD as an organization that is pro lesbian, gay, bi, trans, and queer and creating a safe and empowering space for immigrant youth leaders to come out. Jorge Gutierrez, undocuqueer leader from California who is also on UWD's National Coordinating Committee, talks about the central role that undocuqueer leaders have played over the years shaping strategy and inspiring our movement to take greater risks—such as leading the first civil disobedience actions in 2010. He powerfully shares his story and experience coming out twice—once as queer and another as undocumented. He invites others with the same experience to join him in front of the room. Close to forty leaders come forward. Many of them come out as queer for the first time. They hug each other in tears. The rest of us, also in tears, bear witness and wrap our arms around them. A chant breaks out: "Undocumented, unafraid, queer, queer, unashamed!" The room vibrates with our collective voices. This moment makes explicit our commitment to building an organization that is pro lesbian, gay, bi, trans, and queer.

Felipe leads the presentation of our strategy. In "Dreamspan: The Felipe Report," Felipe reviews the ideas and feedback of UWD's affiliates, showing that in the absence of having a viable path for legislation in Congress, there is a consensus on demanding that President Obama stop the deportations of immigrant youth by using deferred action. How can we pressure him to act before the 2012 presidential election? Leaders break into their affiliate groups to talk about how we can lead a campaign to push Obama to act. They reflect on how our movement has grown. How in 2010 we mobilized like never before. How we got a taste of power and are ready to build a stronger movement.

The affiliates, one by one, share their ideas on how to pressure the president, and then there is an official vote on the strategy. All UWD affiliates vote in favor of demanding that President Obama stop the deportations of immigrant youth. We will pressure him to act by publicly sharing stories of immigrant youth fighting their deportation cases, exposing the injustice and inhumanity of the detention and deportation system, and making the case that the president has the executive authority to use deferred action. UWD staff will work with affiliates on training youth in stopping deportations and collecting the stories of those facing deportation. With every public deportation story, we will ask, "Obama, will you end our pain? Will you stop deporting Dreamers?" The End Our Pain campaign will go live as soon as we get back to our states. We end the meeting feeling clear and determined. It is time to own our power and remind politicians and the country that we are here, stronger than ever.

Before I take off from Memphis, I'm interviewed by Univision national news for their evening program. As chair of the board, representing the leaders of UWD, I use this interview to put the president on notice. Looking straight at the camera, I say that two hundred and fifty undocumented youth from over thirty states convened in Memphis to chart the path forward for our movement. We are united in demanding that President Obama stop deporting undocumented youth. Our movement will hold him accountable to his promise of enacting immigration reforms during his administration. We are not taking no for an answer.

We hit the ground running. Gaby volunteers to take greater responsibility, building the deportation defense program and leading UWD's advocacy strategy. She coordinates with UWD affiliates to bring the stories of those impacted by deportation to members of Congress, DHS, and the White House. We raise the funds to lead "Dream Camp" trainings in Alabama, Oklahoma, New Jersey, Nevada, and Kentucky, where we gather immigrant youth from across the country to empower them with skills to organize, stop deportations, and bring them into the fold of the national campaign to push Obama to act. We train over three hundred immigrant youth. Meanwhile, the Obama administration keeps increasing detentions and deportations, claiming it's focusing on going after "criminals" but deporting anyone who is undocumented, including immigrant youth. We gather over thirty cases of immigrant youth slated for deportation.

We hold press conferences and rallies to bring media attention to these deportation cases, expose the inhumanity and roughness of the ICE and CBP agents, and demand that President Obama stop deportations and provide immigrant youth with deferred action. The pressure we are creating forces the president and DHS secretary, Janet Napolitano, to say publicly that we weren't telling the truth. They give interviews saying that the agency only focuses on terrorists and immigrants with serious criminal charges and that immigrant youth should stop pressuring the president because only Congress can provide a solution.

As an organizer, I've learned that politicians who don't fear you will just ignore you. But when we hear them say, on television, that we are lying, we know that our strategy is working. The truth of our stories is getting through because it is TRUE, and we are working to expose the administration that says it's only deporting "high-priority immigrants" while at the same time deporting us in record numbers. The pressure we put on the administration forces Secretary Napolitano to convene a meeting with immigrant rights advocates, and for the first time, UWD is invited to join. The caveat is that the administration won't meet with anyone who is undocumented. The UWD National Coordinating Committee leaders vote to send Natalia Aristizabal, a formerly undocumented youth and organizer with Make the Road New York, and Idamarie

Collazo from Indiana to represent us. Natalia and Idamarie bring a folder with over thirty cases of undocumented youth facing deportation.

During the meeting, Secretary Napolitano insists that only immigrants with serious "criminal" charges are the target of deportation and that undocumented youth are not a priority. She claims to not know of any such cases. Natalia, who is afraid of nothing, pushes back: "With all due respect, Secretary, you are deporting undocumented youth. Here are their stories," she says, handing her the folder. Secretary Napolitano can't refuse it. She commits to having her staff review the cases. After the meeting, many of the youth in detention facilities are released. We win this argument privately and publicly.

This same scenario is repeated over and over again in a battle for the truth—administration officials and the president saying that immigrant youth aren't being deported and us showing that we are. Instead of just taking the president's words at face value, our work also forces the media to report on our movement's demand for the president to stop deportations. Reporters ask the president if he will consider using his executive power to enact immigration reforms. In interviews, the president pushes back on our demand, claiming he does not have the power to stop deportations. What he doesn't know is that we have done our homework. We have studied the law ourselves and have talked to immigration-and constitutional-law and immigration-policy experts. We know that under the law, he has the power to take executive action and grant deferred action to undocumented youth. It is only a matter of his own political will. We keep up the pressure. That same summer, we mobilize three hundred immigrant youth to head to Washington DC for the US Senate's first hearing on the DREAM Act. This hearing had been scheduled for September 2001, but after the 9/11 terrorist attacks, it was cancelled. We partner with the office of Senator Durbin, the leading champion for the DREAM Act in the Senate, to share the stories of undocumented youth. Even though we know the bill has no chance of moving forward that year, we use the hearing to build support for the bill and to focus attention on the fact that the president is deporting immigrant youth. Our efforts also move Senator Durbin. We work closely with his staff to stop deportations, and he increasingly presses the administration on the need for deferred action until Congress has the votes to pass the DREAM Act.

The pressure we have been putting on the administration pushes them to issue a memo providing guidance on how ICE agents should use their authority, or prosecutorial discretion, to refrain from deporting immigrants with close family or educational, military, or other ties in the US. On June 17, a few weeks after the Senate DREAM Act hearing, ICE director John Morton states in the memo nineteen factors that should be considered by ICE agents before ordering deportation, including "the circumstances of the person's arrival in the United States and the manner of his or her entry, particularly if the alien came to the United States as a young child; the person's pursuit of education in the United States, with particular consideration given to those who have graduated from a U.S. high school or have successfully pursued or are pursuing a college or advanced degrees at a legitimate institution of higher education in the United States."[54] This is a significant win but not the end goal, as ICE agents can still use their discretion to disregard the memo's guidance. Nonetheless, the administration's memo is a sign that our power is growing and our strategy is working.

While our movement is growing in influence, we are also making progress in building the organization. The board of directors decides to hire UWD's first executive director. I'm finishing graduate school at the same time we start the hiring process. Walter has a few more classes left before graduating. He takes a pause from graduate school to work full-time at the North Star Fund, a social justice fund that supports community-organizing organizations in New York City. Now with a work permit in hand, and at the encouragement of some board members, I decide to apply for the executive director role. I don't really know what I'm getting into, but I feel confident and clear about the vision we share with UWD cofounders and leaders. My commitment to a world where immigrants can live without fear and to building the power of the immigrant youth movement fuel my courage to throw my name in the hat.

I share with the board of directors my intention to submit my application. Walter and I recuse from the hiring process because of conflict of interest. A few weeks after my first interview, I get an email from the board notifying me that another candidate and I are finalists and will have one more interview. I'm excited to have made it to this step in the process, but I also feel deeply insecure. I feel as if I'm drowning in an ocean of self-doubts and feelings of inadequacy. I've never built or led a national network on this scale before. Can I do this? The board of directors thinks so. They choose me to be the first executive director of United We Dream. I step into this leadership role with humility, knowing that I have a lot to learn, and a deep sense of responsibility and accountability to the members of UWD and the future generations of immigrant youth leaders. As I take on the role, Walter steps down from the board of directors, opening the space for new leaders to join. We see this as being in alignment with our vision and as a necessary step for the integrity of our leadership and the organization. As we anticipated, ICE agents are not following the guidance from the Morton memo. UWD's deportation defense program is working on over two hundred cases of immigrant youth in deportation.

We are determined to escalate our efforts to expose the truth and push the president. Our plan is to find every opportunity to confront Obama with our demand. We mobilize three hundred immigrant youth to the US Capitol and hold a rally outside of the White House, where undocumented youth facing deportation chain themselves together. Everyone wears red T-shirts that say OBAMA DEPORTS DREAMERS. END OUR PAIN, holding signs and banners with a similar message: OBAMA DEPORTS DREAMERS and OBAMA STOP DEPORTING DREAMERS. The volume of our action and skillful press work lead to the protests getting lots of attention and shape the media coverage about Obama's reelection campaign and his credibility with the immigrant and Latine voters he needs to win. Across the country, undocumented youth keep up the drumbeat by sharing their stories publicly. This momentum also inspires Jose Antonio Vargas, a Pulitzer Prize–winning journalist, to share his story of being queer and undocumented in a deeply personal and moving essay published in the *New York Times*. Jose's story brings greater national visibility and attention to our fight.

In July, UnidosUS, the country's largest Latine civil rights organization, announces that President Obama will speak at their big annual event. We see this as an opportunity to keep pressuring the president to act. Gaby, who represents UWD with other advocacy organizations, secures tickets for UWD leaders to attend the event, and we ask UnidosUS to partner with us in having a meeting with the president before the event where he could hear directly from Mercedes, an undocumented student from Tennessee who is facing deportation. Our hope is to persuade Obama not only to stop Mercedes's deportation, but to agree to our demand of using deferred action to stop deportations.

The leadership at UnidosUS disagrees with our approach and declines our request to have Mercedes meet with the president. They assure us they will raise the concern of deportations with the president. We are disappointed and frustrated at their decision, but we don't give up on using this event as an opportunity to escalate the pressure.

We strategically use an inside-outside tactic. We fly Mercedes from Tennessee to Washington DC to attend the event, while the youth leaders from the Tennessee Immigrant & Refugee Rights Coalition, who have been working to stop Mercedes's deportation, and our National Coordinating Committee, under the leadership of Felipe, organize a group of leaders that will join Mercedes. Before the event, Gaby meets with all of them to hand them the tickets. The event's dress code is formal attire, so everyone wears suits. But what people at the event don't know is that UWD leaders are wearing red OBAMA DEPORTS DREAMERS T-shirts under their suit jackets.

When the president starts speaking, Mercedes, who is wearing a red graduation gown, stands up holding an orange folder (one of UWD's colors) containing the paperwork from her deportation case. Everyone looks at her confused, wondering what's going on. Obama notices her but continues his remarks, saying, "We are responding to your concerns and working every day to make sure we are enforcing flawed laws in the most humane and best possible way. Now, I know some people want me to bypass Congress and change the laws on my own . . ."[55] This is the same tired line that he cannot act on immigration on his own, but by this point, we've played this game over and over again in meetings and in the press. So before the president finishes his sentence, Felipe, Mercedes, and other UWD leaders among the audience interrupt him, chanting, "Yes, you can. Yes, you can," cleverly using Obama's presidential campaign slogan to push back on his position. Many of the attendees join them, and the chant takes over the room.

President Obama stumbles on his remarks and seems clearly upset, but he continues. “The idea of doing things on my own is very tempting . . . but that’s not how our system works; that’s not how our democracy functions. I need a dance partner, and the floor is empty,”[56] he says, alluding to Congress and the Republicans blocking immigration reform. This is another way politicians try to deflect attention from their own responsibilities—always blaming the other party. But we know that while Republicans are by no means blameless, they aren’t the only ones blocking reforms. We can’t be fooled. We have not forgotten that if five more Democrats had voted for the DREAM Act, it would have passed in 2010. And we also know that President Barack Obama can stop deportations on his own but instead has decided to ramp up the deportation machine. Our message is clear: we see you, and we are not going away.

It’s early 2012, and everyone in Congress is already thinking about the election. Senator Marco Rubio, who is concerned about Republicans alienating Latine voters, delivers a speech on immigration at a Republican Latine event in Miami. He argues that Republicans should help undocumented young people stay in the country. What he doesn’t know is that there are Florida immigrant youth leaders in the audience. Felipe, whom people recognize as one of the Trail of Dreams walkers, is blocked from entering by aides, but he figures out a way to get other leaders inside. Rubio is interrupted by an immigrant youth leader who confronts him about his inaction in Congress.

Two months after the protest, Gaby calls Carlos and me after she learns that Senator Rubio is interested in drafting a bill that would protect undocumented youth from deportation via nonimmigrant visas, not by providing them with a pathway to citizenship. I cut to the chase, telling her Senator Rubio has shown us that we can't trust him, and his bill does not meet our demand for a pathway to citizenship. Gaby, who has developed a relationship with Senator Rubio from the time he served as a Florida state representative, pushes back, suggesting that we at least engage with his office to assess how serious he is. "Let's ride these two horses," Gaby tells us. At the end of our discussion, we agree that this is a strategic opportunity to pressure the White House to act. We reach out to the White House requesting a meeting, while Gaby meets with Senator Rubio's office a few times to talk about the crafting of the bill. We don't keep the conversations with the senator secret, making the White House and Democrats nervous that they may look like they are not taking action, while this influential Republican is, and risk losing credibility with Latine voters.

In the early summer, as we get closer to the November elections, the administration continues its deflection game to publicly say that the president can't take executive action on immigration, encouraging advocates to focus on pressuring Congress. But our diverse movement ups the pressure. The groups that broke off from UWD are fearless and launch a hunger strike and sit-ins at Obama's reelection campaign offices in states like Colorado, where Obama needs the Latine vote to win. Meanwhile, UWD organizations lead over fifteen protests across the country.

We just will not go away, and the White House is feeling the pressure. White House staff—Cecilia Muñoz, domestic policy advisor, and Valerie Jarrett, senior advisor to the president—follow up on our request for a meeting. They say they can't meet with undocumented youth on White House premises, so the meeting is arranged at St. John's Church in Washington DC. Gaby, Carlos, and Lorella Praeli (newly elected NCC leader from Connecticut) represent us at the meeting. The White House staff reiterate that the president cannot bypass Congress. They explain that the position of the president is backed by White House legal counsel. Lorella, who is in her early twenties and is the kind of leader you don't want to mess with, confronts Valerie Jarrett: "With all due respect, I disagree. The president does have the power." Can you imagine that? An undocumented young woman feeling her power so much that she can stand up like that? We don't take no for an answer and request that our legal counsel meet with White House legal counsel.

We have a plan. In addition to using protests and public events to pressure the administration, we also meet with members of Congress to persuade them to publicly ask the president to act (Senators Reid and Durbin speak out), and we work with immigration-and-constitutional-law experts on a legal strategy. Lorella, Neidi, and Gaby reach out to legal experts from across the country to draft a letter outlining the president's executive power on immigration and confirming that he has the legal authority to provide deferred action to immigrant youth. We intend for the letter to add public pressure. Behind the scenes we talk to *La Opinión*, the country's largest Spanish-speaking newspaper, and provide the reporters with an embargoed press release to be published right before our meeting with White House legal counsel. On May 29, 2012, thirty minutes before our meeting, the press release, signed by ninety-six immigration-and constitutional-law experts, becomes public. A *La Opinión* article also covers our plan to ramp up our protests June 11–15. We decided to break the story on *La Opinión* to reach the very Latine voters whom Obama needs to win his reelection.

The meeting is awkward. White House legal counsel is shocked, but we are done with the back-and-forth. We are legally right, and we are growing in political power, and it is time for us to make our move. On behalf of the immigrant youth movement, four powerful undocumented women—Neidi, Lorella, Gaby, and Erika Andiola, an undocumented leader from Arizona in our national leadership committee—give the White House an ultimatum: The White House has until mid-June to respond to our demand. If they don't by then, we will be ready to escalate with actions in Arizona, Nevada, Florida, Colorado, and other states.

We convene a national call to recruit as many immigrant youth leaders as possible to lead actions across the country the week of June 11–15. Immigrant youth leaders from Arkansas, Wisconsin, Texas, and Oklahoma agree to join. UWD leaders will lead sit-ins at Obama's election campaign offices. We also plan to convene in Los Angeles on June 14 to lead an action with Neidi, Carlos Amador, and the UCLA Labor Center Dream Summer program, a fellowship that places youth in apprenticeships at labor and progressive organizations across the country and provides them with training on organizing and movement building. From New York, I lead the work to raise the funds for our national week of action. Our goal is to send T-shirts, banners, and other resources so that groups can plan and execute their actions. For the week of action, Gaby stays in Washington DC in case we hear from the White House, Carlos supports actions as needed across the country, and I head to Los Angeles.

On June 14, I join close to three hundred immigrant youth leaders in Los Angeles, where we have an event for the opening day of the Dream Summer program and an action planned to escalate pressure on the president the next day. In the evening, I get a text from Gaby: "Call me ASAP. I have news." I call her immediately. Gaby tells me that Obama will announce deferred action for immigrant youth at the Rose Garden the next day. I pause. I'm shocked. I can't believe it. I feel like somebody needs to pinch me. "Wait—do you mean we won?" I ask.

"Yes! Yes!" Gaby says, giggling. "We did it! We did it!"

I shout, cry, and jump up and down for joy all at the same time. Gaby is working on getting the details of the policy and will keep us posted. Lorella and Carlos head to DC for the announcement.

I sit on the bed in my hotel room in shock. I call Walter, José Luis, Carlos, and Julieta. "Can you fucking believe it?" I shout, crying.

"We fucking did it," José Luis tells me. He is crying too. We are all in awe of our power, but at the same time, we feel cautious. What if the president decides to change his mind? And we don't know the details of the policy yet. The anxiety of our immigrant experience kicks in. We can't celebrate until it happens. I confidentially share the news with Mami and my brother. I tell them that we can't be sure until the president makes an announcement. "But you won't go through what I went through," I tell my brother. "You will be able to go to college, work, and live without worrying about deportation." My brother can't believe it. He is full of joy.

"Thank you for all you did," he tells me.

"I told you that God would give us a miracle," Mami says.

"Mami, this is not a miracle; the movement made this happen. Our movement did this!" I tell her.

The following day, on June 15, immigrant youth leaders convene outside of the Los Angeles federal Metropolitan Detention Center. The crowd is so large that the busy intersection is shut down. Immigrant youth wearing blue and purple T-shirts that say UNDOCUMENTED. UNAFRAID. chant, "Undocumented, unafraid," celebrating this victory as a testament to the power of our movement and sending the message to Obama that we will hold him accountable for the implementation of the program.

And on the East Coast, from the Rose Garden of the White House, President Obama announces the Deferred Action for Childhood Arrivals (DACA) program and sets August 14 as the date for implementation. DACA provides undocumented youth with deferred action for two years, at which point immigrants can apply for a renewal, which would provide them with temporary protection from deportation and a work permit. The application fee for applying and renewal is set by the DHS at $495. DACA allows immigrant youth to live without the fear of deportation, to work, and to go to college. The president is doing the exact thing he had spent a year saying that he could not do, and we forced him to do it.

DACA represents the most significant victory for the immigrant justice movement in over thirty years. We win protection from deportation and work permits for 1.2 million undocumented young people, transforming their lives and those of their families. But it is a bittersweet moment because DACA leaves many members of our community out. Even though we demanded deferred action for all undocumented youth, the White House develops eligibility criteria that mirror the DREAM Act. To qualify, immigrants must have arrived in the US before their sixteenth birthday, have continuously lived in the US since June 2007, be physically present in the US on the day of the DACA announcement (June 15), have not been convicted of a felony or significant misdemeanor, be enrolled in school or have graduated from high school or have a GED, and be younger than thirty-one.

Julieta and Jose Antonio do not meet the criteria because of their age. Julieta has dedicated more than a decade of her life to the movement's work, and yet she can't benefit from our victory. It's heartbreaking. But we are clear that our fight does not end here. We know that with DACA, we are building power to win protections for all people in our community. This has always been part of the strategy. We will come back for more.

We don't have much time to celebrate. We meet in DC to plan for the day when immigrant youth can start submitting their applications to the DHS. We launch a national campaign to educate the community about the program, how the movement achieved this victory, and the criteria for eligibility. We also prepare to lead trainings across the country to empower UWD affiliates to lead DACA-application community clinics, where they can support immigrant youth and families navigating the application process; raise awareness about the role of the movement in winning the program; and recruit young immigrants into efforts to get out the immigrant and Latine vote on Election Day and to join our movement to keep fighting for more.

On August 12, UWD and state immigrant rights organizations host DACA-application events. Thousands of people attend. In Washington DC, we host a press conference and an information session with hundreds of immigrant youth. In Chicago, the state immigrant rights coalition hosts an event at the Navy Pier. Over ten thousand people form lines to begin the process of application. Thousands also join DACA events in Los Angeles, San Francisco, Houston, Phoenix, Denver, and New York City. The huge number of people coming out to the events to seek DACA information is surprising for the administration. They are not prepared for the scale of the response. The immigrant rights organizations in New York press the city to step up. In response, the New York City council announces $3 million to provide legal assistance to those applying for DACA.

A few weeks later, Walter and I head to Texas for a training for hundreds of immigrant youth and pro bono lawyers. On our way to the airport, we pass the offices of Make the Road New York in my neighborhood of Jackson Heights. A sea of people—entire immigrant families—are waiting in a line that goes around several blocks. All I can do is cry. "Look at our gente," I tell Walter. We are both in awe. We know we won, and still it feels so surreal. We've made history!

Over the course of the next several months, I travel with UWD leaders and staff across the country hosting trainings. I meet with immigrant parents, youth, and educators and get to know them and their stories as we share meals and even sleep on their couches. For me, this is a moment to show our power and inspire our community to see that together we can win protection for everyone. I also work with UWD leaders to partner with philanthropic institutions across the country to raise funds to enable families to pay for the application and legal fees. I'm running around like a chicken with its head cut off, doing the work of multiple people. But this is not sustainable. The great thing after DACA is that we can now hire volunteer immigrant youth leaders to lead the implementation of our victory. I move with the leadership of UWD to launch organizing fellowships, recruiting and training hundreds of immigrant youth in Texas, Florida, Arizona, and various other states across the country to support DACA-eligible immigrants' applications while empowering them to join our movement for justice. The mass implementation campaign, Own the Dream, is also supported by the leadership of Carmen Caneda, a former staff member of SEIU, and Adam Luna, one of our closest allies and a former staff member of America's Voice, an immigrant rights advocacy organization, who both join our team. Carmen and Adam help UWD manage hundreds of organizers and volunteers, leading the implementation of DACA and maximizing the partnerships with local governments, colleges, and other institutions to support as many DACA-eligible youth as possible. Carmen and Adam save my sanity and UWD. They will go on to become my close friends and mentors.

Lorella Praeli, NCC leader from Connecticut, becomes our new advocacy director as Gaby steps aside. And we also grow our digital capacity by bringing on board an immigrant youth leader from Arizona, Celso Mireles. Celso leads the digital strategy to reach millions of immigrant youth and their families with information about their rights and DACA eligibility. In 2017, our movement will lose Celso to a tragic accident. His artistic and innovative spirit made our organizing and movement stronger. Rest in peace and power, Celso.

DACAmented immigrant youth are now able to pursue work and education opportunities they didn't have access to before, and thousands of them join social justice organizations and labor unions and pursue their dream jobs as educators, doctors, nurses, journalists, and more. DACA is a success. It's not only because it provides protection from deportation for DACA-eligible immigrants, but also because it's an antipoverty program. UWD partners with the Center for American Progress, the National Immigration Law Center, and Professor Tom Wong of the University of California, San Diego, who is himself formerly undocumented, to lead an assessment of the impact of DACA. We learn that close to seven hundred thousand undocumented youth benefit from DACA, with most beneficiaries living in California and Texas. Over 90 percent of them report that DACA has allowed them to pursue educational opportunities, and 69 percent of them report moving to better jobs after DACA, empowering them to reach financial stability. Over 60 percent of them help their families pay the bills, often as the only ones in their families with a work permit.[57] Thousands of them now have access to loans for homes and cars and for starting businesses. The goal of any social justice fight isn't to win an election or even a new policy; it is to change the lives of real people, and there can be no doubt that we do that.

The work doesn't end with the implementation of DACA. There is also a need to continue building power and to show that DACA was just the beginning. Without taking a break, we create United We Dream Action, our advocacy arm that allows us to do more political work, and we jump into training hundreds of young people to talk to Latine voters and mobilize them to vote. Immigrant youth members of our advocacy arm reach out to voters in person and over the phone. Obama is reelected for four more years with the support of 71 percent of the Latine electorate.[58] Democrats gain a few more seats in the Senate, but Republicans take control of the House of Representatives.

We "won" our campaign for DACA but are also committed to protecting our parents and the rest of the undocumented community from deportation, so we go right back to putting pressure on the president and Congress. In early 2013, we launch the 11 Million Dreams campaign to pressure Obama and Congress to provide a pathway to citizenship, holding a strategy meeting and training with close to two hundred UWD leaders in Washington DC. While at the strategy meeting with our members, I get a call from White House staff, inviting me to meet with the president, along with immigrant rights advocates. My first thought is to ask if another leader who is either undocumented or a DACA recipient can join me. But the invitation is not transferrable, and they can't have two representatives from the same organization. I talk to UWD staff and leaders, and we decide that I should go in representation of our network.

I have twenty-four hours to prepare. This is the first time we are meeting with the president after the enactment of DACA, so we agree on sharing with him our firsthand experience with the positive impact of DACA in immigrant communities, while also pressing him on the reality that ICE is still deporting people in high numbers, and we need him to stop deportations and family separations. In between meetings with our leaders, I realize I have nothing but jeans, sneakers, and T-shirts to wear. I feel embarrassed to wear jeans for this meeting! But I also don't have time to get a different outfit. I feel stressed. I never have an easy time finding clothes and shoes that fit me—shopping for a short woman with curves and small feet can take days! Plus, the meetings and trainings with our leaders are more important.

Carmen, who by now knows me well, takes me aside. "This is an important meeting," she tells me in a calm and steady voice. "We will get you an outfit, and don't forget your power lipstick." Carmen reaches out to Hafid Dumet, an undocuqueer leader with Connecticut Students for a Dream, who is also volunteering with our operations team. Hafid is a financial genius and a get-shit-done kind of person. He also has a great sense of fashion. Hafid rushes out of the meeting and comes back with just the right outfit. My community comes through for me once again.

The following morning, I wear a black pantsuit with a yellow blouse and black high heels. I don't forget to wear my red power lipstick. When I arrive at the security booth of the White House, I'm told to wait for an escort. The White House has done a background check and cleared me with security, but because I'm not a US citizen, I am not allowed to go into the White House alone. I must always be accompanied by an escort, except when I'm in the meeting with the president. A young white guy with a great smile greets me politely and guides me to the meeting room. I feel quite relieved that I have an escort. Otherwise, I'd surely get lost!

We are meeting in the Roosevelt Room in the West Wing—right across from the Oval Office. Before we enter the room, we are asked to leave our phones outside. My sweaty and shaky hands place the phone in one of the small cubbies outside the room. Almost tripping in my new very high heels as I walk into the room, I think of Maya Angelou's words: "You don't go alone. Bring your people with you."[59] I walk into the room, bringing my family, UWD leaders, and undocumented community.

The windowless room has a fireplace at the center and a large cherrywood conference table with fancy brown leather chairs. On the table, tags with our names indicate our assigned seats. I'm next to Valerie Jarrett, whose chair is next to the president's. There are about fifteen other immigrant rights advocates and union leaders around the table. Eliseo Medina, secretary treasurer of SEIU and former leader with United Farm Workers, and Janet Murguía, president of UnidosUS, are seated across from the president's chair. Awkwardly, we all anxiously wait for Obama's arrival.

When Obama walks into the room, I follow everyone in standing up. It feels like being in church when the priest calls on the congregation to rise. I'm struck by his height and his very long legs. With a candid smile, he greets us and moves to take his seat. Janet and Eliseo speak first. I go next. Before I speak, I ground myself in the courage and stories of our undocumented community. I thank him for the administration's work in the implementation of DACA. The US Citizenship and Immigration Services has been greatly receptive to our recommendations on how to best disseminate information with the community and process applications. I share my family's story and how my brother benefited from DACA, allowing him to live without the fear of deportation and to work to save up for college. I tell him that my parents, however, still live in fear of deportation, just like millions of other people in the community. I describe the deportations that UWD is still fighting and press him on the need for his administration to stop deportations. By now, the Obama administration is on its way to deporting more than two million people, far more than any other administration before his. My job in this meeting is to push the president to protect more people in my community.

I have gone from being undocumented and ashamed to speaking the truth directly to the president of the United States. He looks right at me and insists his administration is not targeting families for deportation and that our movement must push Republicans to act. *Here we go again.* The Obama administration thinks that more deportations will bring Republicans to the table to negotiate a bill. But of course, Republicans weren't ever going to come to the table, and the only result is record-setting deportation numbers. Obama's political strategy is a terrible failure with cruel consequences for immigrant communities.

In the months to come, we keep pressing the president and Congress to pass legislation so that, once and for all, deportations can stop and undocumented people can have a pathway to citizenship. We plan rallies and vigils, and we also lead the reunification of families at the US-Mexico border to expose the inhumanity and cruelty of the immigration system that separates entire families. UWD leaders and organizers in partnership with organizations in the US and Mexico work on Operation Butterfly, an action envisioned by the leaders of the network's national committee to reunite three undocumented youth with their mothers, who had been deported. On June 11, 2013, UWD leaders Renata Teodoro from Brazil, Evelyn Rivera from Colombia, and Monserrat Padilla from Mexico reunite with their mothers at the US-Mexico border in Nogales, Arizona, after not seeing each other for many years.[60] Separated by a huge metal border fence, they hug each other in tears. Their mothers caress their face, hair, and arms with devotion, love, and heartbreak in their eyes. The reunification captures national media attention, and it is reported on the front page of the *New York Times*, sparking a conversation about the inhumanity of US immigration policies and the need for the Obama administration and Congress to act.[61]

In the weeks to come, the Democrat-controlled Senate passes a package of immigration reforms, but the Republican-controlled House of Representatives does not. With Congress blocking legislation, we once again focus on the president and demand he use administrative action for our parents. We launch the We Can't Wait campaign, following Democrats and Obama everywhere they go to pressure the administration to act. We lead actions, and marches, calling the president the deporter in chief. We put pressure on Democrats at the state level, pushing them to sign letters asking the president to stop deporting our parents and to grant them deferred action.

While we continue growing our movement and increasing the pressure on the president, we also build solidarity with Black and brown youth leaders and organizers leading movements for racial, gender, economic, and climate justice. We know that the systems and laws that criminalize and incarcerate Black and brown people are the same that dehumanize, detain, and deport immigrants. We've experienced it. We, our families and communities, have been violently separated, racially profiled, exploited in the workplace, jailed, deported, and killed by law enforcement. Together, we share a vision of this country where our communities are free to live and thrive.

On July 13, 2013, George Zimmerman is found not guilty in the killing of Trayvon Martin, a seventeen-year-old Black youth who was walking home from a 7-Eleven in Sanford, Florida, when Zimmerman shot him to death. In response, the Dream Defenders, a Florida-based racial-justice organization led by Black and brown youth that marched from Daytona Beach to

Sanford when Trayvon Martin was killed, makes a national call to take over the Florida State Capitol, demanding justice for Trayvon and an end to stand-your-ground laws, which allow people to shoot and kill in public even if they can walk away safely from a situation. We join them because we are in this together. What hurts one community hurts all of us. Immigrant youth leaders from Florida and other states join the Dream Defenders in occupying the state capitol for thirty days.

The senseless killing of Trayvon Martin and the jury's verdict on Zimmerman spark a movement across the country. People lead marches, rallies, and vigils, demanding justice and an end to the systemic racism and violence killing Black people. Black women organizers Alicia Garza, Patrisse Cullors, and Opal Tometi come together to coin and launch #BlackLivesMatter. At UWD, we know that this moment calls on us not only to join the Dream Defenders at the state capitol, but also to do the work to organize our own immigrant communities in solidarity with Black lives. We issue a solidarity statement and host community events and calls to talk about why the fight for Black lives is also our fight. Some in the immigrant rights movement criticize us. They think us demanding justice for Black lives could weaken the immigrant justice movement and ignite further violence against immigrant communities. Stay in your lane, some of them tell me.

I'm not surprised at the criticism. I know the internalized racism and anti-Blackness that exists in immigrant communities. I'm reminded that when Amadou Diallo, a Black immigrant student, was killed in New York, some in the Latine immigrant communities thought this didn't impact them, because they weren't Black or "criminals," and when Muslim communities were targeted by law enforcement and deportation after 9/11, they said this had nothing to do with them, because they were not Muslim or "terrorists." Yet racial profiling, police violence, incarceration, and deportations have affected all of us, with a disproportionate impact on Black immigrants. This moment is a reminder about the work we must do in our communities to create change. UWD leads sessions with our members about how to fight anti-Blackness and to learn about the narratives, systems, and laws that hurt Black and brown communities. I engage in similar conversations with immigrant rights leaders and advocates. These conversations stretch my emotional muscles. They leave me feeling drained but also hopeful about the capacity of humans to transform. This is not easy work, but it is necessary to win freedom and justice for all.

Our work doesn't end when the marches and protests stop. What the news doesn't report is that we keep organizing people, and along with Black and brown youth leaders and organizers from across the country, we create the Freedom Side collective. Our group is inspired by the young people who were part of the Freedom Summer project of 1964 who traveled to Mississippi, risking their lives to register Black voters and fight for the civil rights and freedoms of Black communities. Together, we envision a world where we are safe to pursue our dreams and a country with a true democracy that represents us all. We organize our communities to demand fully funded public education for all, an end to deportations and the school-to-prison pipeline, equal opportunity and protection under the law, and the right to vote.

By 2014, the Obama administration is deporting more than one thousand undocumented immigrants a day! Our actions escalate. We disrupt the president at events, and immigrant youth get in the road and block deportation buses filled with migrants to protect them. We scream out to the immigrants inside the vehicles that they are loved—after all, they could be our friends or parents. Youth lead sit-ins, blocking busy intersections by the

White House and rally at congressional offices. The broader immigrant justice movement also ups the pressure, with organizations like the National Day Laborer Organizing Network (NDLON) leading protests targeting the president under the demand #Not1More Deportation. People in the administration, and even some senior-level advocates, are getting angry at us for continuing to push so hard. We hear that they think we are being ungrateful for the changes the administration has already made.

We don't stop. As we protest in the streets and all over the media, Lorella, UWD's advocacy director, is behind the scenes, along with other advocates, representing our movement in meetings and negotiations with White House staff. In the third week of November, she tells us that she's heard confidentially that the president will meet our demand. Did we just win again?! We feel proud and powerful.

On November 20, the president announces the Deferred Action for Parents of Americans (DAPA) program, protecting about three million undocumented parents. Only parents that have children who are US citizens or legal permanent residents are eligible. My parents only qualify because my green card was approved earlier in the year. But it leaves millions of parents, including those of immigrant youth leaders that fight for DAPA, in limbo. It is a moment of joy and renewed determination to keep fighting for all those who have been left out.

The White House invites UWD to Las Vegas for the president's official announcement. Lorella and I organize a group of immigrant youth leaders to attend with us. I bring Mami, and Lorella brings her mom, who also qualifies for DAPA. We stand in front of the stage. Mami and I hold hands, and when the president talks about DAPA, Mami starts to cry. Lorella and I look at each other and our mothers in tears. "The movement made this happen," Mami tells me. We look forward to the day that people can start applying.

Painfully, that day never comes. Republicans, fueled by a white nationalist and anti-immigrant movement, challenge DAPA in the courts, arguing the program violates the Constitution, and a Republican-appointed judge rules in their favor. The case goes to the Supreme Court, where Republican-appointed justices have enough votes to keep that ruling in place, and DAPA dies as immigrant youth and their parents sit in the Supreme Court gallery, watching in tears. This is a painful blow to our movement. I'm heartbroken. Many of us fall into depression. Nevertheless, we don't let this loss defeat us. We know our movement is not defined by DAPA. Our fight is beyond a policy demand; it is a fight for freedom, dignity, and justice. Our work continues, and we remain focused on building the power we need to hold those in government and other institutions accountable and win the change we seek.

13

HERE TO STAY

United We Dream leaders lead a protest outside the Supreme Court as part of a campaign to defeat President Donald Trump's attacks on DACA in the courts. 2019. (Courtesy of United We Dream)

> *"A document doesn't define who we are. We were people before DACA and will still be people after DACA."*
>
> —Angelica Villalobos, UWD leader, Dream Action Oklahoma

On Election Day in 2016, United We Dream Action members, allies, and their families gather across the country to watch the election results. Immigrant youth leaders who volunteered countless hours to increase voter participation in Florida, Texas, Oklahoma, California, Arizona, Kansas, Connecticut, and New Mexico host events and watch parties in their communities. We all worked day in and day out to mobilize Latine and immigrant voters to the polls. We gave it all to protect our families and communities from Trump's mass-deportation agenda. Although we feel exhausted, we are also joyful to celebrate our work and follow the election results in community for what we hope will be a night of celebration.

I'm in our office in Washington DC with staff from our advocacy arm and youth leaders from Maryland, Virginia, and DC, along with some of our parents, allies, and friends. Mami, my tías, and my college friends Jonathan, Andreana, and Selene join me as well. The crowd is hopeful, and we've turned our office into a "watch party" with decorations, food, and everything. At this point, we've built strong relationships with key reporters and congressional staff, so we invite them, too, to get firsthand reactions from immigrant youth leaders once a winner is decided. We are wearing our branded orange T-shirts, chatting, and taking selfies as we watch the early results stream on CNN. We believe the electoral polls indicating that Donald Trump will lose the election and with it his dreams of mass deportations. Our spirits are full of hope.

But on the other side of a glass wall from the party, in a small room, the staff and I are carefully watching the election returns with concern that is rising by the minute. The five of us can hear the music and the laughter, we can smell the food and even feel the beat from the speakers, but we aren't actually part of the same celebration. Maybe this is a metaphor for what leadership really feels like.

I never imagined that I'd be a leader in a social justice movement and the executive director of a powerful national organization with over one million members. For each of us in this small room, the responsibility we feel for our community, staff, and movement is heavy. As a network, United We Dream has become arguably the most influential immigrant justice and youth organization in the country—an engine of transformational experiences for hundreds of young people every month.

And while building this level of power was hard work, survival was maybe even harder. So many people tried to undermine our work over the years, to put us in our place, or to shut us down. Looking at the people in that room, and thinking of Julieta, who is holding it down in Houston, Texas, and Adrian Reyna, an immigrant youth leader also from Texas, who thanks to DACA joined UWD's staff to lead the organization's digital and technology strategy, and is now abroad speaking about our work at TEDxBerlin, I think about how we all have survived the cruelty of politics and history-making for over a decade. Of course, we can't talk about most of this stuff with the staff and volunteers on the other side of that glass wall, and certainly not with the media.

The truth is that my plan was to leave the organization and launch a leadership-transition process in early 2017. I believe that a good organizer is always training their replacement so that the next generation of leaders can use their own gifts to do even more. I know that leadership must cycle or organizations get stagnant, and the organization is ready for its new chapter. But as the night goes on, it becomes clear that Donald J. Trump, the man who has declared war on us immigrants, will be the next president of the United States. We look at the TV screen and our phones in disbelief. Another senior staff member and I look across the table at each other, and with slumped shoulders, he says, "Now we can't leave; we have to protect our people." Even though many social justice leaders around us thought Donald Trump couldn't really win, we had an entire action plan prepared just in case he did—talking points, a schedule of staff and community calls, deportation defense teams ready to go, press releases, and social media content and actions. Some people thought we were crazy for doing it, but as immigrants, we know that we must always prepare for the worst-case scenario. But despite having a plan, I feel overwhelmed and paralyzed by fear. I cannot get myself into action mode. I stand there, stunned, my mind racing. Will we survive a Trump presidency? How will we protect our loved ones and the immigrant community from deportation? Trump has called us "criminals," "rapists," "animals," "illegals," and more. He's promised to "build a wall," to hunt down undocumented immigrants, lead mass deportations, and kill DACA, which protects my brother, Jonathan, and over six hundred thousand immigrants from deportation. I fear for the safety of my family, my friends, and the immigrant community.

When I join everyone else in the bigger room, I look around and see our leaders crying and hugging each other. We are all exhausted from the years of fighting, and the thought of what is about to hit us is overwhelming. Mami comes up to me in tears. She asks me, "Mija, que vamos hacer?" For the first time in my journey as an organizer, I feel helpless. In tears, I look into Mami's eyes. I can't assure her that we will be safe. But there is one thing that I can promise her: "We will fight back." Thankfully, the weight of this moment is not only on me. UWD is a leaderful organization. Amid the shock and fear, Greisa Martinez Rosas, an immigrant youth leader from Texas who is a DACA recipient and UWD's deputy director, calls everyone in the Washington DC office into a circle. Greisa has a unique ability to bring people together at a soul level, and she leads us in singing a movement song from a poem written by Jamaican American activist and poet June Jordan. "We have come too far. We won't turn around." Greisa's voice grounds me and fortifies my spirit.

In our circle, people share how they feel. Many feel shocked and disoriented, but when one of the leaders says, "Marchamos!" everyone gets energized. The moms around us repeat, "Marchamos!" We march to the White House for an impromptu rally. We know that the most important thing is to SHOW immigrant communities across the country that we will respond to Trump with vigilance and action. We also move into implementing our plan. We issue our response to the outcome of the election and convene our members across the country. I know that coming together, even if only on the phone, will help all of us move through the fear, trauma, and uncertainty of the moment. On the calls, immigrant youth, many of them crying, report that their communities are afraid. Immigrants fear deportation, family separation, and the loss of DACA. Entire families depend on DACA recipients with work permits. DACA makes it possible for them to access driver's licenses and better jobs and to help their families financially. The impact of Trump's immigration agenda will be devastating. But we remind each other that we are not alone. We will protect each other and our community. UWD and the immigrant justice movement will defend immigrants from Trump's attacks.

In the days post-election, UWD receives reports from immigrant youth who have attempted suicide due to the fear of Trump's actions on immigration. We support them and their families with mental and emotional health resources. And we launch the UndocuHealth program, partnering with social workers and the National Latinx Psychological Association (NLPA), to provide information about mental health tools and services and promote the overall well-being of immigrant youth and their families. We are committed to taking care of our communities and not letting Trump take away our health and joy. But I'm heartbroken at the pain, grief, and trauma that Trump and the outcome of the elections perpetuate on our communities.

I'm also angry—angry that the country's electoral system uses the racist Electoral College to elect the president, making Donald Trump the winner even though he didn't get the majority of votes. I'm angry at all the voters who supported the candidate that promised to deport my family and millions of immigrants. I'm angry that the majority of white voters, including nearly half of white women, voted for a white supremacist candidate to protect their place and power at the top of the hierarchy of American society.[62] I'm angry at the Democratic Party for not using their power to reach out to Black, brown, and youth voters in meaningful ways, for not having the political will to protect people from deportation, and for not passing legislation with a pathway to citizenship. We wouldn't be here if Democrats would've passed immigration reforms when they controlled the White House and Congress. We wouldn't be here if the Democratic Party wouldn't have caved to Republicans whose only interest is deportations and keeping America white.

I'm also angry at myself for longing for this country to embrace me. Even though I know this country has never wanted the Indigenous people of this land, Black people, and people of color, I still feel rejected and unwanted. I increasingly feel uncomfortable and unsafe around white people. Is it possible I know white folks who voted for Trump? The results of the election confront me, once again, with the reality that there are millions of people in this country who do not want people like me here. Yet this country is our shared home.

In the weeks to come, I move beyond my anger. I weep, grieve, and I move into action grounded in love. Love for my family, my community, and the millions of people who share values of equity, justice, and freedom for all. UWD hosts community gatherings across the country to remind immigrant youth and their families they are not alone. We train them on deportation defense and on how to lead local sanctuary campaigns to push city and state governments to defend immigrants from deportation. We launch the Here to Stay Network, where thousands of allies join the effort to fight deportations and volunteer their homes to provide sanctuary for undocumented immigrants. We get ready for the first weeks of the administration by organizing a national rally in Washington DC in coalition with immigrant rights, labor, and progressive organizations.

As we prepare for the new Trump administration, so do they. Trump's campaign was led by known white nationalists who are now set to become part of the government. Steve Bannon, a media executive who aligns with a white supremacist ideology, is announced to become Trump's chief strategist. Stephen Miller, one of the most extreme figures in the Republican Party, is set to become the administration's top advisor on immigration. It is reported that in leaked emails, Miller asked right-wing news outlets to write stories that connect real-life scenarios to *The Camp of the Saints*, a fiction novel published in 1973 by Jean Raspail that has a cultlike following. The novel portrays the "end of the white world" after refugees "take over." The book is filled with horrifying xenophobic descriptions of immigrants as "kinky-haired, swarthy-skinned, long-despised phantoms" and as "teeming ants toiling for the white man's comfort." For us, it's clear Trump is getting ready to assemble the team to bring to life his mass-deportation dreams.

In his first week as president, Trump prioritizes many of his immigration campaign promises. He issues executive orders to ban Muslims from coming to the US; starts the construction of a wall along the US-Mexico border; and makes all undocumented immigrants a priority for deportation. For those who thought Trump didn't mean what he said during the campaign, the first week of his administration is proof that he meant every single word. Thousands of people protest Trump's actions at the airport and in the streets. It is a reminder that we are not alone. In the following months, ICE and CBP agents hunt people down in their homes and at school drop-offs, hospitals, and other public spaces such as courthouses for detention and deportation. Trump terminates DACA and temporary protected status (TPS) for some immigrant groups; issues a zero-tolerance immigration policy, separating over five thousand children from their parents and caging them; and dismantles the country's refugee program.

The new administration also designs the public-charge rule to deny immigrants visas, green cards, and entry to the country based on whether they are likely to use public benefits. In the four years Trump holds office, more than twenty immigrants, including children, die in detention, and detention camps become COVID-19 death traps.[63] And a report reveals that since 2018, ICE officials have been aware of hundreds of immigrant women who have been forcibly sterilized while in detention[64]—a tactic rooted in eugenics with a long history of use against Black and brown people in the US.

The ending of the DACA program allows for those already with DACA to continue renewing every two years, but it blocks new applicants from applying to the program, denying deportation protection, work permits, and access to higher education for thousands of high school students and young immigrants, dooming them to live in fear and uncertainty. This is a painful loss for our movement. We fear for all of those in our community with and without DACA. I'm afraid for my brother's future. But we fight back in spite of the fear.

Immediately after DACA is terminated, we work with our legal partners to challenge Trump's decision in the courts and pressure Congress to protect immigrants from deportation by passing legislation. Courageous DACA recipients are part of lawsuits challenging the administration's decision. We launch the DACA Renewal Fund, raising thousands of dollars to provide financial assistance to families in need of support for DACA renewal fees. By June 2020, our efforts successfully protect DACA when the Supreme Court sides with DACA recipients and blocks the Trump administration's plan to dismantle the program. But Republicans don't stop the legal attacks on DACA, and the future of the program continues to be uncertain. The Supreme Court could decide to hear the challenges on DACA again. A positive outcome is hard to see with a Supreme Court that has three justices appointed by Trump. The legal battle led by Republicans to dismantle DACA is torturous and traumatizing for DACA recipients and their families. But as Angelica Villalobos, a leader from UWD's affiliate Dream Action Oklahoma, reminds us, "We will still be people after DACA."[65]

Despite the attacks from the Trump administration, immigrant youth reclaim our humanity, belonging, and place in this country by organizing and mobilizing people from different backgrounds to stand in defense of immigrants. We proudly proclaim that this is our home, and we are here to stay, even as our voices shake. This defiant and hopeful "here to stay" spirit is inspired by a history of "good trouble," as SNCC leader and Representative John Lewis used to say, and our courageous efforts to build social justice movements to push this country to truly embody values of equity and justice. We don't let Trump and his administration take away our belonging, hope, joy, and determination to fight for change.

In the summer of 2018, during the peak of the administration's family-separation policy, we work together with a broad coalition of civil rights and progressive organizations to defend families. With the leadership of the National Domestic Workers Alliance, Move On, and various immigrant and civil rights organizations, we launch the Families Belong Together campaign to mobilize people against family separation and push back against the administration. Thousands of Americans join protests in over seven hundred cities, condemning the administration's policy. The images of children being ripped away from their parents and of children held in cages cold and alone are met with outrage and strong opposition. Polls show that the majority of Americans oppose family separation.[66] The backlash forces the administration to end the policy. Although rogue ICE and CBP agents continue to separate families, our movement exposes the cruelty of the policy and delegitimizes the administration and its deportation force.

By fall of 2018, immigrant youth come together to celebrate UWD's ten-year anniversary in Miami, Florida. On the opening day, I get to see Dennis, an immigrant youth leader from Houston, Texas, for the first time since his release from detention. Dennis is an undocumented student at Austin High School in Houston who fled violence in Honduras. Like me, he was bullied by other students for his accent and for being an immigrant. One of the bullies shouted racial slurs and threw a bottle of Gatorade at him. In self-defense, Dennis pushed the bully and ran. Dennis reported the altercation, but instead of addressing the bullying as a school-discipline issue, school police arrested Dennis for pushing the bully, charged him with assault, and took him to the Harris County jail. The Harris County police collaborated with ICE by sharing Dennis's immigration status, and he was held in jail until ICE agents showed up to get him. Dennis was sent to an immigrant detention camp over seventy miles away from his family and was slated for deportation.

Teachers, classmates, UWD members, and immigrant justice advocates organized school walkouts to demand Dennis be freed from detention and allowed to stay in the US, his home. His teachers and UWD leaders traveled to Washington DC to meet with members of Congress to ask for their support in pressuring ICE to stop Dennis's deportation. After two months of public pressure, ICE released Dennis. But his deportation was only put on hold until the courts decide on his asylum case. He is required to have monthly check-ins with ICE. Dennis was accepted to three universities and entered the University of Houston. He became a volunteer youth leader with UWD's local Houston group and joined Summer of Dreams, UWD's leadership and organizing training program. He is eager to learn skills and strategies to stop deportations and end the school-to-prison-to-deportation pipeline so that others do not experience what he did.

Wearing his orange UWD T-shirt that says UNAFRAID, Dennis stands on stage in front of one thousand immigrant youth leaders. He begins, "I don't know if you can tell, but I'm really nervous, but even though I'm really nervous, I don't care anymore . . . I'm here because of people like you and others who share their stories . . . To all of you who are beginning your journey here at this [meeting], this is your home, your family, your fellow justice warriors. I hope you leave here taking this spirit of home back to your cities. I am because you are." I watch him from the crowd, in awe of his courage and leadership. Dennis is uncertain about his future, but he has transformed from a shy high school student to a fierce leader in our movement. I think, *This is why United We Dream exists.*

Meanwhile, we keep pressuring Congress to provide permanent protections and a pathway to citizenship for immigrant youth. Even though we know that the chances of legislation moving in Congress are low, we take the risk because the future of DACA is uncertain, and only Congress can pass a permanent solution. The pressure of our movement pushes Democrats to work on a proposal, the American Dream and Promise Act, which includes a pathway to citizenship for immigrant youth, with and without DACA, and immigrants with temporary protected status.

The American Dream and Promise Act becomes the first immigration bill in thirty years to not include increased deportations and detention in exchange for a pathway to citizenship for immigrants, representing a significant milestone.

Republicans, however, hold majorities in both the House of Representatives and Senate, and they demand that the proposal include $1.5 billion for a border wall, Trump's campaign promise and priority, and changes to the visa lottery system to restrict legal immigration from majority Black and brown countries. During a negotiation meeting about the proposal between the White House and Republican and Democratic congressional leadership, Trump grows frustrated with members of Congress for including protections for immigrants from Haiti, El Salvador, and African countries who have been impacted by the termination of TPS. Trump asks lawmakers, "Why are we having all these people from shithole countries come here?"[67] insisting that the US should instead favor immigrants from Norway. The negotiation and the legislation do not move forward. But we are not deterred. We are not defined by legislation, and regardless of who is in Congress or the White House, we know we need to continue organizing to win freedom and dignity for our communities.

In 2019, UWD convenes our leaders in Phoenix, Arizona, to strategize and continue growing the movement. Youth leaders—a mix of undocumented, documented, and US citizens representing Maryland, Connecticut, Texas, Florida, Oklahoma, New Mexico, and Arizona—come together in the offices of local UWD affiliate Living United for Change in Arizona (LUCHA). The members and leaders from LUCHA have lived through and fought back against racist policies and the targeting of Latine and immigrant communities led by xenophobic local politicians like Sheriff Joe Arpaio, so our meeting begins with learning from

Arizona leaders. LUCHA leaders Alejandra Gomez and Abril Gallardo, and Karina Ruiz from Arizona Dream Act Coalition, another UWD affiliate, share lessons. We also invite Neidi, who is organizing in the labor movement, to join us. She can't come in person because the meeting coincides with her wedding day, but she offers to join via Zoom. That's what we do for the love of our community and the commitment to building power to improve people's lives. With her wedding dress hanging in the background, Neidi shares lessons from her experience organizing immigrant youth and workers. The takeaway from the conversation is that the answer to the moment we face is to organize. There is no shortcut. In community and together, we find belonging and are more powerful. By bringing more people into the movement, we grow our power to protect each other and create change.

Neidi and the amazing leaders of United We Dream's Oklahoma affiliate group Dream Action Oklahoma (DAOK) bring attention to a protest led by Japanese American survivors of the internment camps. They rally outside of Fort Sill, a military base in Lawton, Oklahoma, which the Trump administration is planning to use as a detention camp for some of the over one thousand children separated from their parents.

Fort Sill has a long history as a site of violence, terror, and trauma. During World War II, it was used as an internment camp for Japanese Americans, and in the 1800s, it served as a jail for Native Americans. It is also where Apache chief Geronimo and families from his tribe were held and killed.

As the plans from the government become public, Japanese Americans and Native Americans whose families and ancestors were killed and imprisoned in Fort Sill, as well as Black, brown, Latine, and white people, come together to call on the federal government to shut down this plan. A few weeks later, leaders and members from local Oklahoma organizations—the American Indian Movement; Black Lives Matter-Oklahoma City; Dream Action Oklahoma (who call themselves the Oklahomies); and Tsuru for Solidarity, an organization of Japanese American internment-camp survivors—lead a second protest outside of the military base. Together, we mobilize hundreds of people to descend on Oklahoma City.

The evening before the protest, we gather with UWD immigrant youth leaders and allies, young and old, in the ballroom of a local hotel. Every hug, every greeting, every smile, and every person fills the room with a feeling of community, belonging, and hope. This is the magic that happens when people come together to take collective action. There are people chatting, laughing, and making new friends. Some young people from Colorado with black CHINGA LA MIGRA T-shirts are taking selfies. Native American leaders and immigrant youth from UWD are busy making signs in the middle of the room. Buddhist monks in black robes chat over tea. The youngest UWD leaders, who are middle school students, sit on the floor in the corner trying to finish their homework before the big day, and I remember our finance genius, Hafid, helping a college student on an accounting assignment.

At the front of the room, Serena Prammanasudh, at the time executive director of Dream Action Oklahoma and a child of immigrants, welcomes everyone. Mary Topaum, a leader and member of the Cherokee tribe and director of the American Indian Movement, an organization that has been active in Oklahoma since the 1970s, shares with us the story of how her tribe was forcibly displaced by our government and relocated to Oklahoma in the 1800s after gold was found in the Cherokee homeland—the states of Alabama, Georgia, Tennessee, and North Carolina. Oklahoma was the end point of the Trail of Tears.

Mary leads us in a moment of recognizing the land we are

standing on and acknowledging the four directions of the compass. She gestures toward each in turn: The east, the direction of beginnings. The north, the direction of hardship and discomfort. The west, the direction of endings. The south, the direction of growth. Mary says, "We understand that the ones coming from the south are Indigenous people; they're our relations. Everyone here, that's what I call you—*mitakuye oyasin*. All my relations . . . The children being separated from their families are our children. They are all our children."

Reverend Sheri Dickerson, a queer Black nonbinary activist and clergy member and executive director of Black Lives Matter-Oklahoma City, reminds us that Black people, too, have been impacted by a long history of family separation, state violence, and incarceration.

Mike Ishii, cofounder of Tsuru for Solidarity, shares his own experience as an internment-camp survivor: "When I see the children in cages, separated from their families, I see myself when I was child." Mike and his family were among 120,000 Japanese Americans forcibly removed from their homes and imprisoned in camps around the country by the United States government. Seven hundred Japanese Americans were imprisoned in Fort Sill, ninety of them Buddhist priests. Mike shares the story of Kanesaburo Oshima, a father of eleven, imprisoned at Fort Sill. Oshima, out of desperation, tried to climb the fence of the camp and was shot and killed by government agents.

The day of the march, more than seven hundred Black, Indigenous, brown, AAPI, and white people chanting "Close the camps" and "Never again" march outside of Fort Sill in sweltering heat. People hold signs that say CLOSE THE CAMPS, NONE OF US ARE FREE UNTIL WE ARE ALL FREE, ABOLISH PRISONS, ABOLISH ICE, and WHAT WILL YOU DO WHEN IT'S YOUR KIDS? We march toward the main gate of the military base where twenty Buddhist monks lead us in a moment of silence and prayer to honor the lives lost there and the children who died at the hands of our government in detention camps: Jaklin, Constantine, Felipe, Yanela, and Valeria. The monks chant the "Heart Sutra" in rapid succession. The "Heart Sutra" teaches that everyone in the universe exists autonomously, but only interdependently. Then a group of Indigenous and white allies block the entrance to the base. They form a human chain, their arms interlaced, and sit down on the hot pavement while chanting and sharing why they are willing to risk arrest by local police. The police do not arrest anyone, but our march is covered by local and national press.

Two weeks later, Republican senator Jim Inhofe from Oklahoma announces that plans to imprison refugee children at Fort Sill have been halted. Although our collective efforts do not fully end the separation of families, this win is a step toward building more power to protect our communities. Every win, even when small, must be recognized and celebrated.

By the end of the Trump presidency, we are exhausted. We've been hit by mass deportations, hate, family separation, death at the hands of ICE and CBP agents, police violence against Black and brown bodies, and the COVID global pandemic. But we never lose our sense of agency and power to act and push for change. We find energy and hope in each other and in solidarity with communities across the country. We march with women and LGBTQ people, join Indigenous communities in the Standing Rock demonstrations, take part in the Black Lives Matter protests sparked by the killing of George Floyd by a white cop in Minneapolis, and lead mutual aid efforts to take care of poor and working-class communities of color disproportionately impacted by the pandemic. We find resilience in our collective care and in our Indigenous ancestors that survived much worse. The end of this presidency does not mean the end of a growing white nationalist and authoritarian movement that is against my existence—our existence. But we know that the only way forward is by organizing and building more power. It was organizers who led the movements to abolish slavery, end segregation, and win women's right to vote. It is clear that our movement must continue fortifying our communities with collective care, organizing more people, building electoral and economic power, and disrupting the false narratives that dehumanize immigrants.

In 2024, Trump wins the presidential election again. Fewer people voted in comparison to the 2020 election, but Trump wins the popular vote as well. I'm reminded that we are in a much bigger struggle—a struggle for a truly inclusive, multiracial democracy that centers equality and justice. Our movement is sobered by the fact that Trump, a white supremacist authoritarian candidate, made gains across different voter groups, including Latine voters, making clear the work we must do in our own Latine and immigrant communities to reject white supremacy, anti-Black racism, authoritarianism, and misogyny. And I also know that the way people voted expresses a frustration among most Americans who feel our current system has failed them and are struggling to survive in an economy that only benefits the wealthy. We are reminded that elections alone won't save us, especially in a country where our elections can be bought by the rich and corporations and where our government allows for voter suppression and mass voter misinformation in the media and on online platforms. Yet elections are important, as they limit or expand the political terrain social justice movements have to push for change. But elections are only one of many strategies we must use to defend our communities and win a pluralist and inclusive vision of this country. Our work continues. We are grounded in love and the belief that the power of people, solidarity, and community will protect us and get us closer to a more inclusive and just country. We save us.

14

AMERICA THE POSSIBLE

Cristina and her family at her citizenship ceremony in Federal Plaza, New York, 2019 (courtesy of Greisa Martinez Rosas)

> *Let us make an oath to fight for the soul of America—"the land that never has been yet—and yet must be" (Langston Hughes)—with Revolutionary Love and relentless optimism.*
>
> —Valarie Kaur

In November of 2018, Walter and I become eligible to apply for citizenship after eight years of being in the process to adjust our immigration status. We don't look like the people the founders of this country envisioned as US citizens. Then, only white men who owned property were considered citizens protected under the Constitution. In that vision, women, Indigenous and Black people, and the rest of us were destined to second-class citizenship or no citizenship at all. If not for the fight for inclusion and justice led by Indigenous people, women, and Black and brown communities, we would still be living under that vision.

As a citizen, I can petition for my parents to become permanent residents. It's bittersweet because although I can also petition for my brother, who is a DACA recipient, his petition would take over a decade to be processed. The reality is that unless Congress acts, my brother will continue to be vulnerable to deportation for the foreseeable future. Having citizenship also means that I can finally vote. The stakes of the election are high. The country will decide on four more years of Trump or a change in direction. I can't wait for the day when I can vote to defeat Trump.

As I put together my application with the support of my immigration lawyer friends, I become increasingly fearful that the US Citizenship and Immigration Services (USCIS) will deny it. Under the Trump administration, more immigrants are denied citizenship, and applications take an average of 8.8 months to be processed, which is 50 percent more time than they took to be processed under the Obama administration.[68] The long delays are due to Trump's new policy to tighten an already "extreme vetting" process, and the Department of Justice officially creates a section in its immigration office to strip away citizenship from naturalized immigrants.[69]

In some states like Florida, the waiting time for applications is more than two years. Immigration agents who review applications and conduct interviews are trained to see applicants as "liars" and "criminals." I fear that a charge of "disorderly conduct" I got as a teenager for hanging out at a local park in Queens after it was closed could disqualify me from meeting the "good moral character" requirement. I also fear that my involvement in social justice movements could be held against me. After more than a decade of work empowering immigrant and Latine communities, fighting for immigrant, racial, gender, and economic justice, holding our elected officials accountable, increasing voter participation in elections, and pushing this country to live up to its promise of equality and justice for all, *I am still afraid* that I may be kicked out of the place I consider home. Even after getting my citizenship, every time I travel outside of the US and need to pass through US Customs and Border Protection, I fear I might be denied reentry.

In April 2019, after nearly nine months of nervously waiting to hear from the USCIS, I finally get a notice for an interview with an immigration agent. Walter gets a notice for his interview about a month before me, and we move separately in the process. Part of the interview with an agent also includes a civics test for which the applicant must study a booklet with a hundred questions. The applicant is then asked ten random questions from the booklet and must be able to answer six out of the ten correctly. The booklet reviews the country's founding history and values, the role of the Founding Fathers, the form of government, and how democracy works in the US. The irony is that through my lived experience, I have learned that the story we are told about this country, our values, and our democracy is far from the reality that we live. The booklet emphasizes that Americans need to participate in our democracy by voting and getting involved in community and civic organizations. I've studied US history in college, in organizing trainings, and on my own. Yet I'm still nervous about failing the civics test and being denied citizenship. I study for weeks, writing down the questions and answers on index cards and having Walter and my brother test me. I know the immigration agent that will interview me holds the power to grant me or deny me citizenship, so I memorize the answers to the questions exactly as they are written in the booklet. I fear any small mistake or wrong word could be a reason to be denied citizenship.

For the day of the interview, I ask my friend and chosen sister Sussan Lee to come with me. She is the daughter of Korean immigrant parents, an immigration lawyer, and a board member of UWD. She has my back in case the immigration agent tries to intimidate me or breach my rights.

From the get-go, when the agent, who is a petite white woman in her sixties, calls my name, she shows us she is the boss. She has an accent and is probably an immigrant herself, but I can't figure out where she is from. With a stern face, she looks us up and down and asks Sussan who she is. "I will only talk to the applicant," the agent tells her. We follow her to her office, and when I'm about to take a seat, she says, "I didn't tell you you could sit." She asks Sussan to sit in the back of the office and tells her she can't speak on my behalf. "Now you can sit," she tells me.

The officer reviews my application carefully and looks at her computer, verifying information. When we get to the part of the application where the applicant has to provide the name of civic or community organizations they are a part of, she chastises me. "You are a part of too many groups! This is just too many!" she tells me in an irritated way. I am stunned and outraged that she is berating me for engaging civically, as encouraged in their booklet, and for working to make this country a better place! But I remain calm and don't say a word. I am afraid that any movement, word, or nonverbal communication could be held against me. This petite white woman in a red blazer behind her black desk has the power to decide whether I will become a citizen of this country. After a long interrogation about my travel history, my taxes, and my community involvement, and after taking the citizenship test, I'm told I can expect my answer in the mail. A few weeks later, I receive a letter confirming my application is approved, with a date for the naturalization ceremony.

In September 2019, after twenty-one years of living in this country, I am finally recognized as a US citizen. On the day of my ceremony, I am full of mixed feelings. I join more than fifty other immigrants at Federal Plaza to take the oath and get our US citizenship certificates. Before we take the oath, we have to watch a video message from Trump welcoming new citizens into America and reminding us that we have an "obligation to teach [American] values to others."[70] That this man who praises and aligns with white supremacists and neo-Nazi groups and promotes antidemocratic values is reminding us of American values is hypocritical. It fills me with righteous anger.

When I take the oath, I commit to continuing to push this country to live up to its aspirational values of justice and equality for all. I know this America is possible. An America where people see each other's humanity, building a community of belonging and solidarity. The America where millions of people from all backgrounds speak up against injustice, march to defend women's rights, end the Muslim ban, keep immigrant families together, and fight for workers' rights, Black lives, and climate justice. The America where everyday people defend immigrants and refugees from deportations and do the work to keep families together. The America that spoke up for Walter and, in doing so, paved the way for our love and family to exist. This America is possible because I have seen it and felt it. This America is here. It is up to us, you and me, to nurture it and fight for it.

EPILOGUE

If you find a book you really want to read but it hasn't been written yet, then you must write it.

—Toni Morrison

My younger self never imagined writing a book. Growing up in Ecuador with a family that had very little and as an undocumented immigrant in the United States, I didn't come across stories where I could see me, my life, or people like my family. I wrote this book because my younger self yearned for stories and spaces that would make me feel welcomed, safe, powerful, and worthy. That would make me feel at home. I wrote this book for that younger self.

Dear One,

How do you feel at home when you're constantly on the move? When forces outside your control are constantly trying to mess with you, your friends, and your family until you've got no choice but to pack up and leave again? Or when you feel like everything's finally coming together and then a cop or immigration agent comes and rips you or someone you love from your life into a jail cell? You can't even take comfort in yourself because it seems everything around you is saying you have the wrong kind of face, skin that's too dark, an ass that's too big or too small or whatever trend happens to be torturing us. When guys think you're too loud. When others think you're too quiet. When you enter a room and with their looks, people tell you you don't belong there.

When all you feel is fear and shame and all you want is a place to feel safe and secure. A place protected from the rain and wind, warm with the comforting aroma of our abuela's soup wrapped around us like a shawl. A place where you can look in the mirror and love what you see, feel the electric energy of laughing so hard with your friends that our sides hurt. You and all humans want this. It's part of our DNA. Your yearning for that feeling of home and belonging is natural and is right.

White supremacy, misogyny, all of that bullshit behind so many of the systems that shape our world are designed to keep us on edge, feeling uprooted, forever homeless, forever hopeless.

So when we see and feel injustice and pain, it's only sensible to feel powerless. I mean, just think about all the money, time, and energy put in to keeping us feeling this way! Just imagine how much we could change the world if our roots could grasp fertile soil. I'm telling you, Dear One, you can find hope and your power. You can find home no matter how overwhelming things may be.

Home is a practice. You can find home remembering where you come from. Your history and your roots. Remember you come from ancestors who built nations, invented languages and the calendar, and survived genocide, violence, and poverty. Their ingenuity, courage, and resilience led to you. Despite what the haters may say about you—"illegal," "animal," "taker," "ugly," "criminal," and just "not enough"—remember you are a beautiful manifestation of your ancestors' dreams. You are beautiful just as you are. And you, and everyone on this planet, are worthy of freedom and dignity.

You can find home remembering that even though some human beings create violence, hate, and systems and laws of harm and oppression, many more are capable of transforming and healing with love, accountability, and compassion. I learned this by coming to love myself first. Loving who I am, where I come from, how I look, and my dreams. Loving myself is an everyday practice, especially when so much around us tells me people who look like me are not wanted and worthy. Loving myself helped me find home within myself, despite being told I am not worthy of calling this place home.

But don't get it twisted. Real talk, it ain't only about you.

Healing and transformation are not only individual work. Being alone on a deserted island isn't the kind of home I'd want to have. We cannot survive, create change, and thrive on our own or by ourselves. The work to bring healing, transformation, and change to this world happens in community. We organize and build power to change this world in community and solidarity with others. In community, you will realize that you are not alone, and that others share your experiences, fears, worries, and dreams. In community you will realize we are not powerless.

Before finding my community of activist students in college and organizers in the immigrant justice movement, I thought that to survive as an undocumented immigrant I had to make myself small, be under the radar, and never speak up, dream, or even believe that I was worthy of rights, dignity, and freedom. Queens College students fighting for student rights and equal access to higher education helped me realize that regardless of immigration status, I had the right to demand equality and justice. Immigrant justice organizers transformed the way I thought about myself and what's possible. I became a believer in my worth and the right of everyone to a life with dignity, and that a world where we all belong and thrive is possible. In community, you will find belonging and feel at home regardless of where you are and even when you feel homeless. Only in community will we survive pandemics, climate crises, human suffering, and pain. Only in community will we find ways to live despite the odds.

You can find community in your blood family—your parents, siblings, tías, tíos, abuelas, and abuelos, who love you and root for you. You can also find community in your chosen family of friends and kindred spirits. I know that not every family relationship and place around us is healthy, and you'll have to experience some hard-earned lessons to find your boundaries, but you can find home in the people who see your humanity, who love you with your virtues and imperfections, with whom you will share moments of joy and wonder, who will help you grow and be a better human every day, and who will take action to protect you. My community of blood and chosen family helped me move from being undocumented, afraid, and ashamed to feeling unashamed and empowered. I went from feeling alone to finding a community and breaking through the shadows to the center of a movement for justice.

My community has helped me get through tough moments. Without my community of social justice organizers and immigrant youth leaders, I don't know how I could have overcome the fear and devastation I felt when Trump was announced as the winner of the election in 2016 and once again in 2024. This community gave me the hope, spiritual grounding, and certainty I needed in that moment. My chosen family has celebrated with me every single win and victory (personal and for the movement) with good music and sweaty dancing, and they created the space for me to be vulnerable about my personal and leadership mistakes and growth. They encourage me to keep learning, hold compassion for myself, and keep growing. They have helped me survive heartbreak, relationship betrayals, and breakups, and get through bad hangovers or the many times I've made mistakes. In the end, when shit gets real and hard, community is all we've got. My wish is that my experiences might help you see that you're not alone, and that you will take some time to tell a young person in your life how you struggled, found your own community, and found your own power.

Welcome home, Dear One. I love you.

ACKNOWLEDGMENTS

The birthing of this book was possible because of my community. There are so many of you to thank.

Mami and Papi, thank you for the sacrifices and risks you took to protect our family and give us a chance at a better life. And for sharing your stories with me, helping me re-remember our life in Quito. Your courage and hard work inspired these pages. May this book honor you, mis abuelas y abuelos, and all our ancestors. To my siblings, Jonathan and Estefania, thank you for your love and encouragement. Ñañita, you answered every time I called on you during the writing process. Your spirit is always with me. Mil gracias.

Writing this book was a multiyear project. During this time, I also became a mom. I could not have birthed both, my first child and first book, without my love, Walter. Thank you for helping me survive postpartum and the writing process. I couldn't have finished this book if not for your time and devotion to caring for our family and our home. And amid all that you were holding, thank you for also helping me sew the pieces of this story together and reviewing the manuscript. Your storytelling, immigrant youth movement picture archive, and feedback made so many of the stories in these pages come alive.

To Itzae, holding you and watching you grow fueled my commitment to write a book that would contribute to making the world a better place for you and all children. I hope to make you proud. Te amo! Santi, my faithful writing companion, your sweet presence always brought me comfort. Without you I would have forgotten to take breaks and even go to the bathroom!

Gracias a mis tías, primas, y primos por todo el apoyo. Thank you for allowing me to capture a part of your stories—our story. Anita, thank you for answering my texts and calls at random times of the day to talk about our early years in this country and our high school experiences, and for helping me find and edit the family pictures used for the book. We are here. Sobrevivamos, loca!

To Carmen Caneda and Adam Luna, I'm deeply grateful for your partnership in dreaming of this book. You held my hand throughout the entire process, from our visioning conversations to the book proposal and reviewing the manuscript. Your feedback, suggestions, and coaching made this book better. Carmen, you are truly a fairy godmother to so many of us. You worked your magic to connect me with Gail Ross, my agent. Gail, thank you for believing in my story and voice, even when I was still in search of it.

To my editor, Elisabeth Dyssegaard, thank you for believing in this book and supporting me in the process of finding my voice, and also for helping me find a space away from home to write when I desperately needed it. You were incredibly patient and generous with me! To the broader team at St. Martin's Press, thank you for your careful look at every single word and the beautiful cover. This book is ready for showtime because of you.

Finding my voice took some time. In the process, I was blessed to have the support and guidance of inspiring women. Rinku Sen, thank you for encouraging me to write and making it possible for me to attend my first writing retreat with other women of color at Hedgebrook. I'm still in awe of having had the opportunity to be in a retreat with you, Michelle Alexander, Sujatha Jesudason, Amna Akbar, and our instructor, Daisy Hernández. Chaiti Sen, thank you for your mentorship and coaching as I launched into the writing process. And for holding me accountable to my daily writing goals! Nikki Marron, thank you for pushing me, always gently, to stay in the story, to not rush. Your attention to every single line of the early drafts of this manuscript and feedback were invaluable.

There were many ups and downs in the process of finding my voice. It wasn't easy. I had to shed my self-doubt, impostor syndrome, and insecurities as a non-native English speaker. When I reached writer's block and my insecurities won over, I thought to myself that it was time to give up. But my dear friend, la mera mera trailblazer Chicana writer Sandra Cisneros, who has forged the path for Latina writers, didn't let me. In the coziness of her home, I handed her my manuscript. I was terrified. She went on to tell me, "You sound like you are wearing a very uncomfortable suit. This is not your voice. Why don't you get in your pajamas and write from that place? . . . Animo! Tu Puedes!" Sandra, thank you for reviewing these pages and teaching me to tell the story through all my senses. Gracias for reminding me that there is only one of me on this planet and therefore only I can tell my story. Sally Kohn, your assignment to write a letter to my younger self changed everything. It gave me so much clarity. My voice was unleashed! Thank you for your coaching and support.

My deepest gratitude to my friends and movement colleagues who encouraged me and shared their feedback on the manuscript, ensuring the accuracy of the stories shared in this book: Rosa Esteves, Azmina Jasani, Jonathan Gilad, Andreana Tsakanikas, Diana Robinson, Selene Muñoz, Greisa Martínez Rosas, Lorella Praeli, Matias Ramos, Gaby Pacheco, Isabel Sousa Rodriguez, Jose Luis Marantes, Josh Bernstein, Julio Salgado, Carlos Amador,

Natalia Aristizabal Betancur, Julie Dinnerstein, Sussan Lee, and Neidi Dominguez Zamorano. Thank you for making time to talk and answering my many emails and texts.

There were many legal minds that made my journey and the telling of this story possible. Thank you Yasmine Farhang, Bryan Pu-Folkes, Jiyoon Kim, Holly Schadler, David Isaacson, and Mike Trister. Mike, I know you are smiling from heaven.

This book was made possible with the generous support from Open Society Foundations, Ford Foundation, Unbound Philanthropy, and the Pop Culture Collaborative. Thank you Alvin Starks, Andrew Maisel, Taryn Higashi, Adey Fisseha, Mayra Peters-Quintero, Anita Kashu, Javier Valdés, Bridgit Antoinette Evans, and Rupa Balasubramanian. I'm grateful for your support.

To the leaders, members, and staff of United We Dream, past and present, and all the youth, educators, and parents who have fueled the immigrant youth movement, this book is a humble offering to honor your work, courage, and leadership. Thank you for all you have done and still do to advance immigrant justice. Si Se Puede!

NOTES

1 Mae Ngai, *Impossible Subjects: Illegal Aliens and the Making of Modern America* (Princeton, NJ: Princeton University Press, 2004).

2 Ruth Milkman, Deepak Bhargava, and Penny Lewis, *Immigration Matters: Movements, Visons, and Strategies for a Progressive Future* (New York: New Press, 2021), 8–9.

3 Brian Naylor and Tamara Keith, "Kamala Harris Tells Guatemalans Not to Migrate to the United States," NPR, June 7, 2021, https://www.npr.org/2021/06/07/1004074139/harris-tells-guatemalans-not-to-migrate-to-the-united-states.

4 David Suggs, "The Long Legacy of the U.S. Occupation of Haiti," *Washington Post*, August 6, 2021, www.washingtonpost.com/history/2021/08/06/haiti-us-occupation-1915/.

5 Selam Gebrekidan, Matt Apuzzo, Catherine Porter, and Constant Méheut, "The Ransom: Invade Haiti, Wall Street Urged. The U.S. Obliged," *New York Times*, May 20, 2022, www.nytimes.com/2022/05/20/world/haiti-wall-street-us-banks.html.

6 Kathryn Prociv and Phil Helsel, "Tropical Storm Iota Sweeps Central America with Humanitarian Crisis Looming," NBC News, November 16, 2020, www.nbcnews.com/news/weather/hurricane-iota-nears-landfall-central-america-category-5-humanitarian-crisis-n1247907.

7 Albinson Linares, "'We're Defeated': Climate Migrants Fleeing Storm-Stricken Central America Struggle to Find Refuge," NBC News, April 5, 2021, www.nbcnews.com/news/latino/central-american-climate-migrants-face-countless-barriers-seeking-refu-rcna525.

8 Charles Kamasaki, "US Immigration Policy: A Classic, Unappreciated Example of Structural Racism," Brookings, March 26, 2021, www.brookings.edu/articles/us-immigration-policy-a-classic-unappreciated-example-of-structural-racism/.

9 Andrea Bernstein, "Who Is Jared Kushner?" *New Yorker*, January 6, 2020, www.newyorker.com/news/news-desk/who-is-jared-kushner.

10 Daniela Gerson, "My Grandparents' Immigration Lies Shaped My Father's Views of Justice," *New York Times*, April 26, 2021, www.nytimes.com/2021/04/26/opinion/dreamers-undocumented-immigration-holocaust.html.

11 Dara Lind, "The Disastrous, Forgotten 1996 Law that Created Today's Immigration Problem," *Vox*, April 28, 2016, https://www.vox.com/2016/4/28/11515132/iirira-clinton-immigration.

12 Jennifer Van Hook, Julia Gelatt, and Ariel G. Ruiz Soto, "A Turning Point for the Unauthorized Immigrant Population in the United States," Migration Policy Institute, September 2023, www.migrationpolicy.org/news/turning-point-us-unauthorized-immigrant-population.

13 Saket Soni, "Post-Hurricane Rebuilding Will Be Done by Undocumented Workers—And They Need Protection," *Los Angeles Times*, October 12, 2017, www.latimes.com/opinion/op-ed/la-oe-soni-hurricane-recovery-undocumented-immigrants-20171012-story.html.

14 Jeffrey S. Passel and D'Vera Cohn, "Industries of Unauthorized Immigrant Workers," Pew Research Center, November 3, 2016, www.pewresearch.org/race-and-ethnicity/2016/11/03/industries-of-unauthorized-immigrant-workers/.

15 Annette Bernhardt, Ruth Milkman, and Nik Theodore, "Broken Laws, Unprotected Workers: Violations of Employment and Labor Laws in America's Cities," National Employment Law Project, September 21, 2009, www.nelp.org/insights-research/broken-laws-unprotected-workers-violations-of-employment-and-labor-laws-in-americas-cities/.

16 Sam Dillon, "Queens Sophomore Slashed by 2 Youths for Gold Chain," *New York Times*, February 8, 1994, www.nytimes.com/1994/02/08/nyregion/queens-sophomore-slashed-by-2-youths-for-gold-chain.html.

17 Sarah Mervosh, "How Much Wealthier Are White School Districts Than Nonwhite Ones? $23 Billion, Report Says," *New York Times*, February 27, 2019, www.nytimes.com/2019/02/27/education/school-districts-funding-white-minorities.html.

18 Hannah Dreier, "He Drew His School Mascot and ICE Labeled Him a Gang Member," ProPublica, December 27, 2018, https://features.propublica.org/ms-13-immigrant-students/huntington-school-deportations-ice-honduras/.

19 Amanda Petteruti, "Education Under Arrest: The Case Against Police in Schools," Justice Policy Institute, November 2011, https://justicepolicy.org/press/school-resource-officers-are-a-waste-of-resources-says-new-report/.

20 Samantha Michaels, "Black Kids Are 5 Times Likelier Than White Kids to Be Locked Up," *Mother Jones*, September 13, 2017, www.motherjones.com/politics/2017/09/black-kids-are-5-times-likelier-than-white-kids-to-be-locked-up/.

21 Eliza Gray and Nate Rawlings, "New York 'Stop and Frisk' Ruling: When Violated Rights Lead to Federal Intervention," *Time*, August 13, 2013, https://nation.time.com/2013/08/13/new-york-stop-and-frisk-ruling-when-violated-rights-lead-to-federal-intervention/.

22 Dreier, "He Drew His School Mascot."

23 Jie Zong and Jeanne Batalova, "How Many Unauthorized Immigrants Graduate from U.S. High Schools Annually?," The Migration Policy Institute, April 2019, www.migrationpolicy.org/research/unauthorized-immigrants-graduate-us-high-schools.

24 William C. Kidder and Jay Rosner, "How the SAT Creates Built-in Headwinds: An Educational and Legal Analysis of Disparate Impact," *Santa Clara Law Review* 131, 2002, https://digitalcommons.law.scu.edu/lawreview/vol43/iss1/3/.

25 Mariana Viera, "The History of the SAT Is Mired in Racism and Elitism," *Teen Vogue*, October 1, 2018, www.teenvogue.com/story/the-history-of-the-sat-is-mired-in-racism-and-elitism.

26 "From the Archives: George W. Bush's Oval Office Speech on 9/11," NBC News, September 11, 2019, www.nbcnews.com/now/video/from-the-archives-george-w-bush-s-oval-office-speech-on-9–11–68719685777.

27 Moni Basu, "15 Years after 9/11, Sikhs Still Victims of Anti-Muslim Hate Crimes," CNN, September 15, 2016, www.cnn.com/2016/09/15/us/sikh-hate-crime-victims/index.html.

28 Maia Jachimowicz and Ramah McKay, "Special Registration Program," Migration Policy Institute, April 1, 2003, www.migrationpolicy.org/article/special-registration-program.

29 Doris Meissner, Donald M. Kerwin, Muzaffar Chisthi, and Claire Bergeron, "Immigration Enforcement in the United States: The Rise of a Formidable Machinery," Migration Policy Institute, January 2013, www.migrationpolicy.org/sites/default/files/publications/pillars-reportinbrief.pdf.

30 Dalia Mogahed and Erum Ikramullah, "American Muslim Poll 2020," Institute for Social Policy and Understanding, October 1, 2020, www.ispu.org/american-muslim-poll-2020-amid-pandemic-and-protest/.

31 Muzaffar Chishti and Jessica Bolter, "Two Decades after 9/11, National Security Focus Still Dominates U.S. Immigration System," Migration Policy Institute, September 22, 2021, www.migrationpolicy.org/article/two-decades-after-sept-11-immigration-national-security.

32 Katie Worth, "Closing the Schoolhouse Door," The Village Voice, January 22, 2002, www.villagevoice.com/closing-the-schoolhouse-door/.

33 Amelie G. Ramirez, Kipling J. Gallion, Rosalie Aguilar, and Erin Surette Dembeck, "Mental Health and Latino Kids: A Research Review," Robert Wood Johnson Foundation, September 12, 2017, https://salud-america

.org/wp-content/uploads/2017/09/FINAL-mental-health-research-review-9–12–17.pdf.

34 Jim Dolan, "Father of 10-Year-Old Boy Who Took His Own Life Demands Change from School Board," ABC 7, June 6, 2023, https://abc7ny.com/peekskill-10-year-old-boy-suicide-school-bullying/13352622/.

35 Fernanda Echavarri and Marlon Bishop, "'No Mexicans Allowed': School Segregation in the Southwest," NPR Latino USA, March 11, 2016, www.latinousa.org/2016/03/11/no-mexicans-allowed-school-segregation-in-the-southwest/.

36 DeNeen L. Brown, "The Determined Father Who Took Linda Brown by the Hand and Made History," *Washington Post*, March 27, 2018, www.washingtonpost.com/news/retropolis/wp/2018/03/27/the-determined-black-dad-who-took-linda-brown-by-the-hand-and-stepped-into-history/.

37 Catherine Winter, "A Supreme Court Case 35 Years Ago Yields a Supply of Emboldened DACA Students Today," APM Reports, August 21, 2017, www.apmreports.org/story/2017/08/21/plyler-doe-daca-students.

38 "1982: Plyler v. Doe," Library of Congress, https://guides.loc.gov/latinx-civil-rights/plyler-v-doe.

39 "Public Education for Immigrant Students: Understanding *Plyler v. Doe*," American Immigration Council, October 2016, www.americanimmigrationcouncil.org/sites/default/files/research/public_education_for_immigrant_students_understanding_plyer_v_doe.pdf.

40 Julian Borger, "There Were No Weapons of Mass Destruction in Iraq," *The Guardian*, October 7, 2004, www.theguardian.com/world/2004/oct/07/usa.iraq1.

41 Laura Wides-Muñoz, "A Family in Missouri Had a Life for 15 Years. Then They Were Torn Apart," *The Guardian*, January 30, 2018, www.theguardian.com/us-news/2018/jan/30/a-family-in-missouri-had-a-life-for-15-years-then-they-were-torn-apart.

42 Shawn Fremstad, Hayley Brown, and Hye Jin Rho, "Meatpacking Workers Are a Diverse Group Who Need Better Protections," Center for Economic and Policy Research, April 29, 2020, https://cepr.net/meatpacking-workers-are-a-diverse-group-who-need-better-protections/.

43 Missy Ryan, "US Chases Identity Theft in Biggest Work Raid Ever," Reuters, August 9, 2007, www.reuters.com/article/us-immigration-swift-usa/u-s-chases-identity-theft-in-biggest-work-raid-ever-idUSN1344776020061213/.

44 Virgie Hoban, "'Discredit, Disrupt and Destroy': FBI Records Acquired by the Library Reveal Violent Surveillance of Black Leaders, Civil Rights Organizations," Berkeley Library, University of California, January 18, 2021, www.lib.berkeley.edu/about/news/fbi.

45 Peter Nicholas, "Democrats Point the Finger at Obama's Chief of Staff for

Immigration Reform's Poor Progress," *Los Angeles Times*, May 21, 2010, www.latimes.com/archives/la-xpm-2010-may-21-la-na-immigration-20100521-story.html.

46 Frederick Douglass, "West India Emancipation Speech," University of Rochester Frederick Douglass Project, New York, 1857, https://rbscp.lib.rochester.edu/4398.

47 Valeria Fernández, "Arizona's 'Concentration Camp': Why Was Tent City Kept Open for 24 Years?," *The Guardian*, August 21, 2017, www.theguardian.com/cities/2017/aug/21/arizona-phoenix-concentration-camp-tent-city-jail-joe-arpaio-immigration.

48 Terry Greene Sterling and Jude Joffe-Block, "How Activists Fought Joe Arpaio's Immigration Roundups," *High Country News*, April 30, 2021, www.hcn.org/articles/books-how-activists-fought-joe-arpaios-immigration-roundups/.

49 Julie Pace, "Obama: Immigration Overhaul Is Unlikely Soon," NBC News, April 28, 2010, https://www.nbcnews.com/id/wbna36838545.

50 John Morton, "Memorandum for All ICE Employees," U.S Immigration and Customs Enforcement, Department of Homeland Security, June 30, 2010, https://www.ice.gov/doclib/news/releases/2010/civil-enforcement-priorities.pdf.

51 Peter Slevin, "Deportation of Illegal Immigrants Increases under Obama Administration," *Washington Post*, July 26, 2010, www.washingtonpost.com/wp-dyn/content/article/2010/07/25/AR2010072501790.html.

52 Dara Lind, "The Gutsy Decision that Saved Harry Reid's Career and Made Him a Hero to Latinos," *Vox*, May 27, 2015, https://www.vox.com/2015/3/27/8301387/harry-reid-dream-act.

53 Nikita Stewart, "'I've Been to the Mountaintop,' Dr. King's Last Sermon Annotated," *New York Times*, April 2, 2018, https://www.nytimes.com/interactive/2018/04/02/us/king-mlk-last-sermon-annotated.html.

54 John Morton, "Memorandum for All Field Office Directors," Department of Homeland Security, June 17, 2011, https://www.ice.gov/doclib/secure-communities/pdf/prosecutorial-discretion-memo.pdf.

55 *Obama Interrupted at NCLR Conference*, video recording by United We Dream, July 25, 2011, https://www.youtube.com/watch?v=Qk-7cCLB8ng.

56 Catherine E. Shoichet, "Obama: 'I Need a Dance Partner' on Immigration Reform," CNN, July 25, 2011, https://ufw.org/CNN-International-Obama-I-need-a-dance-partner-on-immigration-reform.

57 Zenén Jaimes Pérez, "A Portrait of Deferred Action for Childhood Arrivals Recipients," United We Dream, October 2015, https://unitedwedream.org/wp-content/uploads/2015/10/DACA-report-final-1.pdf.

58 Mark Hugo Lopez and Paul Taylor, "Latino Voters in the 2012 Election,"

Pew Research Center, November 7, 2012, https://www.pewresearch.org/race-and-ethnicity/2012/11/07/latino-voters-in-the-2012-election/.

59 *Maya Angelou's 1992 Commencement Address at Spelman College*, https://www.youtube.com/watch?v=70RH-h7QfP0.

60 Rebekah Zemansky and Julia Preston, "Immigrants Reach Beyond a Legal Barrier for a Reunion," *New York Times*, June 11, 2013, https://www.nytimes.com/2013/06/12/us/divided-immigrant-families-reunite-at-arizona-fence.html.

61 *New York Times*, front page photo, June 12, 2013, https://www.facebook.com/UnitedWeDream/photos/a.322493024478526/525201024207724/.

62 Jon Huang, Samuel Jacoby, Michael Strickland, and K. K. Rebecca Lai, "Election 2016: Exit Polls," *New York Times*, November 8, 2016, https://www.nytimes.com/interactive/2016/11/08/us/politics/election-exit-polls.html.

63 Hannah Rappleye and Lisa Riordan Seville, "24 Immigrants Have Died in ICE Custody During the Trump Administration," NBC News, June 9, 2019, https://www.nbcnews.com/politics/immigration/24-immigrants-have-died-ice-custody-during-trump-administration-n1015291.

64 Victoria Bekiempis, "More Immigrant Women Say They Were Abused by ICE Gynecologist," *The Guardian*, December 22, 2020, www.theguardian.com/us-news/2020/dec/22/ice-gynecologist-hysterectomies-georgia.

65 Angelica Villalobos, "Home Is Here" campaign, https://homeishere.us/stories/angelicas-story/.

66 Dylan Matthews, "Trump's Family Separation Policy Is Very Unpopular—Except Among Republicans," June 18, 2018, https://www.vox.com/policy-and-politics/2018/6/18/17475740/family-separation-poll-polling-border-trump-children-immigrant-families-parents.

67 Lauren Gambino, "Trump Pans Immigration Proposal as Bringing People from 'Shithole Countries,'" *The Guardian*, January 11, 2018, https://www.theguardian.com/us-news/2018/jan/11/trump-pans-immigration-proposal-as-bringing-people-from-shithole-countries.

68 "Historical National Median Processing Time (in Months) for All USCIS Offices for Select Forms by Fiscal Year," US Citizenship and Immigration Services, fiscal years 2019 to 2024, https://egov.uscis.gov/processing-times/historic-pt.

69 Nicole Narea, "How Trump Made It That Much Harder to Become a US Citizen," *Vox*, September 3, 2020, www.vox.com/2020/9/3/21408528/trump-naturalization-backlog-citizenship-voting.

70 Donald J. Trump, "President Trump's Message for New Citizens," *AZ Central*, October 24, 2017, https://www.azcentral.com/videos/news/politics/arizona/2017/10/24/president-trumps-message-new-citizens/106882110/.

ABOUT THE AUTHOR

Cristina Jiménez is an award-winning community organizer and a leading voice in movements for social justice. She is the cofounder and former executive director of United We Dream, the largest immigrant youth–led organization in the country, where she steered national and state campaigns for immigrant justice, playing a leadership role in the campaign to win and implement the Deferred Action for Childhood Arrivals program (DACA). Jiménez is the director of Shared Future, a new national initiative seeking to build a consensus on what unites us, immigrants and nonimmigrants, as Americans. She received a 2017 MacArthur Fellowship and a spot on the 2018 *Time* 100 Most Influential People list. Jiménez came to the US from Ecuador in 1998 and grew up undocumented in Queens, New York.